Faithful Science

To Jennet,

lovely to meet you
at the Creation
conference, 2022.

Yours in Christ,

Alistair

Faithful Science

Teaching Intelligent Design to Evangelical Students

ALISTAIR J. MCKITTERICK

RESOURCE *Publications* · Eugene, Oregon

FAITHFUL SCIENCE
Teaching Intelligent Design to Evangelical Students

Resource Publications
An Imprint of Wipf and Stock Publishers
199 W. 8th Ave., Suite 3
Eugene, OR 97401

www.wipfandstock.com

PAPERBACK ISBN: 978-1-6667-3045-6
HARDCOVER ISBN: 978-1-6667-2201-7
EBOOK ISBN: 978-1-6667-2202-4

JANUARY 27, 2022 9:42 AM

Contents

List of Figures

Preface

I HAVE BEEN INTERESTED in the science and faith debate for over thirty years and for the last fifteen have been an active supporter of the intelligent design movement. This book is my response to concerns about secular ideologies that influence schools, universities and the media more generally. Science is typically taught without reference to God and in a way that separates science from discussion about design in the natural world. Secular science presupposes it offers a sufficient explanation to account for all natural phenomena: any appeal to God is unnecessary and done only for theological reasons, not scientific ones. Belief in God is seen as an optional extra for those identified as people of faith: many who see themselves as people of science feel they have outgrown faith. A sharp division has developed between theology and science, the private and public, subjectivity and objectivity, opinion and truth. Those who hold a Darwinian worldview believe they have reason and evidence on their side and do not feel the need to engage in discussions about a God they don't believe exists and have no need for in their scientific worldview.

The intelligent design argument questions the sufficiency of the secular, materialist worldview. It challenges the Darwinian narrative as a scientific theory (it is really a naturalist story to which certain evidence is brought in for support). It offers scientific evidence demonstrating the inadequacy of materialism to explain what is best explained as design. The fact that the universe had a beginning, the fine-tuning of the physical constants, the information stored in DNA, the sudden appearance of different plants and animal body plans, and the extraordinary reality of consciousness all point away from naturalist explanations and point instead towards intelligent design.

Christian participants in the research project found learning about intelligent design liberating. It gave them greater confidence to engage in conversation with those holding a Darwinian worldview. They recognized the controlling influence that materialism has on the public and places of education and found in intelligent design a language they could better use to integrate faith in the Christian God with science. I want to acknowledge my gratitude to the research project participants: they were sincere, articulate and fully engaged with the interviews and focus group. They were everything that a researcher could have wanted. I also owe a great deal to the church leaders that facilitated the research by providing the location and lunch for the two-day course. Their diligence in planning and support were exemplary acts of trust and courage in me and in the value of the course for their church members.

I am very grateful for being able to attend the Summer Seminar run by the Discovery Institute based in Seattle. I was fortunate enough to meet many key figures in the intelligent design movement there and through my involvement with what became the Centre for Intelligent Design in the UK. Each encounter affirmed my growing conviction that the intelligent design argument responds to a real need in Western society and provides a means of re-engaging science with the God of creation.

I wish to thank my supervisors at Spurgeon's College, Philip McCormack and Joshua Searle, for their wisdom and guidance. I am indebted to my friend and former colleague Neil Tinson who generously gave of his time formatting and proofing the text. I also thank David and Sue Pickard who encouraged me as the research project progressed. And finally, and with the greatest gratitude, I want to thank my wife Emily for her wonderful love and unfailing support for these many years, and particularly these last few in achieving my doctorate. I dedicate this work to her.

Abbreviations

AG: Assemblies of God Church

AR: Action Research

ARCS: Action Research: Church and Society

CoRE: Commission on Religious Education

DfE: Department for Education

DID: Discovering Intelligent Design

DNA: Deoxyribonucleic Acid

GDPR: General Data Protection Regulation

ID: The Intelligent Design movement

ITDEM: Identify, Think, Do, Evaluate, Modify

MGT: Muted Group Theory

NOMA: Non-Overlapping Magisteria

NTPG: New Testament and the People of God

OARS: Oxford Argumentation in Religion and Science

Open UP: Open University Press

PedAR: Pedagogical Action Research

POMA: Partially Overlapping Magisteria

PRS: Philosophy and Religious Studies

QCA: Qualifications and Curriculum Authority

RE: Religious Education

SDA: Special Divine Action

TAR: Theological Action Research

Introduction

HOW CAN CHRISTIANS ENGAGE ATHEISTS in meaningful conversations that open them up to the Gospel? The aim of this book is to test the hunch that intelligent design is a good strategy for evangelical Christians to use when evangelizing those whose worldview excludes God. It was observed by many of my students (and from my own experience) that certain people are harder to engage with the Gospel as they often use questions of science as a barrier to discussing God. Their confidence comes from the belief that science has provided a sufficient explanation for life, the universe and everything. This view is reinforced in popular media, schools and academia. Most are not aware of the extensive scientific evidence opposing the Darwinian worldview. This evidence shows the inadequacy for Darwinism to account for the diversity and abundance of life. Far from following the evidence wherever it leads, many Darwinists are holding tight to their faith in materialism despite the scientific evidence.

This is not a religion-versus-science debate. Opposing Darwinism has commonly been done from a religious (usually creationist) perspective where the argument quickly turns into defending the historicity of Scripture or why Christians hold a variety of views on the matter. The intelligent design argument does not start from any religious text or philosophy: it focuses on the lack of scientific support for the Darwinian narrative. The intelligent design argument is open to the possibility that mind might be the best causal explanation for certain evidence in the natural world. Materialists are closed to this possibility which prevents them from following the scientific evidence when it points toward the existence of God. The strategy of the intelligent design argument is to cause materialists to reconsider their materialist assumptions in light of scientific evidence. Intelligent design is a science-versus-science argument (or better, theistic science versus atheistic science) argument. Instead of precluding the possibility of God from the outset, it argues that the most coherent approach to science is one that is open to finding design in nature.

My research shows the positive effect on evangelical Christians from learning about intelligent design, seen in their increased confidence to evangelize those with a Darwinian worldview. This book is an account of how I came to that conclusion. In keeping with it being a professional doctorate, the first chapter starts by articulating the question and why I was motivated to research it. I introduce my methodology and discuss my own role and influence in the research project, namely that of a college lecturer working with higher education students and latterly with those who signed up for the Discovering Intelligent Design course.

Teaching and researching intelligent design as a theology lecturer meant having a clear understanding about God, science, and the world he created. Must science confine itself to studying chance and necessity, or can it identify the effect of mind in nature? Would God contradict his own physical laws if he were to act miraculously in the world today? These questions about how science and theology relate together are discussed in chapter 2. I drew from a typology developed by Tenneson, Bundrick and Stanford to group different positions along a spectrum: Conflict, Compartmentalism, Complementarism, and Concordism. Unlike the creationism and scientism positions that present science and theology in conflict with each other, intelligent design is seen as the most integrated position between the two disciplines: they are in deep concord with each other. Theistic evolutionists align with a Darwinian narrative, whereas intelligent design argues that Darwinism does not fit the facts. Theistic evolutionists typically shy away from the miraculous intervention of God in the world: intelligent design argues that there is scientific evidence in the natural world for exactly that. A sketch of intelligent design (and some of its detractors) emphasises different definitions of science and the role that presuppositions play in determining whether the search for design in nature can be considered properly scientific.

The research draws from two academic traditions. As a professional doctorate, it integrates theory with practice through action research and reflexive awareness. As a ministry doctorate, it frames that research as practical theology involving theological reflection and Christian praxis. Chapter 3 outlines my research methodology. Whereas action research is often done through a self-reflective lens where success is gauged through meeting personal goals or values, I used a method more appropriate for researching the effectiveness of teaching a scientific program, namely Norton's Pedagogical Action Research. Norton locates her approach as meeting the needs of those wanting to bring about improved practice in education as well as encouraging social change. I found teaching intelligent design to be an effective pedagogical intervention in a higher education context for bringing about improved confidence for evangelical Christians seeking to evangelize those with a materialist or Darwinian worldview. I conclude the chapter by demonstrating the value of using a model of practical theology (in this case Richard Osmer's model) for reflecting theologically on a change of practice and formulating theologically-motivated praxis arising from the reflection.

Chapters 4 and 5 follow Norton's pedagogical action research model through two cycles to provide the data for theological reflection. The anacronym ITDEM summarizes the action taken: identify the problem, think about how to tackle it, do it, evaluate it, and modify future practice. Students not feeling confident discussing matters of science in ministry contexts provided the problem to be addressed. This was correlated with relevant surveys predominantly in Europe and America about how people relate science and faith. The research project involved designing a science curriculum appropriate to be taught to theology students. I based the course on Kemper, Kemper and Luskin's helpful textbook called *Discovering Intelligent Design*. The delivery was initially in my place of work, Moorlands College, to students that signed up for it as an extracurricular activity. Their responses were evaluated through interviews and satisfaction surveys and this evaluation modified my future practice by locating the second delivery of the course in a local church, making it more accessible to part-time students by running it over two Saturdays rather than over several midweek afternoon sessions.

Chapter 5 describes the second cycle of Norton's pedagogical action research, the two-day Saturday School, where the main data gathering took place from interviews with volunteering participants. I used thematic analysis on the transcripts to identify the participants' main themes. These were that *the church does not encourage engagement between science and faith*, that there is *unquestioning certitude of Darwinism in school* as a result of which *young people are vulnerable to losing Christian faith*. They argued that we need to *recognize the Darwinian consequences* in society, that the intelligent design course *enabled participants to engage in conversational evangelism*, and that it empowered participants to *respond to the challenge of Darwinism* through apologetic debate.

A distinguishing feature of this research project was to complement the pedagogical action research with a cycle of a model of practical theology, namely Richard Osmer's model. This christocentric model provided a structure to reflect theologically on the thematic analysis. Chapter 6 describes Osmer's Sagely Wisdom phase where I draw from several academic disciplines to understand more deeply why participants found engagement with Darwinism difficult. Darwinism is commonly presented as fact in schools and academic institutions, and cultural elites construct a materialist symbolic worldview to support it. As we become more conscious of, and confront, the moral consequences of such a worldview, we recognize the muting effect it has on the Christian's theistic worldview. I highlight the damaging Darwinian campaign to deny children's instincts to see design in nature and suggest a strategy for presenting theistic science as common sense to enable evangelicals to evangelize more confidently those holding to a secular worldview through initiating conversations about science.

In chapter 7 I reflect theologically on my findings and argue that teaching intelligent design is analogous to the Parable of the Sower (Matt. 13:1–9). This prime parable is a model for understanding why many reject the scientific evidence for intelligent design or are afraid to endorse its finding. It gives encouragement to those who feel marginalized for holding to its teachings and suggests that there is a spiritual context of competing worldviews. Like the parable itself, intelligent design invites the hearer to respond to the invitation or recognize that in rejecting it there are factors of spiritual deception, persecution, worry, and wealth at play.

Practical theology involves going from theological reflection to faithful praxis, and in chapter 8 I outline several applications of the research. The benefits of teaching intelligent design should be appropriated by seminaries and Bible colleges to enable evangelicals to evangelize with greater confidence. It is hoped that intelligent design would be used within schools to support the suggested change of Religious Education to a more worldview-oriented approach. However, the evidence for intelligent design can be just as well shared in smaller groups outwith an academic context and the hope is to develop online training courses that will enable more people to develop their skills in sharing this information.

The research is concluded, summarised, and critically reflected upon in chapter 9. I have indicated ways that my research might be generalizable to some extent, including a suggestion for its inclusion in the Oxford Argumentation in Religion and Science (OARS) project. The hope is that the evidence for intelligent design will be presented in different formats in many contexts to enable conversations and debates that lead to the preaching of the Gospel of Jesus Christ.

1

Research Question

[The] ability to transform research into action can meet the needs of employers and society, demonstrate improvements in practice and help society adapt well to the ever-increasing pace of change in the twenty-first century.[1]

THE RESEARCH QUESTION

The research question for this thesis is "To what extent, if at all, does teaching intelligent design to evangelical students contribute to their confidence and ability to share their faith?"[2] I address this question as a lecturer at Moorlands College in response to a problem encountered by my students of science being used as a reason not to believe, or no longer to believe, in the Gospel. My research is part of a professional

1. Carol Costley and John Fulton, eds., Methodologies for Practice Research: Approaches for Professional Doctorates (London: SAGE, 2019), xix–xx.

2. For this project, I will use Olson's definition of an evangelical to be anyone "who is sincerely, passionately committed to the gospel of Jesus Christ as that is conveyed to us through the inspired narratives of the Bible"; cited in Roger E. Olson, *How to Be Evangelical without Being Conservative* (Grand Rapids: Zondervan, 2008), 13; a more widely used definition is that of Bebbington's four characteristics of conversionism, activism, biblicism, and crucicentrism in D. W. Bebbington, *Evangelicalism in Modern Britain: A History from the 1730s to the 1980s* (London: Unwin Hyman, 1989), 3; although note the critique in Brian Harris, 'Beyond Bebbington: The Quest for Evangelical Identity in a Postmodern Era', *Churchman* 122, no. 3 (2008): 201–19; the term should be distinguished from fundamentalist as argued in 'British Evangelicals Are Not Fundamentalists', Religion & Society Research, 19 July 2012, http://www.religionandsociety.org.uk/research_findings/featured_findings/british_evangelicals_are_not_fundamentalists.

doctorate in practical theology "designed to meet the specific needs of a professional group [. . .] and which develops the capability of individuals to work within a professional context."[3] The contribution to knowledge comes from the development of my capacity to respond to this context-specific need.[4]

In this introduction I outline the motivation and rationale for the project. Part of that rationale is an outline of my own context as a tutor and lecturer to evangelical students of applied theology, and my interest in the intelligent design argument. It provides the contextual basis for why this question is important for me to research. The motivation for the study derives from the concerns from students' ministries (discussed more fully below), and this context locates an area for evaluation: did the students benefit from the changes I made in my practice? The research project was a way of engaging with evangelical Christian students to gain an understanding from them of how a change in my professional practice as a theology lecturer at an evangelical college might address a student concern raised from the context of their ministries. The responses of those I interviewed point towards the research having a broader relevance, and the methods used might therefore be relatable to others as a way of responding to similar concerns.[5] It is recognized that there is no neutral point of observation, and that as a participant in the research project I have inevitably influenced the outcomes.

The thesis was complex and developed my capacity as a researcher in areas outside of my expertise.[6] I benefitted from the input of various seminar discussions on methods and methodologies for guiding me through the process of conceptualizing and articulating the research process. One important learning point was to focus on the right voices. Priority was given to the voices of those participating in the research, and they provided the content upon which to reflect theologically. It was also important to bring my own theological evaluations as an expression of the values of the professional context in which the study was done. In

---

3. S. Hoddell, *Professional Doctorates* (Staffordshire: UK Council for Graduate Education, 2002), 62; cited in T. A. Maxwell, 'Philosophy and Practice–Why Does This Matter?', in *Methodologies for Practice Research: Approaches for Professional Doctorates*, ed. Carol Costley and John Fulton (London: SAGE, 2019), 5.

4. Maxwell, 6.

5. David Kember, *Action Learning and Action Research: Improving the Quality of Teaching and Learning* (London: Routledge, 2000), 35.

6. Maxwell, 'Philosophy and Practice—Why Does This Matter?', 5.

this way the literature that I interact with throughout the thesis can be extended.

The nature of the discussion is academic and transdisciplinary. Consequently, the way in which the research is structured needed to be carefully considered. As Costley says, the "'turn' towards practice-based research calls for a new relationship between theory and practice."[7] The topics to consider, she argues, include "awareness of the research aims," "an imperative to communicate results of the research to non-academic audiences," "transdiciplinarity," "criticality," an awareness of the position of the researcher, and the "ethics, values, trust and power" associated with the researcher, the organization and participants in the research.[8]

ACTION RESEARCH AND THE RESEARCH QUESTION

The research question ("To what extent, if at all, does teaching intelligent design to evangelical students contribute to their confidence and ability to share their faith?") developed over time. The start of the process was instinctive and unrefined. As Dick argues, this is quite common: "[a]n action research study can begin with quite imprecise research questions."[9] McNiff considers that it need not even begin with a hypothesis, but just an "idea." "The research process is the developmental process of following through the idea, seeing how it goes, and continually checking whether it is in line with what you wish to happen."[10]

McNiff and Whitehead argue that, for it to count as action research, the question should begin with "how do I . . . "[11] They argue that the researcher must be at the centre of the research. This is consistent with their preferred "living theory" approach to research.[12] "In living theory

---

7. Carol Costley, 'Research Approaches in Professional Doctorates: Notes on an Epistemology of Practice', in *Methodologies for Practice Research: Approaches for Professional Doctorates*, ed. Carol Costley and John Fulton (London: SAGE, 2019), 30.

8. These topics are drawn from a bulleted list in Costley, 30.

9. Bob Dick, 'Action Research: Action and Research', in *Doing Good Action Research* (Southern Cross University, 2002), 5.

10. Jean McNiff, 'Action Research for Professional Development', 2002, 6, http://www.jeanmcniff.com/ar-booklet.asp.

11. Jean McNiff and Jack Whitehead, *All You Need to Know about Action Research* (London: SAGE, 2006), 8.

12. Jack Whitehead, 'Living Theories', in *The SAGE Encyclopedia of Action Research*, ed. David Coghlan and Mary Brydon-Miller (London: SAGE, 2014).

approaches researchers focus on themselves and their own learning."[13] Other kinds of questions (and they list questions that have quantitative expectations such as "Is there a relationship between room temperature and degree of concentration?") are not considered appropriate as "they produce answers about quantity" rather than focusing on quality.[14]

Norton argues for a broadening of what counts as action research. She gives several examples of action research questions within higher educational contexts that focus on students and are different to McNiff and Whitehead's approach, such as "Are there any problems about using journals for your psychology essays?"[15] Norton argues that students expressing their concerns about problems they are having is a valid starting position for an action research project: it "fit[s] very comfortably with the action research model of professionals starting from practical questions that are embedded within their working context."[16] My decision to use Norton's pedagogical action research is discussed in the methodology chapter below.[17]

The research question for this project fits Denscombe's third type (listed in Bryman) that evaluates an experience or event as in "does y exhibit the benefits that it is claimed to have?"[18] In this thesis, the experience was teaching intelligent design to evangelical students, and the evaluation was initially in terms of the effectiveness of the intervention in bringing about the desired effects of increased student confidence and ability in sharing their faith and, later on, in terms of how such qualitative research, interdisciplinary dialogue, and theological reflection (using a model of practical theology) has transformed and developed my own professional practice. Costley argues that professional doctorates are suited to the kind of study that is situated in contexts of application "where theory can be drawn out of practice."[19]

---

13. Jean McNiff and Jack Whitehead, *Action Research: Principles and Practice*, 2nd ed. (London; New York: RoutledgeFalmer, 2002), 89.

14. McNiff and Whitehead, 86.

15. Lin Norton, *Action Research in Teaching and Learning: A Practical Guide to Conducting Pedagogical Research in Universities* (London: Routledge, 2009), 74.

16. Norton, 78.

17. Norton, *Action Research in Teaching and Learning*.

18. Alan Bryman, *Social Research Methods*, 4th ed (Oxford: Oxford University Press, 2012), 9.

19. Costley, 'Research Approaches in Professional Doctorates: Notes on an Epistemology of Practice', 23.

Key issues for professional doctorates are that a widening concept of knowledge is understood as emanating from, developed in and providing change for professional contexts. Professional doctorates provide a way of addressing knowledge that is to an extent outside disciplinary cultures and can offer alternative views and values that have resonance with practice, thereby engaging higher education more coherently with learning at work.[20]

DEVELOPMENT OF THE RESEARCH QUESTION

Action research begins with identifying a problem to consider, or an issue to address. It is "something that catches one's eye or ear, arousing interest and curiosity."[21] The stimulus for the research project was expressed concerns from students in tutorials or during lectures of science being used as a reason why some of those they minister to or grew up with rejected Christianity. One student reported how some young people in a group he led asked how he could still believe in God if he knew about the Big Bang.[22] Several students experienced the topic of science as problematic for others in terms of coming to faith as a Christian or associated with a decline in faith or affiliation to church particularly within the millennial and gen-Z generations. There was an espoused sense of congruency between their belief in God and their understanding of science (seen in student comments such as "God created everything, so science is just the study of what God made") but their enacted theory was that science was a problem to young believers, seen in their practice of encouraging young people to "put their faith in God instead of in science."[23] One student explained that his A-level Religious Studies teacher believed that "science

---

20. Costley, 29.

21. Norton, *Action Research in Teaching and Learning*, 4.

22. For similar narrative accounts in youth ministry, see Andrew Root, *Exploding Stars, Dead Dinosaurs, and Zombies: Youth Ministry in the Age of Science* (Minneapolis: Fortress, 2018).

23. Personal comments to me from tutees. For the use of Schön's terms, see Jan Fook, 'Reflective Models and Frameworks in Practice', in *Methodologies for Practice Research: Approaches for Professional Doctorates*, ed. Carol Costley and John Fulton (London: SAGE, 2019), 61; Zoë Bennett et al., *Invitation to Research in Practical Theology* (Abingdon; New York: Routledge, 2018), 36.

disproves religion and gave demons as an example of a biblical idea which for her had been disproved by science."[24]

The initial assumptions in conducting the research included the belief that students were intelligent communicators of the Gospel, and that the difficulties they faced in certain ministry situations were not due to their lack of love for neighbour, lack of understanding of their own faith, or lack of ability to share their understanding. In many other encounters they were able to share their faith confidently and effectively.

Initially, my intention was a pragmatic one, namely to try something that might work to address the presenting problem from the student body: "there is a concern with applications—what works—and solutions to problems."[25] As the process of listening to the students continued, and as I reflected upon both their reactions to the changes implemented and my own sense of involvement, I began to develop a greater sense of these changes being transformative.[26] What began as a hunch and "giving it a go" developed into a theologically-rich reflection resulting in transformed praxis. As Bennett et al. write, "the hallmark of a genuine epiphany is that the person who "sees" must themselves make a move."[27]

One approach to this research would be to reflect upon the meanings that students made of the problems they encountered. Qualitative research (and indeed practical theology) can be done simply through carrying out a narrative description of a situation.[28] That descriptive task could also be undertaken from an explicitly theological perspective using one of several theological reflective methods.[29] However, appropriate for a professional doctorate, my aim was not simply to understand the situation deeply, but to change it.[30] As Kember puts it, "Understanding a

24. Personal correspondence from one of my tutees.

25. John W. Creswell and J. David Creswell, *Research Design: Qualitative, Quantitative, and Mixed Methods Approaches*, Fifth edition (London: SAGE, 2018), 48.

26. Creswell and Creswell, 46–47.

27. Bennett et al., *Invitation to Research in Practical Theology*, 31.

28. D. Jean Clandinin and F. Michael Connelly, *Narrative Inquiry: Experience and Story in Qualitative Research* (San Francisco: Jossey-Bass, 2000); see also Jane Leach, 'Pastoral Theology as Attention', *Contact* 153 (2007): 19–32; although note the argument in Andy Wier, 'From the Descriptive to the Normative: Towards a Practical Theology of the Charismatic-Evangelical Urban Church', *Ecclesial Practices* 4, no. 1 (17 May 2017): 112–32, https://doi.org/10.1163/22144471–00401002.

29. Elaine L. Graham, Heather Walton, and Frances Ward, *Theological Reflection: Methods* (London: SCM, 2005).

30. Inevitably, putting things this way echoes Marx's critique of philosophy. See

problem, through interpretive work, can be a useful step but solving the problem requires action."[31] This coheres with Norton's understanding of a good starting point for educational action research.

> In the case of educational quality enhancement through action research, the topic is something of interest to the teacher so there is motivation for them to conduct the study. The topic can be some innovation they feel is worth introducing into their teaching. It can be a problem they want to solve or an issue they want to tackle. It can often be a concern that they have been aware of for some time, but which has lain dormant because they were unsure how to tackle it.[32]

Although the focus of the research is a change in my professional practice introducing a form of action research in pursuance of my own Christian values, that, of course, does not mean that the action research cannot have more than one dimension. Chandler and Torbert outline the various possible dimensions of action research. Far from narrowing the focus, they argue for a plurality of foci when doing action research, and that identifying more than one dimension to one's research is a sign of strength of the project. Their proposal is that "including more of the 27 types of research as part of any given project, organizational design or institutional procedure will improve eventual outcomes."[33] They argue that action research "aims not only to understand past events, but also present phenomena, particularly the ongoing dynamics of human interactions in which one is a participant, as well as future intentions and the forward design of joint organizing."[34] Aspects of their multi-dimensional approach is seen in my own first-person reflections and evaluations, the second-person voices and reflections of intersubjective participants, and the constant interaction with the formal voices of appropriate literature as a form of validity testing.[35] This reflective research process considers

---

Bryan S. Turner, 'Introduction: A New Agenda for Social Theory?', in *The New Blackwell Companion to Social Theory*, ed. Bryan S. Turner, Blackwell Companions to Sociology (Chichester: Wiley-Blackwell, 2009), 4.

31. Kember, *Action Learning and Action Research*, 21.

32. Kember, 24–25.

33. Dawn Chandler and Bill Torbert, 'Transforming Inquiry and Action: Interweaving 27 Flavors of Action Research', *Action Research* 1, no. 2 (October 2003): 135, https://doi.org/10.1177/14767503030012002.

34. Chandler and Torbert, 134.

35. Chandler and Torbert, 139–42.

the past context, the present interaction of second-person action taken, and the forward dimension of planning and anticipating (or what Coleman describes as "for me," "for us," and "for them").[36]

REFLECTIVE PRACTICE AND REFLEXIVITY

A key question to reflect upon was the extent to which I might be imposing my own values on to the college and students, a concern addressed through reflexivity. Fook provides an integrated definition combining both reflection and reflexivity as being:

> initiated by a process of unearthing and examining deeply held assumptions embedded in experience, in order to redevelop the meaning of this experience and reformulate new guiding principles (more congruent with fundamental values) for practice. This in turn should enable a more ethical and compassionate engagement with the social world.[37]

Bryman notes that "reflexivity is a notoriously slippery concept" that is often associated with postmodern epistemologies and with a "greater awareness and acknowledgement of the role of the researcher as part and parcel of the construction of knowledge."[38] He offers a brief critique of the concept and identifies Lynch's term "methodological reflexivity" as most appropriate for social research.[39] This view of reflexivity encourages the researcher to be aware of assumptions, sources of bias, and concepts such as positionality or standpoints to ensure that the researcher is self-conscious about decisions taken and interpretations made. Reflexivity of this kind is seen especially in the evaluation stages of the action research cycles and the Sagely Wisdom phase of Osmer's model of practical theology.

Issues discussed during supervisory sessions included the risk that I might use intelligent design to argue for a particular (evangelical)

36. Gill Coleman, 'Action Research', in *Methodologies for Practice Research: Approaches for Professional Doctorates*, ed. Carol Costley and John Fulton (London: SAGE, 2019), 159.

37. Fook, 'Reflective Models and Frameworks in Practice', 64.

38. Bryman, *Social Research Methods*, 394.

39. Lynch identifies six broad categories and several subcategories of the term; for "methodological reflexivity," see Michael Lynch, 'Against Reflexivity as an Academic Virtue and Source of Privileged Knowledge', *Theory, Culture & Society* 17, no. 3 (1 June 2000): 29, https://doi.org/10.1177/02632760022051202.

theological position, and whether my position as a lecturer in theology provided motivation to raise the status of theology over against its scientific rivals in the academic hierarchy. The history of the debates between theology and science have often been framed in terms of ridicule or redundancy (such as the way the Huxley and Wilberforce debate was reported, or the way that the 1960's film *Inherit the Wind* portrayed the arguments presented in the Scopes Trial). Through my own educational journey from studying physics to studying theology I encountered several instances of such a reaction. However, the research supervision process helped me to maintain a clear motivation for the project as primarily educational with the aim of supporting the students in the college.

Reflexivity on my position in college included an awareness of comparing my own view with how my colleagues engaged the students with concepts of science. Any such comparison or analysis becomes political within an organization, and it was important to reflect on tensions that might arise through my research.[40] The debate with respect to science over the interpretation of Genesis features in a level 5 doctrine assessment where students are encouraged to demonstrate awareness of the scientific significance of different interpretative stances towards Genesis. The suggested reading included a range of texts on the interpretation of Genesis from those advocating a creationist position (such as Paul Nelson) to those reading Genesis through a theistic evolutionary lens (such as Howard J. Van Till).[41] However, the primary focus of the assessment question is hermeneutical and theological, appropriate for a doctrine module assessment, and an understanding of the science associated with, for instance, evolution or the age of the earth was not necessary. Student responses oriented around decisions about the inspiration of Scripture, divine accommodation to ancient culture, and the relationship of history to typology. Students' critical reflections were directed towards their presuppositions concerning the authority of Scripture for preaching and how that might affect their doctrine of humanity being created in the image of God. In conversation with my colleague who teaches this module it was established that my intention to teach intelligent design would not be perceived as a challenge to his approach to teaching the subject,

---

40. David Coghlan and Teresa Brannick, *Doing Action Research in Your Own Organization*, 2nd ed. (London: SAGE, 2005), 70–71.

41. See, for example, J. P. Moreland and John Mark Reynolds, eds., *Three Views on Creation and Evolution*, Counterpoints (Grand Rapids: Zondervan, 1999).

and I received encouragement to pursue my research topic from all my colleagues.

My aim as a researcher-teacher was to address the student-led concern about science through education and to find an opportunity to teach science to my students in a relevant and constructive manner. As well as meeting modular learning outcomes, my role is to equip future Christian ministers and leaders to impact the church and the world,[42] and the educational good of teaching at an applied theology college includes equipping students to engage with the people that they serve, in this case regarding their concerns with science.[43] My reflection on the way the college encouraged students' critical engagement with science was as mediated through prior theological discussions on Scripture. Debates were presented from different Christian perspectives, and the scope of the discussion tended towards how these different positions could still fall within an evangelical remit. It did not, in my view, address the concerns of the way science is experienced as a problem within a ministry context. It fell short, it seemed to me, of "raising their consciousness or advancing an agenda for change to improve their lives."[44] Responding to the perception of science as a problem required a conceptual approach to the topic and a strategy to implement change: it meant "transforming the abstract theory into concrete action plans and then acting in the direction the theory leads and producing accounts of practice to show how the critique enabled them to implement change towards improvement."[45]

McNiff and Whitehead raise the issue of whose voice should be heard; those researched or those doing the research?[46] They point to the problem of power dynamics "as to who is regarded as a legitimate knower, whose practice is to be studied, and whose knowledge counts."[47] They typify the power problem as being between reluctant "elites who like to keep things

42. 'Our Values—Moorlands College', accessed 17 April 2019, https://www.moorlands.ac.uk/our-values/.

43. For an excellent discussion of the good in education see Paul Gibbs, 'Is Higher Education Inherently Good, Educative Practices Intrinsically Good and Universities Instrumentally Good? What Should We Hope For?', in *Higher Education and Hope*, ed. Paul Gibbs and Andrew Peterson (London: Palgrave Macmillan, 2019), 224–32.

44. Creswell and Creswell, *Research Design*, 47.

45. McNiff and Whitehead, *Action Research*, 34.

46. McNiff and Whitehead, 32.

47. McNiff and Whitehead, 33.

that way" and claims to democracy as a "moral commitment."[48] Following the third of Habermas' typology of research, McNiff and Whitehead advocate the use of research where people learn how to change by first learning to understand their social situation. "People could not comment on their experience unless they understood how that experience was shaped by their own situatedness."[49] They could not be free, McNiff and Whitehead argue, until they become aware of the "historical and cultural forces which had influenced them."[50] This research project followed their advice by attempting to locate the relationship between science and religion within its theoretical and social context, and by attending carefully to the voices of those participating in the research. Indicators of success would include the extent to which (if at all) participants felt they had experienced some measure of empowerment in the way they related to the those they ministered to. That is, in keeping with the research question, did those participating in the research feel more confident in sharing their Christian faith with others in ministry contexts?

SUMMARY

This first chapter introduced the research question, the motivation for studying it, and the professional context in which it was to be studied. It discussed some aspects of positionality within my working environment and has shown why the question has not been adequately addressed already. It has introduced some initial reflexive questions and given some defence of why it was appropriate to address the problem through action research. The next chapter locates the relationship between science and theology within a broader academic context with a view to identifying why teaching intelligent design was a suitable response to the problem identified.

48. McNiff and Whitehead, 32–33.
49. McNiff and Whitehead, 33.
50. McNiff and Whitehead, 33.

2

Science and Theology

It is the full-blooded metaphysical question of whether science could in any circumstances accept the intervention of God. Is science of its very nature anti-theistic?[1]

IN THIS CHAPTER I discuss the relationship between science and faith and the reasons for choosing intelligent design as a response to the student need identified in the last chapter. What is intelligent design and how does it relate to other Christian understandings of science? Why did I decide to teach the intelligent design argument to evangelical students? I have indicated my own interest and involvement in the introduction and this chapter gives a rationale for choosing to teach intelligent design in the college. It provides the background theory to the question of whether intelligent design is a proper subject to teach, and how it relates to other, more established, approaches to the subject of the relationship of science to theology.[2] It also locates intelligent design philosophically along a spectrum of positions relating science with theology, and provides justification for using it as the teaching content of the pedagogical action research model followed.

1. Roger Trigg, *Rationality and Religion: Does Faith Need Reason?* (Oxford: Blackwell, 1998), 79.
2. Bryman, *Social Research Methods*, 23.

PARADIGMS OF SCIENCE AND THEOLOGY

Teaching intelligent design to Christian evangelical students is situated within a dispute between the disciplines of science and religion. Many today hold that science and the Christian faith are inevitably in conflict. The topic of Darwinian evolution is a focus for that conflict because of its competing claims about God's involvement in the creation of life and the question of origins. This conflict was famously illustrated in the debate between Wilberforce and Huxley in Oxford in 1860 at the thirtieth annual meeting of the British Association for the Advancement of Science when, in answer to Wilberforce's demeaning point about his opponent's ape ancestry, Huxley is reported to have replied:

> If then the question is put to me whether I would rather have a miserable ape for a grandfather or a man highly endowed by nature and possessed of great means of influence and yet employs these faculties and that influence for the mere purpose of introducing ridicule into a grave scientific discussion, I unhesitatingly affirm my preference for the ape.[3]

It is worth noting, however, that Rev Wilberforce was himself a Fellow of the Royal Society and had written that his opposition to Darwin's ideas came "solely on scientific grounds."[4] He insisted it was insufficient to simply deny Darwin's arguments on the grounds that it contradicted Scripture.

An important work on "Ways of Relating Science and Theology" was by Barbour.[5] His fourfold categorization (conflict, independence, dialogue and integration) has been the basis for many others, including the model used below.[6] A similar fivefold typology relating religion with culture came from Niebuhr's five classifications.[7] These two approach-

3. 'The Great Debate', Oxford University Museum of Natural History, accessed 20 July 2020, https://oumnh.ox.ac.uk/great-debate.

4. For further information, see 'The Great Debate' published by the Oxford University Museum of Natural History, www.oum.ox.ac.uk/learning/pdfs/debate.pdf, accessed 20/1/2019.

5. Ian G. Barbour, 'Ways of Relating Science and Theology', in *Physics, Philosophy, and Theology: A Common Quest for Understanding*, ed. Robert J. Russell, William R. Stoeger, and George V. Coyne (Vatican: Vatican Observatory, 1988), 21–48.

6. See his chapter 1, Ways of Relating Science and Religion, Ian G. Barbour, *Religion in an Age of Science* (London: SCM, 1990); this is helpfully found online at https://www.religion-online.org/book/religion-in-an-age-of-science/.

7. H. Richard Niebuhr, *Christ and Culture* (San Francisco: Harper, 1951).

es were developed by Murphy into equivalent expressions for the relationship of theology with science.[8] Tenneson, Bundrick, and Stanford,
building on Barbour and Murphy's work,[9] have surveyed eight other
contemporary schemes of relating science to theology and developed a
well-tested model that has been used extensively as a way of identifying
the attitudes and stances people hold on this topic, and I have structured
my discussion of where teaching intelligent design is located using their
paradigms.[10] I give reflexive comments below as to how my understanding of what I am doing relates to them. Their five paradigms are:

1. Conflict: Science over Theology

2. Conflict: Theology over Science

3. Compartmentalism

4. Complementarism

5. Concordism

Conflict

Harvard psychologist Stephen Pinker epitomized the first conflict paradigm in a well-quoted claim:

> To begin with, the findings of science entail that the belief sys-
> tems of all the world's traditional religions and cultures—their
> theories of the origins of life, humans, and societies—are fac-
> tually mistaken. [. . .] We know that the laws governing the
> physical world (including accidents, disease, and other misfor-
> tunes) have no goals that pertain to human well-being. There is
> no such thing as fate, providence, karma, spells, curses, augury,
> divine retribution, or answered prayers . . . In other words,

8. See Michael Tenneson, David R. Bundrick, and Matthew S. Stanford, 'A New
Survey Instrument and its Findings for Relating Science and Theology', *Perspectives
on Science and Christian Faith* 67, no. 3 (September 2015): 220n11 where they cite
Murphy's typology but with their classifications. 'a. *Theology requires the rejection of
science where the two conflict. b. Science requires the rejection of theology where they
conflict. c. Theology subsumes science. d. Science and theology are separate. e. Theology
affects science.*'

9. Nancey Murphy, 'A Niebuhrian Typology for the Relation of Theology to Science', *Pacific Theological Review* XVIII, no. 3 (1985): 16–23.

10. Tenneson, Bundrick, and Stanford, 'A New Survey Instrument and its Findings
for Relating Science and Theology', 205.

the worldview that guides the moral and spiritual values of an educated person today is the worldview given to us by science. Though the scientific facts do not by themselves dictate values, they certainly hem in the possibilities. By stripping ecclesiastical authority of its credibility on factual matters, they cast doubt on its claims to certitude in matters of morality.[11]

Pinker defines his position as "scientism" and argues that it is the only reasonable view for an intelligent, informed person to hold.[12] A similar stance is taken by the cosmologist Krauss in opposing the possibility of theological values impinging on public life. He refers to the "fact that religion and science are often in conflict."[13]

> It's ironic, really, that so many people are fixated on the relationship between science and religion: basically, there isn't one. In my more than 30 years as a practicing physicist, I have never heard the word "God" mentioned in a scientific meeting. Belief or nonbelief in God is irrelevant to our understanding of the workings of nature.[14]

Coyne and Dawkins both frame the relationship between science and religion as being in conflict and typify Tenneson et al.'s first conflict paradigm of Science over Theology. Coyne argues it is not simply a clash of competing worldviews but "a war between rationality and superstition."[15] Dawkins likewise suggests that anyone making concessions towards religion is emulating Neville Chamberlain.[16] Coyne insists that the existence of scientists who are Christians does not demonstrate that these two ways of understanding the world are compatible. "Scientists of faith happen to

11. Steven Pinker, 'Science is Not Your Enemy', *The New Republic*, 7 August 2013, https://newrepublic.com/article/114127/science-not-enemy-humanities.

12. A similar understanding of the term is commonly found in UK schools: see Berry Billingsley, 'Teaching and Learning about Epistemic Insight', *School Science Review* 98, no. 365 (2017): 61.

13. Lawrence M. Krauss, 'All Scientists Should Be Militant Atheists', *The New Yorker*, 8 September 2015, https://www.newyorker.com/news/news-desk/all-scientists-should-be-militant-atheists.

14. Krauss.

15. Jerry A. Coyne, *Faith versus Fact: Why Science and Religion Are Incompatible* (New York: Penguin, 2015), xii.

16. Richard Dawkins, *The God Delusion* (London: Bantam, 2006), 67.

be the ones who can compartmentalize two incompatible worldviews in their heads."[17]

The second conflict view, Theology over Science, is sustained, Clague argues, by those who oppose what he calls "conventional science" because of their belief that "the Bible is an accurate scientific and historical document."[18] He suggests that biblical literalists draw support for their view by highlighting attacks on religion by Dawkins or Hitchens as a way of attracting support for a literalist view of Genesis. They augment this conflict approach by putting forward "superficially plausible alternative scenarios that are compatible with validity of the literal account of creation in Genesis."[19] Clague draws attention to the similar tactics of the militant atheist and biblical literalist, calling them "comrades-in-arms" because they draw strength from each other's opposition.

The conflict paradigms described above do not represent a majority position of those actively engaged in scientific research, as evidenced by the scientific data on the beliefs of scientists in academia. In a landmark study published in the *Journal for the Scientific Study of Religion*, Ecklund, Park and Sorrell argue that, of 275 "natural and social scientists at the top twenty one US research universities," most do not frame the relationship between religion and science as being "in conflict."[20] In a similar study including UK scientists, Ecklund et al. conclude that the idea that scientists see science and religion in simple opposition is not sustainable.

> In contrast to the pervasive conflict narrative, which assumes that science and religion are intrinsically in tension with one another, it is striking that a substantial majority of physicists and biologists in the eight regional contexts studied do not adhere to this view. The conflict thesis would posit that most scientists would characterize the science-religion relationship as one of conflict and take the side of science, yet the UK and the US are the only nations where support for this view approaches one-third of scientists.[21]

17. Coyne, *Faith versus Fact*, 14.

18. Alan Clague, 'Militant Atheism and Biblical Literalism: Comrades-in-Arms for Promotion of Disharmony between the Science and Theology of Creation', *Pacifica* 23, no. 1 (1 February 2010): 85, https://doi.org/10.1177/1030570X1002300105.

19. Clague, 86.

20. Elaine Howard Ecklund, Jerry Z. Park, and Katherine L. Sorrell, 'Scientists Negotiate Boundaries Between Religion and Science', *Journal for the Scientific Study of Religion* 50, no. 3 (2011): 552.

21. Elaine Howard Ecklund et al., 'Religion among Scientists in International

I have never been persuaded by either of the conflict views, although they are commonly represented by science writers. Having gained a degree in physics, I understood very well the interest and creativity associated with scientific study and felt little of the sense of conflict described above. However, as mentioned above, many of my students experienced responses in their ministry contexts that assumed just such a conflict, and it provided part of the motivation for my research.

Compartmentalism

These conflict views contrast with the more amenable "live and let live" approach such as Stephen J. Gould's widely adopted Non-Overlapping Magisteria position (often termed NOMA) understood as a truce between the disciplines.[22] This stance corresponds to Tenneson et al.'s compartmentalism paradigm: theology should be excluded from any discussion of science not because they are in conflict but because the two disciplines are "logically distinct and fully separate."[23] Once it is recognized that nature has nothing to do with moral truth, Gould argues, religious people are free to have moral discussion "on our own terms,"[24] by which he means without appeal to any scientific authority.

David Wilkinson, a Methodist minister and Fellow of the Royal Astronomical Society, illustrates this compartmentalist approach in opposing the simplistic conflict models of science and theology. Wilkinson critiques the philosophy of the new atheists as being "dominated by the conflict model of science and religion, and a reductionism which believes that science can explain everything."[25] Christian apologetics are needed to defend Christianity from "the work of Richard Dawkins and his fellow new atheists and the sleight of hand which couples science with atheism."[26] Apologetics, he argues, operates at the level of implica-

Context: A New Study of Scientists in Eight Regions', *Socius: Sociological Research for a Dynamic World* 2 (31 August 2016): 5, https://doi.org/10.1177/2378023116664353.

22. Stephen Jay Gould, *Rocks of Ages: Science and Religion in the Fullness of Life.* (New York: Random House, 1999), 65.

23. Gould, 59.

24. Stephen Jay Gould, 'Nonoverlapping Magisteria', *Natural History* 106 (March 1997): 22.

25. David Wilkinson, *Science and Apologetics: How Can We Defend Our Faith in the Light of Modern Science?*, Thinking About . . . (Christians in Science, n.d.), 2.

26. Wilkinson, 2.

tions and interpretations. Wilkinson warns of reducing the apologetic approach to that of rational engagement alone because it "does not represent Christian faith."[27] God is not the kind of thing to be proved like a mathematical theorem. Instead, what is needed are "pointers to a deeper story of the universe, and an invitation to talk some more."[28]

McGrath also takes a nuanced approach within this compartmentalist category. Although he recognizes that a "general anti-theistic worldview [. . . is] widespread in scientific culture and beyond,"[29] he thinks less about separate and equal spheres of interest and more in terms of the limitation of scientific enquiry and the need to go "beyond" the natural world to answer the deep and fundamental questions of life. He cites with approval Einstein's rejection of "an irreconcilable conflict between knowledge and belief" and agrees with him that humanity needs more than what the scientific method can offer.[30] In his 2014 Boyle lecture, McGrath argues that science cannot explain everything and that, by its own nature, it has limits. New Atheism, he argues, "takes a strongly positivist view of science, holding that it explains (or has the potential to explain) everything [. . .] and only the scientific explanation can be valid."[31] The real issue, he argues, was a discussion within science and about the methodology of science: it "is not about 'science versus religion', although it suits the purposes and agendas of some to present it as such, [but instead] is fundamentally about competing interpretations of science, and diverging applications of the scientific method."[32]

McGrath draws from Polkinghorne's use of multiple levels of explanation, where a scientific explanation is seen only to go so far (typically answering the "how?" question) and another domain of reasoning is needed to answer the "why?" question.[33] The example given is the physi-

27. Wilkinson, 2.

28. Wilkinson, 5.

29. Alister E. McGrath, 'A Blast from the Past?: The Boyle Lectures and Natural Theology', *Science & Christian Belief* 17, no. 1 (2005): 26.

30. Alister E. McGrath, *Enriching Our Vision of Reality: Theology and the Natural Sciences in Dialogue* (London: SPCK, 2016), 8–9 citing Albert Einstein, *Ideas and Opinions* (New York: Crown, 1954), 41–9.

31. Alister E. McGrath, 'New Atheism—New Apologetics: The Use of Science in Recent Christian Apologetic Writings', Boyle Lecture (St Mary-le-Bow, Cheapside, 2014), 6.

32. McGrath, 2.

33. Polkinghorne writes "Science has achieved its great success precisely by bracketing out questions of meaning, value and purpose and limiting itself solely to the

cal account of "how" the convection of water in a heated kettle leads to a change of phase producing steam, whereas the "why" question can explain that the kettle was boiling in order to make a cup of tea. By analogy, the two levels of explanation, science and religion, are not competing but rather complement each other: "friends, not foes."[34] McGrath is critical of Gould's NOMA terminology and suggests the term POMA (Partially Overlapping Magisteria) because of his experience of "cross-fertilization" of methods and subjects.[35] But it is still the language of complementarity between the disciplines that governs the way the relationship is framed: he cites Collins saying that "the principles of faith are [. . .] complementary with the principles of science."[36] Or, in McGrath's own words, "[s]cience dismantles the world so that we can see how things work; the Christian faith reassembles them so we can see what they mean."[37]

McGrath sets out his concerns in his Boyle lecture. The problem he sees is that the New Atheists have "set the terms of the debate" as being the rationality (and morality) of Christianity.[38] In responding to them, Christian apologists (and he includes himself) have unhelpfully accepted that Christianity should be defended in those term resulting in it being perceived as "excessively rational, lacking any real concern for beauty (to mention one obvious point)."[39]

As a historian of theology, McGrath sees the intelligent design movement as recapitulating the failed strategy of those seventeenth- and early eighteenth-century Boyle lectures (upon which his own 2014 Boyle lecture is a reflection). Initially intended as a "confutation of atheism," they became a "liability" to the Christian faith and led, in the end, towards "atheism, heresy or agnosticism, rather than to authentic Christian

---

question of the processes by which things happen." J. C. Polkinghorne, *Science and Religion in Quest of Truth* (New Haven; London: Yale University Press, 2011), 70.

34. McGrath, 'New Atheism—New Apologetics: The Use of Science in Recent Christian Apologetic Writings', 6.

35. Alister E. McGrath, *The Dawkins Delusion?: Atheist Fundamentalism and the Denial of the Divine* (London: SPCK, 2007), 18.

36. Francis S. Collins, *The Language of God: A Scientist Presents Evidence for Belief* (London: Pocket Books, 2007), 6; cited in; McGrath, *The Dawkins Delusion?*, 19.

37. McGrath, *Enriching Our Vision of Reality*, 14.

38. Alister E. McGrath, 'New Atheism—New Apologetics: The Use of Science in Recent Christian Apologetic Writings', *Science & Christian Belief* 26, no. 2 (October 2014): 112.

39. McGrath, 112; McGrath believes his rebuttal of Dawkins was overly cognitive in its approach. See McGrath, *The Dawkins Delusion?*

faith."[40] The reason for this decline in efficacy was, McGrath argues, that
the argument from natural theology pointed towards Deism, rather than
supporting the "specifics" of the Christian faith.[41] The Newtonian view of
a mechanical solar system tended to pull away from the Christian belief
in an immanent God towards one of the distant watchmaker and, eventually, the complete absence of God. Paley's natural theology was accused of
being a "false gospel" by John Henry Newman for taking the focus away
from orthodox Christianity and on to notions of contrivance in nature.[42]

McGrath argues that the rise of Darwinism has meant that clas-
sical approaches to apologetics have been undermined and are now
self-defeating.

> So my concern, broadly stated, is this: in developing a natural
> theology along the lines of the original Boyle lectures, are we
> just making life more difficult for Christian belief in today's
> very different situation? Have we created something that may
> achieve short-term gains, yet prove destructive in the longer
> term? To put this in a much more focused way: does a natural
> theology which makes an appeal to God's wisdom, perfection or
> goodness end up making the existence of imperfections within
> nature a disconfirmation of faith, where once it was little more
> than an anomaly or puzzle? And does not the Darwinian ac-
> count of natural selection highlight the suffering, destructive-
> ness and wastefulness of the natural order?[43]

In this he is following Haught's argument that any "Paleyesque"
design argument towards God's goodness and providence is countered
by the moral implications of what he calls the "Darwinian recipe."[44] The
kind of natural theology that argued for God's goodness from evidence
of design in nature, based on a shared common sense approach, is seen
by McGrath to be "problematic" in the light of Darwinian evolution.[45]

40. McGrath, 'A Blast from the Past?: The Boyle Lectures and Natural Theology',
28.

41. McGrath, 27.

42. J. H. Newman, *The Idea of a University* (London: Longmans, 1907), 450–454;
cited in McGrath, 29.

43. McGrath, 30.

44. McGrath, 31.

45. McGrath, 33.

Darwinism does not provide "suitable soil for a natural theology centred on intelligent design."[46]

McLeish, like McGrath, preserves the NOMA construct in arguing that science "is blind to purpose—it has no 'teleological' methodology or goals"[47] and that it "cannot articulate stories with goals and values."[48] Notions of purpose, values and teleology, he argues, are the sole preserve of theology, and design is excluded from science.[49] This position runs counter to the sciences of archaeology and forensics which routinely deal with purpose and intention.[50] McGrath wants to change the terms of the debate on to the meaning, beauty and narrative coherence that the Christian faith gives to science, something that materialism cannot offer.

Complementarism

Drawing upon critical realism, Polkinghorne argues that science and religion both explain the same reality but do so using different frames of reference.

> To put it in simple and directly personal terms, my experience as a physicist and my experience as a priest have to be capable of being held together, without compartmentalism or dishonest adjustment.[51]

46. McGrath, 32.

47. Tom McLeish, *Faith and Wisdom in Science* (Oxford: Oxford University Press, 2014), 214.

48. McLeish, 214.

49. McLeish, 214; for an example of using a design argument (fine-tuning principles) within molecular biology, see Steinar Thorvaldsen and Ola Hössjer, 'Using Statistical Methods to Model the Fine-Tuning of Molecular Machines and Systems', *Journal of Theoretical Biology* 501 (September 2020): 110352, https://doi.org/10.1016/j.jtbi.2020.110352.

50. Lucas draws the comparison between the written record and archaeological objects: "the important thing is the intention to record. The archaeological record is full of intentions." Gavin Lucas, *Understanding the Archaeological Record* (Cambridge: Cambridge University Press, 2012), 27–28; for the view that archaeology should be a materialist undertaking without recognizing human intention, see Michael J. O'Brien and R. Lee Lyman, *Applying Evolutionary Archaeology: A Systematic Approach* (New York: Kluwer Academic/Plenum, 2000), 14–15; for a response see Lucas' discussion of Hawkes's ladder; Lucas, *Understanding the Archaeological Record*, 154–55.

51. J. C. Polkinghorne, *Science and Creation: The Search for Understanding* (London: SPCK, 1988), 83.

Polkinghorne prefers the term "complementary" (Tenneson et al's fourth paradigm)[52] to describe the relationship of the mental (in which he includes the spiritual)[53] and material, analogous to the wave-particle duality of light.[54] The mental and the material are equally real and are "complementary necessities."[55]

Polkinghorne addresses at length how God acts in a physical universe whilst being true to himself. The problem is that the universe is governed by an intricate network of laws and constants whilst at the same time all physical interactions occur at the quantum (and therefore indeterminate) level. The laws are fixed, and quantum indeterminacy cannot be bypassed without nature being abrogated. Polkinghorne's complementarian approach insists that physical causes and divine causes are coterminous. God certainly acts in the world, but does so in and through "the operation of Chance and Necessity entwined at the edge of chaos."[56] His key concept is the kenotic theory where God "condescends to act as a cause among causes" rather than distinguishing between divine and natural causation.[57] This is needed to avoid the problem of divine special action in the world, the problem of God "capriciously interfering with created nature."[58] This was the significant insight of Darwinian evolution, Polkinghorne believes, namely that God "is not to be thought of as acting through acts of occasional interference in cosmic history, but is at all times the God of the whole show."[59] There is no design or purpose to detect in nature because the individual atomic and subatomic interactions have "an irrational element in their behaviour."[60]

> The view held by the majority of physicists asserts that there is no cause to be assigned to individual quantum events. It is only the overall statistical character of many events of a similar kind that the theory can predict. If that is right, it provides a

52. Tenneson, Bundrick, and Stanford, 'A New Survey Instrument and its Findings for Relating Science and Theology', 205.

53. Polkinghorne, *Science and Creation*, 91.

54. Polkinghorne, 86.

55. Polkinghorne, 92.

56. Polkinghorne, *Science and Religion in Quest of Truth*, 82.

57. J. C. Polkinghorne, 'Divine Action: Some Comments', *Science & Christian Belief* 24, no. 1 (April 2012): 32.

58. Polkinghorne, 32.

59. Polkinghorne, *Science and Religion in Quest of Truth*, 80.

60. Polkinghorne, *Science and Creation*, 41.

remarkable stopper, in terms of human knowledge, to the search for an understanding through and through.[61]

Divine action arises, he believes, from an interplay between law and chance, between information-providing patterns of behaviour in nature and the freedom given to creatures "to behave according to their natures."[62] Such divine action is seen only with the eyes of faith, because there is no ability to demarcate what is natural, what is of human, and what is of divine agency. "The acts of providence may be discernible by faith, but they will not be demonstrable by experiment."[63] Polkinghorne concedes that God performs what he calls the "radically miraculous" act of the resurrection, but even here this must not be seen as a conflict between science and theology. Instead, it is simply a manifestation of "deep aspects of that nature not discernible through normal experience."[64]

The problem of divine action is central to the argument of theistic evolution. Whatever role God might have played in creation, Peacocke argues, "it would be extremely unwise for any proponent of theism to attempt to find any gaps to be closed by the intervention of some non-natural agent, such as a god."[65] Nature is a continuum, not requiring any non-natural causes to be invoked. Various analogies are proposed for how, in fact, God still is to be considered active in the world and achieve his purposes through the laws of nature and chance events. Polkinghorne recognizes that this form of natural theology is "consistent with the spectatorial God of deism, who simply decreed the order of creation and then watches from a detached distance as its history unfolds."[66] God only acts through the "remorseless consistency and invariance of the laws of physics" and the "unpredictable eruptions of spontaneity" in the world.[67]

The problem of divine action for an understanding of the relationship between science and theology is serious and ongoing. Lloyd surveys several scientists in seeking to understand how God might answer prayer

61. Polkinghorne, 41.

62. Polkinghorne, *Science and Religion in Quest of Truth*, 84.

63. Polkinghorne, 90.

64. Polkinghorne, 96.

65. A. R. Peacocke, *Creation and the World of Science*, The Bampton Lectures (Oxford: Clarendon, 1979), 60–61.

66. Polkinghorne, *Science and Religion in Quest of Truth*, 76.

67. John F. Haught, 'Darwin and Divine Providence', *Sewanee Theological Review* 56, no. 4 (2013): 360–61.

in a non-interventionist world.[68] An extensive examination of the argument by Saunders concludes that squaring the circle between a biblical view of God's Special Divine Action (SDA) and what he calls "modern science" is unlikely.

> *In fact it is no real exaggeration to state that contemporary theology is in crisis.* As we have seen, such a wide range of doctrine is dependent on a coherent account of God's action in the world, and we simply do not have anything other than bold assertions and a belief that SDA takes place.[69]

Concordism

My evangelical perspective meant I never warmed to the theistic evolutionary presupposition that biblical theology had to adopt a closed historical continuum. Bultmann famously articulated this:

> It is impossible to use electric light and the wireless and to avail ourselves of modern medical and surgical discoveries, and at the same time to believe in the New Testament world of spirits and miracles. We may think we can manage it in our own lives, but to expect others to do so is to make the Christian faith unintelligible and unacceptable to the modern world.[70]

I attended Polkinghorne's 1993 Gifford Lecture series in Edinburgh and felt then the strain of trying to accommodate the miraculous into a quantum universe. My evangelical belief in the God who answers prayers, turns water into wine, and raises the dead struggled with Polkinghorne's "bottom-up" approach to theology. Despite his stated intention, Polkinghorne ended up with a remote and less biblical God, although his willingness to adopt less traditional approaches to theological reflection was inspiring.[71] McLeish also critiques Polkinghorne's complementarian

---

68. John B. Lloyd, 'Everyday Intervention', *Theology* 121, no. 6 (November 2018): 413–21, https://doi.org/10.1177/0040571X18794140.

69. Nicholas Saunders, *Divine Action and Modern Science* (Cambridge: Cambridge University Press, 2002), 215; emphasis original.

70. Rudolph Bultmann, 'New Testament and Mythology', in *Kerygma and Myth*, ed. H. W. Bartsch (London: SPCK, 1964), 5; cited in C. John Collins, 'How to Think about God's Action in the World', in *Theistic Evolution: A Scientific, Philosophical, and Theological Critique*, ed. J.P. Moreland et al. (Wheaton: Crossway, 2017), 660.

71. For a summary, see Jordon Hillebert, 'The Faith of a Physicist: Reflections of

approach as a third disjointed strategy that requires God to act in ways imperceptible to science.[72] Instead of adjudicating where the boundaries of domains and epistemologies lie, McLeish proposes a "theology of science" rather than separate domains of "theology and science."[73]

> We need a "theology of science" because we need a theology of everything. If we fail, then we have a theology of nothing. [. . .] Science and theology are not complementary, they are not in combat, they are not just consistent—they are "of each other."[74]

The problem lies with trying to integrate a theology of divine action as understood by the compatibilists such as Peacocke and Haught with a naturalist view of science without making "God-talk superfluous."[75] Haught thinks that theology that has not squared up to the reality of evolution. In the light of Darwin, he argues, "the face of God will inevitably appear different from before."[76] However, Leidenhag argues that theistic evolutionists should "reject" their view of natural divine causation, even though he recognizes that this would inevitably lead towards adopting a "position significantly closer to ID."[77]

Intelligent design fits well with the theology of special divine action and with evangelicalism's view of a prayer-answering, miracle-performing God. Plantinga shows that physical laws of conservation are not broken by God's acting specially in the world in the manner that the intelligent design argument suggests. The universe is not causally closed to God (alleviating the problem of conservation of energy), physical systems cannot be determined due to Heisenberg's uncertainty principle (overcoming Laplacian determinism), and there is no distinction between special and general quantum effects as all collapse outcomes can be considered as divine collapse-causation.[78] There is no physical rationale to deny divine

a Bottom-Up Thinker, John Polkinghorne', The Gifford Lectures, 1 December 2014, https://www.giffordlectures.org/books/faith-physicist-reflections-bottom-thinker.

72. McLeish, *Faith and Wisdom in Science*, 169.

73. McLeish, 170.

74. McLeish, 209.

75. Mikael Leidenhag, 'The Blurred Line between Theistic Evolution and Intelligent Design', *Zygon* 54, no. 4 (December 2019): 920, https://doi.org/10.1111/zygo.12556.

76. Haught, 'Darwin and Divine Providence', 359.

77. Leidenhag, 'The Blurred Line between Theistic Evolution and Intelligent Design', 910.

78. Alvin Plantinga, *Where the Conflict Really Lies: Science, Religion, and Naturalism* (New York: Oxford University Press, 2011), 76–121.

action of the kind that intelligent design proposes on the grounds that God would be "interfering" in his own world.[79]

The relationship between science and theology is reframed through Plantinga's work. He sees a fundamental conflict between, not theology and science, but between naturalism and science. If you are a naturalist, he asks, can you be sure that your cognitive faculties of reason and memory and perception are reliable? "I say you can't."[80] By contrast, he argues that there is deep concord (the fifth of Tenneson et al.'s paradigms) between science and Christian belief. Science provides good grounds for the existence of God in the form of fine-tuning of the cosmos and design arguments from biology: both of these, he notes, are connected with intelligent design.[81]

SCIENCE AND MEANING

Having surveyed how science and theology are commonly understood, where does intelligent design fit into the field of ideas, and what are its key features? Intelligent design arguments are commonly found within some of the authors mentioned, but not usually identified as such. Wilkinson adopts an approach common to intelligent design in evidence he presents, even though he is cautious not to frame it as a proof for God. In addressing the question "where do the scientific laws themselves come from?" he implies that naturalism has no ready explanation: "This is not a 'god of the gaps' argument as science itself assumes these laws in order to work."[82] His intra-science argument infers that neither chance nor law is an adequate answer to the question of the origin of scientific laws. The only other causal explanation is design, and therefore the existence of the laws of physics infers (by the use of the metaphor of law) a law-giver. In a similar vein, McGrath draws from the arguments of Richard Swinburne in arguing that "the capacity of science to explain itself requires explanation—and that the most economical and reliable account of this

79. The term "interference" is attributed to Bultmann's view of a historic continuum; see for instance Alvin Plantinga, 'What is "Intervention"?', *Theology and Science* 6, no. 4 (November 2008): 372, https://doi.org/10.1080/14746700802396106.

80. Plantinga, *Where the Conflict Really Lies*, 314.

81. Plantinga, 194.

82. Wilkinson, *Science and Apologetics*, 1.

explanatory capacity lies in the notion of a creator God."[83] This is not, he asserts, a god of the gaps argument because it draws from what is known, namely "the very comprehensibility of scientific and other forms of understanding," rather than from ignorance.[84] Polkinghorne also makes an impressive argument for the fine-tuning of the physical constants as evidence of divine endowment against the alternative multiverse hypothesis.[85] These inferences to the best explanation on the basis of what is known are shared by intelligent design theorists who adopt the same epistemology.

By treating science as a separate level to religion, McGrath reserves the place of meaning to a theistic metaphysics, in his case the Christian religion. Science, he claims, "can't detect meaning."[86] This claim then creates space for a theological narrative to perceive what was beyond the capacity of science and to construct our identity as "social animals."[87] Science is too limited and reality is "too complex" for one level of enquiry: "we need both a robust theology and an informed science."[88] However, McGrath's depiction of science is too limited. Scientists often present metaphysical claims as coming from the scientific data, rather than leaving it to others. Staune, in his introduction to a text on the relationship of science and meaning, points to the metaphysical claims to meaninglessness from such scientists as Steven Weinberg, Jacques Monod and Francis Crick.[89] Recognizing that this might, to some, be seen as straying outside of their "magisteria," he argues that:

> [I]t is obvious that scientific theories relating to the origins of the universe, the nature of matter, the nature of consciousness, and the evolution of life must have philosophical and metaphysical implications. These theories cannot be completely neutral with respect to the views that different traditions of humanity have passed down to us about man and the world.[90]

83. McGrath, *The Dawkins Delusion?*, 12.

84. McGrath, 12; emphasis removed.

85. Polkinghorne, *Science and Religion in Quest of Truth*, 74–75.

86. McGrath, *Enriching Our Vision of Reality*, 20.

87. McGrath, 20.

88. McGrath, 21.

89. Jean Staune, 'Introduction', in *Science & the Search for Meaning: Perspectives from International Scientists*, ed. Jean Staune (West Conshohocken: Templeton Foundation, 2006), 4.

90. Staune, 4.

Philosophical and metaphysical questions are raised by scientific discoveries, he argues, and should be addressed by them, rather than leaving questions of meaning to those who claim it to be within their magisteria.

> [S]cience has found itself associated with the spread of mean-inglessness, not only for objective reasons (the discoveries of science seem to corroborate the supporters of this viewpoint) but also because the advocates of the presence of meaning in the universe (important Christian scientists, such as Pasteur or Leprince-Ringuet) have been more defensive of the separatist position than their opponents, the defenders of atheism.[91]

Staune believes that the tide is turning against the separation of these disciplines, and that scientific discoveries at the micro and macro level have produced "a new vision of the world" that "revisits the path to meaning."[92] It is in this new view of science that the intelligent design argument locates itself. It is "the 'hard core' of current science [that] allows science and meaning to come together after a long period of separation."[93]

INTELLIGENT DESIGN

This research project involves the teaching of intelligent design. Definitions of intelligent design differ between detractors and advocates, and it is important to allow those within the intelligent design community to define themselves.[94] The UK's Centre for Intelligent Design defines it this way:

> ID holds that certain features of the universe and of life are best explained by an intelligent cause and not an unguided process such as natural selection. The evidence for this is drawn from a wide range of the sciences including biology, geology, cosmology, chemistry, physics and psychology.

---

91. Staune, 4.

92. Staune, 5 citing Bernard d'Espagnat (unreferenced).

93. Staune, 6.

94. See the chapter by D. W. Bebbington in Alister Chapman, John Coffey, and Brad S. Gregory, eds., *Seeing Things Their Way: Intellectual History and the Return of Religion* (Notre Dame: University of Notre Dame Press, 2009).

The Discovery Institute in the US describes the various approaches taken by intelligent design theorists:

> Intelligent design refers to a scientific research programme as well as a community of scientists, philosophers and other scholars who seek evidence of design in nature. [. . .] Intelligent design has applied these scientific methods to detect design in irreducibly complex biological structures, the complex and specified information content in DNA, the life-sustaining physical architecture of the universe, and the geologically rapid origin of biological diversity in the fossil record during the Cambrian explosion approximately 530 million years ago.[95]

The intelligent design movement has developed in several stages. It began with Phillip Johnson's challenge to neo-Darwinian authors who influenced the public understanding of science.[96] The initial phase of the movement was to expose assumptions and poor arguments supporting a neo-Darwinian evolutionary explanation. The second phase was to consider the role of design in science. The third phase is the establishment of research laboratories to use design insights for scientific discovery.[97]

Intelligent design locates itself within the network of ideas in a way that some find difficult to accept. As discussed above, intelligent design is outside of the normal science-versus-faith conflict paradigm because it does not start with a faith commitment to any religious belief. Those who identify with it include agnostics such as Berlinski and Denton, and former atheists such as Flew.[98] It is common for those who oppose intel-

95. Discovery Institute, 2011

96. Some suggest the movement began with the publication of Charles B. Thaxton, Walter L. Bradley, and Roger L. Olsen, *The Mystery of Life's Origin: Reassessing Current Theories* (New York: Philosophical Library, 1984); and Michael Denton, *Evolution: A Theory in Crisis* (Bethesda: Adler & Adler Publishers, 1986); for an overview of Johnson's influence see Donald A. Yerxa, 'Phillip Johnson and the Origins of the Intelligent Design Movement, 1977–1991', *Perspectives on Science and Christian Faith* 54, no. 1 (2002): 47–52; and Walter L. Bradley, 'Phillip Johnson and the Intelligent Design Movement: Looking Back and Looking Forward', in *Darwin's Nemesis: Phillip Johnson and the Intelligent Design Movement*, ed. William A. Dembski (Downers Grove: Inter-Varsity, 2007), 305–14.

97. See for example 'Biologic Institute', Biologic Institute, accessed 15 May 2020, http://www.biologicinstitute.org; and 'The Evolutionary Informatics Lab', Evolutionary Informatics, accessed 15 May 2020, https://www.evoinfo.org/.

98. David Berlinski, *The Devil's Delusion: Atheism and its Scientific Pretensions* (New York: Basic Books, 2009); Denton, *Evolution*; Antony Flew, *There is a God: How the World's Most Notorious Atheist Changed His Mind* (New York: HarperOne, 2007).

ligent design to associate it with creationism, but intelligent design takes no theological stance on the status of revelation (of any religion) and does not argue on the basis of its coherence or otherwise with Scripture. It does not participate in a NOMA schema because it does not accept the dichotomy of material and mental. Intelligent design does not accept equating the term science with methodological naturalism and instead views it similarly to Ratzsch as being "a deeply empirical project aimed most fundamentally at understanding and explaining the natural realm, typically in natural terms."[99] The disputed term, of course, is the word "typically," rather than "exclusively." It opposes a neo-Darwinism narrative as a sufficient explanation for the existence of life in all its variety. As Kojonen puts it, the intelligent design movement "sees its critique of Darwinism as a scientific dissent from a doctrine of evolution which does not fit the facts."[100] It does not provide a meta-narrative itself, and so to that extent McGrath is right that it is not a fully-orbed Christian apologetic argument.

It is a modern form of the arguments from design that "focus upon finding and identifying various traces of the operation of a mind in nature's temporal and physical structures, behaviors and paths."[101] Consequently it runs counter to materialist accounts of nature that exclude *a priori* the possibility of design in nature. It is not the challenge to the sufficiency of neo-Darwinism that singles out intelligent design (as Shapiro and Müller amongst others also challenge it),[102] nor the view that there is design in the cosmos (as theistic evolutionists also believe in that, such as McGrath and Polkinghorne). The distinguishing feature is that intelligent design argues that design is identifiable within nature (and biology in particular) according to properly scientific methods (including the methodology used by Darwin himself). The main methodologies used for the

99. Del Ratzsch, 'Science and Religion', in *The Oxford Handbook of Philosophical Theology*, ed. Thomas P. Flint and Michael C. Rea, Oxford Handbooks in Religion and Theology (Oxford: Oxford University Press, 2009), 55.

100. Erkki Vesa Rope Kojonen, 'Intelligent Design: A Theological and Philosophical Analysis' (Helsinki, University of Helsinki, 2014), 17.

101. Del Ratzsch, 'Teleological Arguments for God's Existence', accessed 6 April 2020, https://plato.stanford.edu/archives/win2010/entries/teleological-arguments/#IntDesIDMov.

102. Robert Shapiro, *Origins: A Skeptic's Guide to the Creation of Life on Earth* (Toronto: Bantam, 1987); Gerd B. Müller, 'Why an Extended Evolutionary Synthesis is Necessary', *Interface Focus* 7, no. 5 (6 October 2017): 1–11, https://doi.org/10.1098/rsfs.2017.0015.

identification of design in nature are the design filter, specified complexity, irreducible complexity, and inference to the best explanation.[103]

OPPOSITION TO INTELLIGENT DESIGN

Many argue that intelligent design should be seen as either religion, or politics, or something other than science. Foster et al. think science is "under siege from the forces of religious irrationalism in the form of the intelligent design movement."[104] Often this is done by simple declaration.[105] A common strategy is to equate intelligent design with creationism, and to equate being anti-Darwinian with being anti-science.[106] Allowing intelligent design into the academy is equated with "astrology, spoon-bending, flat-earth cosmology or alien abductions."[107] In Forrest and Gross' opinion, the movement is manipulative, disingenuous, recycled, old-fashioned, anti-scientific public relations.[108] They present it as a trojan horse, adopting a conspiratorial "wedge" strategy that seeks to "overthrow the system of rules and procedures of modern science and those intellectual footings of our culture laid down in the Enlightenment and over some 300 years."[109] However, intelligent design has not adopted a secretive political strategy, and the wedge strategy was the title of one

103. William A. Dembski, *The Design Inference: Eliminating Chance through Small Probabilities*, Cambridge Studies in Probability, Induction and Decision Theory (Cambridge: Cambridge University Press, 2005); Michael J. Behe, *Darwin's Black Box: The Biochemical Challenge to Evolution* (New York: Free Press, 1996); Peter Lipton, 'What Good is an Explanation?', in *Explanation*, ed. Giora Hon and Sam S. Rakover, Synthese Library 302 (Dordrecht: Springer, 2001), 43–60, https://doi.org/10.1007/978-94-015-9731-9.

104. John Bellamy Foster, Brett Clark, and Richard York, *Critique of Intelligent Design: Materialism versus Creationism from Antiquity to the Present* (New York: Monthly Review Press, 2008), 26.

105. 'American Association for the Advancement of Science (2002) | National Center for Science Education', accessed 27 July 2020, https://ncse.ngo/american-association-advancement-science-2002.

106. Barbara Forrest and Paul R. Gross, *Creationism's Trojan Horse: The Wedge of Intelligent Design* (New York: Oxford University Press, 2004), 8.

107. Mike Archer et al., 'Letter—Intelligent Design is Not Science | Australian Academy of Science', 21 October 2005, https://www.science.org.au/supporting-science/science-policy/submissions-government/letter%E2%80%94intelligent-design-not-science.

108. Forrest and Gross, *Creationism's Trojan Horse*, 6–9.

109. Forrest and Gross, 10.

of Johnson's book.[110] As Johnson argues elsewhere, it is only those who define science as philosophical naturalism that find intelligent design a threat to science.[111] For instance, Hafer writes: "[r]emember that when they say 'materialism,' what they mean is science."[112] Forrest and Gross' critique quickly dated as the scientific basis for design in nature developed in peer-reviewed research,[113] but the association of intelligent design with creationism is still commonly asserted in critiques and reviews.[114] Those who do engage with the scientific evidence of the intelligent design argument often still refer to their interlocuters as creationists.[115] However, the difference in epistemologies between creationism and intelligent design is increasingly recognized. Scientists such as Sternberg and Gelernter, who have publicly identified with intelligent design, have no religious affiliations.[116] The debate is shifting back towards the scientific evidence, rather than political and theological debates, and the level of engagement is strong.[117]

Intelligent design is recognized as a scientific discipline by many who oppose it. Monton, an atheist philosopher of science, argues that "intelligent design needs to be taken more seriously than a lot of its opponents are willing to."[118] He believes that intelligent design arguments

110. Phillip E. Johnson, *The Wedge of Truth: Splitting the Foundations of Naturalism* (Downers Grove: InterVarsity, 2000).

111. Phillip E. Johnson, 'Bringing Balance to a Fiery Debate', in *Intelligent Design 101: Leading Experts Explain the Key Issues*, ed. H. Wayne House (Grand Rapids: Kregel, 2008), 38.

112. Abby Hafer, *The Not-so-Intelligent Designer: Why Evolution Explains the Human Body and Intelligent Design Does Not* (Eugene, Oregon: Cascade, 2015), 22.

113. See, for example, the bibliography available at 'Peer-Reviewed Articles Supporting Intelligent Design', Center for Science and Culture, accessed 27 July 2020, https://www.discovery.org/id/peer-review/.

114. See for instance the phrase "a group of creationist thinkers" in Foster, Clark, and York, *Critique of Intelligent Design*, 8; Eugenie C. Scott, 'Creationism and Intelligent Design', in *How Evolution Shapes Our Lives*, ed. Jonathan B. Losos and Richard E. Lenski (Princeton: Princeton University Press, 2016), 284–99.

115. See for instance John C. Avise, *Inside the Human Genome: A Case for Non-Intelligent Design* (Oxford: Oxford University Press, 2010), 145.

116. Richard Sternberg, 'How My Views on Evolution Evolved', 2008, http://www.richardsternberg.com/pdf/sternintellbio08.pdf; David Gelernter, 'Giving up Darwin', *Claremont Review of Books* XIX, no. 2 (Spring 2019): 104–9.

117. William A Dembski and Michael Ruse, eds., *Debating Design: From Darwin to DNA* (Cambridge: Cambridge University Press, 2011).

118. Bradley John Monton, *Seeking God in Science: An Atheist Defends Intelligent*

should receive careful evaluation because they do have "*some* force—they make me less certain of my atheism than I would be had I not heard the arguments."[119] They are not, he argues, "inherently theistic," although he recognizes that the motivation for those using the arguments is as evidence for the existence of God. His treatment of several arguments from design, including Behe's irreducible complexity, is even-handed and engaging.[120] Despite protestations from others, he concludes that intelligent design theorists like Dembski are fundamentally "pro-science; he's just not pro-naturalism, and hence he's not pro-naturalism-as-a-scientific-methodology."[121] Nagel has followed Monton in challenging what he calls "the dominant scientific consensus" to engage with intelligent design arguments on their own terms.

> Even if one is not drawn to the alternative of an explanation by the actions of a designer, the problems that these iconoclasts pose for the orthodox scientific consensus should be taken seriously.[122]

SUMMARY

The purpose of this chapter was to locate the intelligent design argument within a range of views relating science and religion, and to justify its use within the research project. Since the research question involved teaching intelligent design, it was important to define and outline the benefits of using it compared to other options. Using Tenneson et al.'s paradigmatic approach, intelligent design was identified as being within the concordist paradigm.[123] I defended its status as a suitable scientific argument and indicated how it fits well within an evangelical theology of the action of God within the world.[124] It was a valid concept for me

---

Design (Peterborough: Broadview, 2009), 7.

119. Monton, 7–8; emphasis original.

120. Monton, 105–10.

121. Monton, 112.

122. Thomas Nagel, *Mind and Cosmos: Why the Materialist Neo-Darwinian Conception of Nature is Almost Certainly False* (New York: Oxford University Press, 2012), 10.

123. Tenneson, Bundrick, and Stanford, 'A New Survey Instrument and its Findings for Relating Science and Theology'.

124. Plantinga, *Where the Conflict Really Lies*, 194.

to address the concerns raised by students about how they respond to scientific challenges and arguments.

3

Methods and Methodology

The methodology justifies the methods used, which are the practical activities of research.[1]

THE METHODOLOGY FOR THIS project must provide reasons to accept the methods used as ethical, the findings as reliable, and must satisfy the needs of the professional doctorate research project as being a work of practical theology. The basis for the decision to teach intelligent design to evangelical students was defended in the previous chapter. This chapter considers the rationale for choosing the methods used in the research project that contribute to the overall knowledge claims. As Maguire says, "the trustworthiness of the research is dependent on the trustworthiness of the researcher and their ability to articulate and account for their choices."[2] In this section, then, I discuss the development of the research project before presenting arguments supporting my critical realist approach. I then defend my use of Norton's pedagogical action research and Osmer's model of practical theology.

1. Guro Hansen Helskog, 'Justifying Action Research', *Educational Action Research* 22, no. 1 (2 January 2014): 16, https://doi.org/10.1080/09650792.2013.856769.

2. Kate Maguire, 'Methodology as Personal and Professional Integrity: Research Designing for Practitioner Doctorates', in *Methodologies for Practice Research: Approaches for Professional Doctorates*, ed. Carol Costley and John Fulton (London: SAGE, 2019), 102.

DEVELOPMENT OF THE RESEARCH PROJECT

The design of the research project flowed from the research question and was framed as a change in professional practice in response to a problem. A professional doctorate requires a methodology of integrity defined by Maguire as choices and decisions being taken to achieve "coherence and internal consistency through personal and professional integrity."[3] The research project was conceptualized as an interdisciplinary exercise where theological students would be introduced to scientific arguments. This was a development of my practice of teaching theology students in terms of content (the teaching of intelligent design) and in the way that I received feedback from student-participants.

A formative event in developing the methodology of the research project came when some friends of mine asked for suggestions because their son (who had been brought up in the same church I am a member of) had rejected his Christian faith and identified as an atheist. It so happened that I was going to attend a lecture given by John Lennox at a Christians in Science event in Southampton entitled "God and Stephen Hawking: Whose Design is it Anyway?" and so I invited him to come along, accompanied by his mother and my son of his age.[4] Lennox's presentation challenged Hawking's argument that the universe is self-generating, and made the case that the evidence pointed towards God as the Creator. Lennox responded to several difficult questions and challenges at the end of his presentation. My friend's son was willing to share his thoughts about the event at the time. He expressed that it had disturbed his confidence in the sufficiency of atheism and the inadequacy of Christianity. He had experienced it as a challenge at the point where he had felt most secure, namely in his confidence that science was a reason not to believe in Christianity. My interpretation of the experience was that he experienced it as a challenge not just to an argument about the origin of the universe, but to his worldview.

Lennox's presentation exemplified some of my motivations behind this research project. Like his use of cosmology, the intelligent design argument is a scientific argument with metaphysical implications. Lennox demonstrated its potential to raise questions and provoke reflection

3. Maguire, 103.

4. 'Southampton Previous Events', Christians in Science, accessed 9 August 2020, http://www.cis.org.uk/resources/articles-talks-and-links/general-science-and-faith/central-south-previous-events/.

in those who are confident in their atheism. My perception was that it had more influence in provoking a response than a theological approach would have had. I was inspired by the communicative ability of Lennox and the clarity of the argument. It was directly relevant to the situation of my friend's son, and it provided a valid example to follow in my own context. It also pointed to the complexity of the task of providing scientific content in an accessible manner. It raised the issue of challenging someone's worldview and anticipating a level of resistance as a result. Like Lennox, my positionality with respect to intelligent design would need to be transparent to participants to maintain a methodology of integrity.[5]

Concerns about the incident are also important: did my friend's son respond in the way he did because there was pressure to show appreciation? His attendance was voluntary, but perhaps his responses were constrained by social pressure from being with a parent or having been invited by a lecturer in theology.[6] In my view, the young man came across as sincere and showed a critical ability when reflecting on the lecture. The ethical sensitivities of discussing these things with him with others around meant that I restricted myself to asking for his reflections rather than engaging with his answers. Reflection on the event impacted my research design: an alternative research project I had considered was to interview people that students at my college had identified from their ministries as having similar views to the young man mentioned above. However, the complexity of arranging permissions with gatekeepers would have made this prohibitive.[7] My research design would require that all participants were fully informed of the purpose of responses and would not require permission from gatekeepers.

Maguire suggests reflection on research design through the concepts of resistance and facilitation.[8] Resistance to the kind of change of professional practice proposed comes from several sources. There is the difficulty in fitting in more teaching content for students into an already busy term timetable. Students have obligations to complete assessments

---

5. Maguire, 'Methodology as Personal and Professional Integrity: Research Designing for Practitioner Doctorates', 113.

6. Bryman cites the fourth principle of the *Framework for Research Ethics* that involvement must be entirely voluntary in Bryman, *Social Research Methods*, 146.

7. Paul Oliver, *The Student's Guide to Research Ethics*, 2nd ed. (Maidenhead: McGraw-Hill; Open University Press, 2010), 39–41.

8. Maguire, 'Methodology as Personal and Professional Integrity: Research Designing for Practitioner Doctorates', 103.

and to fulfil placement responsibilities and these must be considered to avoid adding to their burden. Any teaching addition would need to fit around them, as well as fitting into my own teaching commitments. Another source of resistance was the effort of constructing the teaching content for the course. I describe the decision-making process below, but I found the research and comprehension to be a challenge. Whereas I might have anticipated some resistance to the notion of teaching intelligent design from colleagues (not all of whom accept it), instead (as mentioned above) I found only encouragement from them to do so. There was no conflict between the "intended goals of both the researcher and the system," which in this case was Moorlands College.[9]

Facilitators to the design of the research came from the College's encouragement to fulfil the professional doctoral requirements, and my colleagues were supportive and helpful in enabling me to put on the course. My supervisors gave advice about methods of assessing the research. I benefitted from attending research colloquia on the topics of practical theology and qualitative research methods and from the feedback to my methodological presentations from visiting speakers. The leaders of the evangelical church where the main intelligent design course was taught were accommodating and generous in facilitating and publicizing the event. They demonstrated a good deal of trust in my competence as the course leader, in the suitability of the course content, and the integrity of the research afterwards, making their church buildings generally available for me. In follow-up meetings after the research event, they expressed they were "well up for hosting it again."[10]

CRITICAL REALISM

Maguire describes methodology as "how we view knowledge that will influence the methods and the sources of data we choose."[11] My understanding of knowledge and reality is best expressed as critical realism that has a realist ontology and holds that truth claims can be argued for rationally, if not conclusively.[12] This approach was appropriate in address-

---

9. Coghlan and Brannick, *Doing Action Research in Your Own Organization*, 48.

10. Private email correspondence with church leader, 17 December 2019.

11. Maguire, 'Methodology as Personal and Professional Integrity: Research Designing for Practitioner Doctorates', 101.

12. A central point is the rejection of the epistemic fallacy that equates

ing the different aspects of the research question of teaching evangelical students intelligent design, namely: science and religion, qualitative research, and evangelical practical theology.

Losch argues that critical realism is the dominant paradigm for understanding the relationship between science and religion.[13] In contrast to the NOMA approach discussed above, Andrew Wright argues that "critical realism opens up, and indeed demands, rational engagement with religious and secular questions about ultimate truth and the ultimate order-of-things."[14] Barbour, who first proposed the term, believed it meant that, at some points, scientific and theological claims are relatable.[15] In his book relating science with youth ministry, Root describes his approach as "critical realist personalism."[16]

Ward believes that critical realism "frames a theologically informed, qualitative method."[17] Although not the most common epistemology underpinning social science, Greenwood does include critical realism in his "eclectic" list of accepted "theoretical approaches."[18] Challenging perspectives and theories within qualitative research fits the critical realist approach that holds that the world is real and "out there" but that

---

epistemological subjectivity with a lack of ontological objectivity; see Margaret S. Archer, Andrew Collier, and Douglas V. Porpora, *Transcendence: Critical Realism and God*, Critical Realism: Interventions (London: Routledge, 2004), 2; see Alvin I. Goldman, 'Truth and Realism', in *The Nature of Nature: Examining the Role of Naturalism in Science*, ed. Bruce Gordon and William A. Dembski (Wilmington: ISI, 2011), 237–40 for a defence of a realist correspondence theory.

13. Andreas Losch, 'Critical Realism—A Sustainable Bridge Between Science and Religion?', *Theology and Science* 8, no. 4 (November 2010): 394, https://doi.org/10.10 80/14746700.2010.517638; for a more sustained discussion, see Andreas Losch, 'On the Origins of Critical Realism', *Theology and Science* 7, no. 1 (February 2009): 85–106, https://doi.org/10.1080/14746700802617105.

14. Andrew Wright, *Christianity and Critical Realism: Ambiguity, Truth, and Theological Literacy*, New Studies in Critical Realism and Spirituality (London: Routledge, 2013), 2.

15. Ian G. Barbour, *Religion and Science: Historical and Contemporary Issues* (San Francisco: HarperSanFrancisco, 1997), 161; cited in Root, *Exploding Stars, Dead Dinosaurs, and Zombies*, 96.

16. Root, *Exploding Stars, Dead Dinosaurs, and Zombies*, 14.

17. Pete Ward, *Liquid Ecclesiology: The Gospel and The Church* (Leiden: Brill, 2017), 22, https://doi.org/10.1163/9789004347359.

18. Davydd J. Greenwood, 'An Analysis of the Theory/Concept Entries in the *SAGE Encyclopedia of Action Research*: What We Can Learn about Action Research in General from the Encyclopedia', *Action Research* 13, no. 2 (June 2015): 200, https://doi.org/10.1177/1476750315573592.

our perspectives on it are different.[19] "For realists, mental and physical entities are equally real."[20] Since mental ideas and beliefs can be true things in themselves, they not only explain but can also effect changes in behaviours. Ideas, Maxwell argues, are the right kind of thing to cause behaviours and explain those behaviours, even if the mechanisms behind them are sometimes hard to discern.[21] My qualitative research began with an idea and a pragmatic approach of finding out what worked: the thematic analysis of the semi-structured interviews revealed the way participants understood an aspect of society as constructed through power and authority. My project then proposed a warranted interpretation of reality and provides theological impetus for action to change that reality (see chapter 8). The critical realist is interested in a hermeneutical approach to gain increasingly better understandings of what Maxwell calls the "single real world."[22]

A critical realist approach, as Porpora argues, is consistent with an evangelical view of experience and ministry more generally.[23] Losch notes its common use within theology.[24] He quotes Peacocke who argues that Christians "regard themselves as making meaningful assertions about a reality which man can and does encounter."[25] My evangelical professional context does not assume that everyone shares the same beliefs about the world, and critical realism accepts differences in interpretation and is suspicious of claims asserting the prominence of any one view. But nonetheless there is an assumption that ideas have capacity to describe reality truly, if not exhaustively. As NT Wright says, "the only access we have to this reality lies along the spiralling path of appropriate dialogue or conversation between the knower and the thing known," and

19. Helen Cameron and Catherine Duce, *Researching Practice in Ministry and Mission: A Companion* (London: SCM, 2013), 28–33.

20. Joseph A. Maxwell, *A Realist Approach for Qualitative Research* (Thousand Oaks: SAGE, 2012), 8.

21. Maxwell, 9.

22. Maxwell, 16.

23. See Popora's chapter 'Judgemental rationality and Jesus' in Archer, Collier, and Porpora, *Transcendence*, 49–62.

24. Losch, 'Critical Realism—A Sustainable Bridge Between Science and Religion?', 395–96; see Wright's application of this approach in theology in N. T. Wright, *The New Testament and the People of God*, Christian Origins and the Question of God 1 (London: SPCK, 1992), 34–40.

25. Peacocke, *Creation and the World of Science*, 22; cited in Losch, 'Critical Realism—A Sustainable Bridge Between Science and Religion?', 396.

this path can enable us to "speak truly of reality."[26] Or in Osmer's terms, alluding to Andrew Wright, critical realism "holds together ontological realism, epistemological relativism, and judgmental rationality."[27] The term "judgmental rationality" is defined as meaning "that we can publicly discuss our claims about reality, as we think it is, and marshal better or worse arguments on behalf of those claims."[28]

ACTION RESEARCH

In this section I locate Norton's pedagogical action research within the family of action research approaches and then give reasons why I considered it suitable for my research project. Norton defines her pedagogical model as "systematically investigating your own teaching and [. . .] your students' learning [. . . It is] derived from an 'issue' that has arisen in your pedagogical practice [with the] dual aim of contributing to theoretical knowledge and to improving practice."[29] It starts with a problem or issue, rather than, for instance, Huxtable and Whitehead's Living Theory version of pedagogical action research which is motivated "from enquiries of the kind, 'How do I improve what I am doing?'"[30] Norton characterizes their approach as being on the extreme interpretive end of a "positivism–interpretivism dimension,"[31] although Huxtable and Whitehead deny this.[32]

McKernan argues that action research's origins are at least in part from the scientific method associated with the Science in Education

---

26. Wright, *NTPG*, 35–36.

27. Richard R. Osmer, *Practical Theology: An Introduction* (Grand Rapids: Eerdmans, 2008), 74; see Wright, *Christianity and Critical Realism*, 2.

28. Archer, Collier, and Porpora, *Transcendence*, 2; cited in Osmer, *Practical Theology*, 74.

29. 'Pedagogical Action Research (PedAR) | Lin Norton', accessed 22 October 2020, https://www.linnorton.co.uk/pedagogical-action-research; emphasis removed.

30. Marie Huxtable and Jack Whitehead, 'Enhancing Educational Influences in Learning with a Living Educational Theory Approach to Pedagogical Action Research in Higher Education', *Educational Action Research*, 15 June 2020, 1, https://doi.org/10.1080/09650792.2020.1779771.

31. Norton, *Action Research in Teaching and Learning*, 64.

32. Huxtable and Whitehead, 'Enhancing Educational Influences in Learning with a Living Educational Theory Approach to Pedagogical Action Research in Higher Education', 2.

Movement of the early twentieth century.[33] Kurt Lewin's turn to problem solving in the 1940s, and his use of action and reflection spirals, made it a more experimental, democratic, and inductive approach, but still within the realm of scientific research and knowledge generation.[34] Masters traces a steady "separation of theory and practice" associated with "the split between science and practice" which led to action research's decline in the 1950s.[35] An example of the effect of such separation was Toulmin's claim that action research aimed only to improve practices, not theories of reality,[36] which meant that "it could not bring forward new and valid knowledge about this reality."[37] Helskog suggests that a better typology for action research would be "constructive science."[38] Norton notes that pedagogical action research was considered by some to be nothing more than "curriculum development" and not "real" research within psychology departments.[39] It has been understood, she observes, simply as a form of self-reflective improvement of practice, or practitioner enquiry, or a way of seeking practical solutions to pressing concerns.[40] Its association with complexity or "messy" methods means that it can be difficult to manage.[41] Norton's version encourages a more systematic approach, which made it attractive for my project.

33. J. McKernan, *Curriculum Action Research. A Handbook of Methods and Resources for the Reflective Practitioner* (London: Kogan Page, 1991), 8; cited in Janet Masters, 'The History of Action Research', in *Action Research Electronic Reader*, ed. I. Hughes (on-line: University of Sydney, 1995), 1, http://www.behs.cchs.usyd.edu.au/arow/Reader/rmasters.htm.

34. David Bargal, 'Lewin, Kurt', in *The SAGE Encyclopedia of Action Research*, ed. David Coghlan and Mary Brydon-Miller (Thousand Oaks, California: SAGE, Inc, 2014), 501–2.

35. Masters, 'The History of Action Research', 2.

36. Stephen Toulmin, 'Is Action Research Really "Research"?', *Concepts and Transformation* 1, no. 1 (January 1996): 58, https://doi.org/10.1075/cat.1.1.05tou.

37. Helskog, 'Justifying Action Research', 6.

38. Helskog, 6.

39. Lin Norton, 'The Case for Pedagogical Action Research in Psychology Learning and Teaching', *Psychology Teaching Review* 20, no. 2 (2014): 3.

40. Compare with Jean McNiff, 'My Story is My Living Educational Theory', in *Handbook of Narrative Inquiry: Mapping a Methodology*, ed. D. Jean Clandinin (Thousand Oaks: SAGE, 2007), 312.

41. Norton, 'The Case for Pedagogical Action Research in Psychology Learning and Teaching', 5; see also Renata Phelps and Stewart Hase, 'Complexity and Action Research: Exploring the Theoretical and Methodological Connections', *Educational Action Research* 10, no. 3 (September 2002): 507–24, https://doi.

In the second edition of their book, Reason and Bradbury give a well-quoted definition:

> Action research is a family of practices of living inquiry that aims, in a great variety of ways, to link practice and ideas in the service of human flourishing.[42]

They argue that action research is not done at a distance, but rather engages with participants to work out what might change. It "brings together action and reflection, theory and practice, in participation with others, in the pursuit of practical solutions to issues of pressing concern to people, and more generally the flourishing of individual persons and their communities."[43] The connection that Reason and Bradbury make between action research with human flourishing, and the recognition that there is not just one form of it, made it suitable for my evangelical (and therefore teleological) theological context.[44] It questions "the role of ideas" and challenges "the ways in which 'the academy' defines and uses knowledge,"[45] something that fits well with the implications of teaching intelligent design in a higher educational context.

Norton describes action research as "a broad umbrella term for what is actually a wide range of research paradigms and processes, each with its own philosophies and rationales."[46] Suitable data collection methods range from "positivist experimental design to autoethnography" depending on context.[47] Norton notes that her approach is in fact "more positivist than interpretivist,"[48] and she encourages practitioners to "have confidence in a research approach which has a different epistemological

org/10.1080/09650790200200198.

42. Peter Reason and Hilary Bradbury, 'Introduction', in *The SAGE Handbook of Action Research: Participative Inquiry and Practice*, ed. Peter Reason and Hilary Bradbury, 2nd ed (London: SAGE, 2008), 1.

43. Reason and Bradbury, 4.

44. See my forthcoming chapter; Alistair McKitterick, 'The Role of Teleology in Practical Theology', in *Evangelicals Engaging with Practical Theology: Theology That Impacts Church and World*, ed. Helen Morris and Helen Cameron, Explorations in Practical, Pastoral and Empirical Theology (Abingdon: Routledge, Forthcoming).

45. Coleman, 'Action Research', 152.

46. Norton, *Action Research in Teaching and Learning*, 51.

47. Norton, 'The Case for Pedagogical Action Research in Psychology Learning and Teaching', 6.

48. Norton, *Action Research in Teaching and Learning*, 60, 65.

and philosophical stance."[49] Coleman agrees that action research is not a single methodology but rather "an approach that encompasses a range of methods and 'tools' which have some key characteristics."[50] Reason and Bradbury argue that it is characterized by "an orientation to inquiry."[51] Different species of action research emphasize different aspects of the orientation to inquiry, and not all were suitable for my project. Some models emphasize curriculum reform and the role of teachers as researchers in the school environment.[52] Norton uses the term pedagogical action research to distinguish research done in a higher educational context from "other educational contexts," which again made it more relevant to my research context.[53]

Several scholars point to the influence of Shirley Grundy, Stephen Kemmis and Wilf Carr in articulating three main approaches to action research. These are the "socio-technical, the pragmatic-dialogical and the critical-utopian traditions of action research."[54] The socio-technical form aims to influence the values and conceptions of participants through interventions that are carried out by the researcher, often using established theory to inform action. Action research of this kind follows the tradition of Dewey in seeing knowledge as that which is experimentally known and is justified by "getting knowledge and making sure it is knowledge, and not mere opinion."[55] For Dewey, it is the "trying out of ideas" that produces knowledge. The researcher in this mode is seen as the expert,

49. Norton, 65; I am grateful to the encouragement received from Professor Norton in developing my methodology in this way; Lin Norton, 'Personal Communication', 2020.

50. Coleman, 'Action Research', 153.

51. Reason and Bradbury, 'Introduction', 1; emphasis original.

52. Lawrence Stenhouse and John Elliott are particularly associated with this development of action research: see Bridget Somekh, 'Action Research', in *The SAGE Encyclopedia of Qualitative Research Methods*, ed. Lisa M. Given (Thousand Oaks: SAGE, 2008), 5.

53. Norton, *Action Research in Teaching and Learning*, 50; see also the definition given in Lydia Arnold and Lin Norton, 'Problematising Pedagogical Action Research in Formal Teaching Courses and Academic Development: A Collaborative Autoethnography', *Educational Action Research*, 2020, 2, https://doi.org/10.1080/09650792.2020.1746373.

54. Helskog, 'Justifying Action Research', 8; see also Somekh, 'Action Research', 5; Masters, 'The History of Action Research', 3; and Norton, *Action Research in Teaching and Learning*, 53–54.

55. John Dewey, *Democracy and Education*, 1916, 184; cited in Helskog, 'Justifying Action Research', 14.

and participants aim to develop the effectiveness of their practice through the intervention.[56]

The pragmatic-dialogical approach to action research begins more collaboratively and seeks to develop practice through greater use of personal wisdom from all participants, and communication between them is of great importance. Change to practice is owned by the participants who are considered to be more autonomous and deliberative.[57] The emphasis is on the participants' own interpretation of their practice rather than bringing a pre-existing frame of reference. Whitehead's "living theory" approach, which is described by Hammond as providing "an opportunity for practitioners to put forward descriptions and explanations of their own value-laden practice for interrogation within a 'dialogical community,'" is typical of the pragmatic-dialogical approach.[58] The focus is on local and immediate problems rather than on wider issues that might imply social change. It rejects positivism and instead is committed to "open and democratic discussion with full respect for other points of view."[59]

The third type of action research, critical-utopian, or what is also called 'emancipatory action research,' starts with a critique of the social and political context of practitioners and of the social theory behind it.[60] It is more than critiquing the researcher's own practice and positionality; it is giving participants "access to knowledge and the power to resist oppressive institutional practices."[61] Reason and Bradbury argue that "action research without its liberating and emancipatory dimension is a shadow of its full possibility and will be in danger of being co-opted by the status quo."[62] Done well, they argue, action research's goal is "to liberate the human body, mind and spirit in the search for a better, freer

56. Norton, *Action Research in Teaching and Learning*, 53.

57. The terms are from Grundy, cited in Masters, 'The History of Action Research', 4.

58. Michael Hammond, 'The Contribution of Pragmatism to Understanding Educational Action Research: Value and Consequences', *Educational Action Research* 21, no. 4 (December 2013): 604, https://doi.org/10.1080/09650792.2013.832632; citing Jack Whitehead, 'Creating a Living Educational Theory from Questions of the Kind, "How Do I Improve My Practice?"', *Cambridge Journal of Education* 19, no. 1 (1 January 1989): 41–52, https://doi.org/10.1080/0305764890190106.

59. Hammond, 'The Contribution of Pragmatism to Understanding Educational Action Research', 608.

60. Masters, 'The History of Action Research', 5.

61. Somekh, 'Action Research', 5.

62. Reason and Bradbury, 'Introduction', 5.

world."[63] In reviewing these three traditions, I recognize aspects of my approach in each of them (as seen below): experimental intervention, pragmatic collaboration with colleagues, and critical interpretation of social context.

My project began as a rather pragmatic attempt at improving my professional practice by introducing a form of teaching to see if it would have a positive effect in addressing a problem raised by the students. My aim was, as Coleman describes, "to find out more about the issue or question being studied and to be able to positively change or develop it in practice."[64] My approach developed as I tested the effectiveness of introducing the theory of intelligent design into a classroom setting to see if it would have the desired outcomes of giving greater confidence and ability for students to share their faith with those they had found it difficult to do so otherwise. As Berg puts it, "[t]he researcher contributes expertise when needed as a participant in the process."[65] This more interventionist or experimental approach (along the lines of the socio-technical approach) made Norton's pedagogical action research a good fit for my project.[66] My role as a researcher-practitioner tested the effectiveness of teaching intelligent design against criteria of confidence and an improved ability to share their faith, and it produced "knowledge and action directly useful to a group of people" and "[empowered] them at a second and deeper level to see that they are capable of constructing and using their own knowledge."[67] The approach was justified in the way it was seen to develop knowledge and ability amongst participants that was "useful in action,"[68] in this case in building relationships with those whose views on science caused a barrier to evangelism.[69] As Hathcoat

---

63. Reason and Bradbury, 5.

64. Coleman, 'Action Research', 152.

65. Bruce L. Berg, *Qualitative Research Methods for the Social Sciences*, 5th ed (Boston: Pearson, 2004), 202.

66. Norton, *Action Research in Teaching and Learning*, 45.

67. Reason and Bradbury, 'Introduction', 9.

68. Helskog, 'Justifying Action Research', 11.

69. Note that Greenwood also accepts and uses more positivist approaches and considers rejection of them irresponsible and counterproductive; Greenwood, 'An Analysis of the Theory/Concept Entries in the *SAGE Encyclopedia of Action Research*', 212.

and Nicholas put it, "[o]utcome validity demands that the action result-ing from the research lead to some form of resolution to the problem."[70]

Norton's Identify, Think, Do, Evaluate, Modify (ITDEM) cycli-cal model was accessible for a non-specialist and was suitable for my situation where improvement (and self-improvement) was driven by my perception of the problem to be addressed.[71] As the project developed through a second cycle of her model, and as the effect of my interven-tion was revealed through the interviews and focus group, the impor-tance of the social and political context became more apparent to me. I became increasingly aware that "the reality we confront is a complex, dynamic, interactive open system."[72] Participants described the effects of the teaching input in emancipatory terms. Their responses expressed a sense of liberation that the course had empowered their engagement with others and help them to understand their social context better. I had not set out to do action research with a critical-utopian approach (in fact, the paradigm of science and theology that I taught was the most integrative paradigm and least associated with a conflict between the disciplines).[73] Nonetheless, participants expressed the implications of at-tending the course in emancipatory language. It had the effect, in Reason and Bradbury's terms, of "redressing imbalances of power and restoring to ordinary people the capacities of self-reliance and ability to manage their own lives."[74] The structured nature of Norton's cyclical model of ac-tion research, and the use of her model of thematic analysis to reflect on the semi-structured interviews, provided a rigorous method for drawing a narrative account of the experience of the participants.

The reasons for my choice in using Norton's pedagogical action re-search model for my research project, therefore, included the fact that Norton does not believe the threefold framework described above need

70. John D. Hathcoat and Mark C. Nicholas, 'Epistemology', in *The SAGE Ency-clopedia of Action Research*, ed. David Coghlan and Mary Brydon-Miller (London: SAGE, 2014), 305.

71. Norton, *Action Research in Teaching and Learning*, 56, 70.

72. Greenwood, 'An Analysis of the Theory/Concept Entries in the *SAGE Encyclo-pedia of Action Research*', 207.

73. Michael Tenneson, David R. Bundrick, and Matthew S. Stanford, 'Faith and Science Integration: Surveys and Findings', in *Faith & Science Conference: Genesis & Genetics: Proceedings of the 2014 Faith & Science Conference*, ed. David R. Bundrick and Steve Badger (Springfield, MO: Logion, 2014), 319–52.

74. Reason and Bradbury, 'Introduction', 7.

constrain the use of action research in academia,[75] and that this was conducive to my more eclectic approach.[76] She argues that "the process of carrying out pedagogical action research inevitably means we scrutinise our professional practice more closely."[77] Norton believes that pedagogical action research has the potential "to bring about more radical change in which the very nature of higher education should be open to critique and fresh perspectives."[78] This combines what she sees (drawing on Masters) as the more British emphasis on action research focused on improved practice in education, and the more American emphasis on "bringing about social change."[79] Pedagogical action research, she argues, is teacher-led, rather than "outsider"-led research, and is critical in the sense of being sensitive to power dynamics found within the research context. Norton encourages its use in influencing policy decisions within higher education as "a way of challenging existing beliefs, concepts and theories in the scholarship of teaching and learning."[80] These attributes aligned with my project that began with a teacher-led change of practice to try to improve the students' interaction with others regarding science through a process of change, and concluded with proposals for modified future actions ranging from local to more meso and macro level suggestions.[81]

PRACTICAL THEOLOGY AND ACTION RESEARCH

In this section I explain the decision to use a model of practical theology as the third reflective cycle of my research project, and its connection with action research. I then explain the reasons for choosing Osmer's model. Action research operates within the researcher's own values that motivate and justify the reflection process and the modified action taken, and it is governed by clear, ethical principles. For my project, however, there was a need to reflect theologically upon what was going on in the

75. Norton, *Action Research in Teaching and Learning*, 54.

76. For the use of the term 'eclectic opportunist', see Greenwood, 'An Analysis of the Theory/Concept Entries in the *SAGE Encyclopedia of Action Research*', 200.

77. Norton, 'The Case for Pedagogical Action Research in Psychology Learning and Teaching', 7.

78. Norton, *Action Research in Teaching and Learning*, 50.

79. Masters, 'The History of Action Research'; cited in Norton, *Action Research in Teaching and Learning*, 51.

80. Norton, *Action Research in Teaching and Learning*, 60.

81. See Norton's adaption of Fanghanel's framework in Norton, 9–16.

project. This motivation came partly from my professional position as a theological lecturer and the fact that the research project is part of a ministerial doctorate program situated "within the field of practical theology."[82] It came also from my evangelical value of reflecting upon my ministry prayerfully and biblically to provide a theological imperative for my practice.[83] Osmer argues that practical theology should be thought of as "more of a spiral than a circle,"[84] and my use of Osmer's cycle spiralled naturally from my previous use of Norton's pedagogical action research cycle. My project developed interdisciplinary insight as I reflected theologically on the previous action research cycles. Any modification of practice suggested by my research should be directed by a process of theological reflection for it to be considered as spirit-led and faithful praxis.

The decision to follow action research with a cycle of practical theology had coherence due to practical theology's relationship with the origins of action research, namely experiential learning and liberation theology.[85] Indeed, Swinton and Mowat believe that practical theology simply is action research, albeit a particular form of it.[86] Liberation theology's legacy is seeking to deliver people from suffering or political constraints that diminish their ability to flourish as individuals and communities, and action research has inherited that goal of emancipation.[87] Paulo Freire was a pivotal figure both in action research and liberation pedagogy: action research draws from his linguistic practice with the poor in South America, and liberation theology draws from his emancipatory instincts, seeking to empower those who felt excluded from the

82. 'Doctor of Ministry Student Handbook (Part 5): Version 2' (Spurgeon's College; University of Chester, 2016), 8.

83. For a discussion of the term 'theological imperative', see Alistair McKitterick, 'The Theological Imperative Model for Practical Theology', *Journal of European Baptist Studies* 16, no. 4 (September 2016): 15–18.

84. Osmer, *Practical Theology*, 11; emphasis original.

85. For a fuller list of critical influences, see Greenwood, 'An Analysis of the Theory/Concept Entries in the *SAGE Encyclopedia of Action Research*', 203.

86. John Swinton and Harriet Mowat, *Practical Theology and Qualitative Research*, 2nd ed. (London: SCM, 2016), 261.

87. For a helpful overview of the development of participatory and action research out of liberation theology, see M. Brinton Lykes and Amelia Mallona, 'Towards Transformational Liberation: Participatory and Action Research and Praxis', in *The SAGE Handbook of Action Research: Participative Inquiry and Practice*, ed. Peter Reason and Hilary Bradbury, 2nd ed (London: SAGE, 2008), 106–20.

levers of control in their lives.[88] This liberation is often framed in terms of the kingdom of God or the Exodus narrative (which resonates with the critical-utopian form of action research). The connection between practical theology and liberation theology comes, to a large extent, from the methodology arising from Roman Catholic Episcopal conventions that proposed a see-judge-act cycle to reflect on the situation of people in the "base ecclesiastical communities."[89] That cyclical process, stemming from Cardinal Joseph Cardijn, was conceived as a method "to fundamentally reorient one's life toward social justice and solidarity."[90] Cardijn wrote that "it leads to action, to solving problems; it turns to reality to change it and make use of it, to make daily life vast and beautiful."[91] The methodology behind liberation theology "is not static, and [knows that] social change changes both the self and the other."[92] It is community-oriented, dynamic, and emancipatory.

The key theological virtue that emanated from the Catholic Bishop's conference, the notion of God's "preferential option for the poor," has been democratized in more secular forms of action research.[93] For instance, Lykes and Mallona "suggest that a preferential option for the poor and a politically contextualized psychology are critical to developing participatory and action research that more fully realizes the radical changes envisioned by their founders."[94] As Coleman argues:

88. Reason and Bradbury, 'Introduction', 3; see also Nancy J. Ramsay, 'Emancipatory Theory and Method', in *The Wiley-Blackwell Companion to Practical Theology*, ed. Bonnie J. Miller-McLemore, Wiley-Blackwell Companions to Religion (Chichester: Wiley-Blackwell, 2012), 183–86.

89. Chris Howson, 'Liberation Theology', in *The SAGE Encyclopedia of Action Research*, ed. David Coghlan and Mary Brydon-Miller (London: SAGE, 2014), 508.

90. Justin Sands, 'Introducing Cardinal Cardijn's See–Judge–Act as an Interdisciplinary Method to Move Theory into Practice', *Religions* 9, no. 4 (14 April 2018): 3, https://doi.org/10.3390/rel9040129.

91. Joseph Cardijn, *La Pensée de Joseph Cardijn* (Brussels: Vanbraekel Mouscron, 1982), 87; cited in Sands, 4.

92. Sands, 9.

93. See, for example, Carolina Muñoz-Guzmán, 'Liberation Theology in Social Work', in *International Encyclopedia of the Social & Behavioral Sciences* (Elsevier, 2015), 32–38, https://doi.org/10.1016/B978-0-08-097086-8.28051-3.

94. Lykes and Mallona, 'Towards Transformational Liberation', 107.

> [Action research] grew, then, from practices intended to bring about improvement, liberation, greater social and political justice, and so on.[95]

In this project I turned to a model of practical theology after two cycles of pedagogical action research. I drew inspiration from the influences of Freire and liberation theology as I studied the interview transcripts and prayerfully reflected upon the sense of oppression and marginalization expressed by the participants within their social context.

My use of practical theology was motivated by my professional context at Moorlands College where I teach practical theology to evangelical students as part of their degree. Cameron et al.'s Theological Action Research (TAR) model might well have been thought of as a more logical sequitur to my use of action research.[96] They describe TAR as theological from the start and encourage the use of "four voices" of theology (espoused, operant, normative and formal) as a conversational approach of theological reflection aimed at articulating theological concerns and complexities within the situation.[97] Like other models, they encourage interdisciplinary engagement with social sciences, but their scope (as worked out in their ARCS chapters) is aimed at more organizational change with insider and outsider teams having regular meetings to implement agreed praxis, something that went beyond the resources of my project.[98] However, their second person focus (partnering with an insider team) was something that resonated with my focus on the student community.[99] The scale and scope of Osmer's model is more modest than that of TAR. In common with other models, it is designed to equip Christian ministers to respond to complex pastoral or congregational situations through a reflective, interdisciplinary (or multi-disciplinary)

---

95. Coleman, 'Action Research', 155.

96. Helen Cameron et al., *Talking about God in Practice: Theological Action Research and Practical Theology* (London: SCM, 2010), 51.

97. Cameron et al., 29, 53–56.

98. Cameron et al., 64–69; ARCS stands for Action Research: Church and Society; see the discussion in James Sweeney and Clare Watkins, 'Theological Action Research', in *The SAGE Encyclopedia of Action Research*, ed. David Coghlan and Mary Brydon-Miller (London: SAGE, 2014).

99. Cameron et al., *Talking about God*, 41; referring to Reason and Bradbury, 'Introduction'.

and prayerful process.[100] I felt this approach provided a good analogy for my position as tutor and lecturer of my students.

Osmer's model was presented as an appropriate choice for doctor of ministry studies by Spurgeon's College and fitted well within my critical realist approach. Barreto argues that Osmer's model enables the theologian to "learn from practical experience in ministry, to learn from doing,"[101] and describes it as the "consensus model for interpreting situations."[102] Osmer's cycle employs a distinctive christocentric framework,[103] appropriate for my evangelical context.[104] Anderson had earlier shown sensitivity to this concern when he revised his depiction of Browning's model of practical theology and placing what he termed "Christopraxis" at the centre instead of "experience." Anderson's motivation was to help practical theologians recognize that:

> [T]he praxis of Christ was already at work in their lives; theological reflection now took place between this praxis at work and the praxis of Christ as presented in the word of Scripture. The role of Scripture as a normative, apostolic deposit of truth remains critical for a hermeneutic of Christopraxis.[105]

Osmer does something similar in framing the stages of his model with christological concepts. Cartledge describes each phase as having "a basis in biblical texts, focusing on the themes of wisdom, Prophetic Discernment and servant leadership."[106] Cartledge critiques a majority of practical theologians as either using Scripture "in a limited manner or

---

100. For the distinction between these terms, see Osmer, *Practical Theology*, 163–64.

101. Eric D. Barreto, *Thinking Theologically: Foundations for Learning* (Minneapolis: Fortress, 2015), 53.

102. Barreto, 46.

103. Osmer, *Practical Theology*, 74; this was one reason for not choosing either Swinton and Mowat, *Practical Theology and Qualitative Research*; or *Building Deeper Relationship: Using Faith-Based Facilitation* (London: Salvation Army International, 2010).

104. Root's approach to practical theology also emphasizes christopraxis, but he does not provide a structure to follow, as Osmer does. Andrew Root, *Christopraxis: A Practical Theology of the Cross* (Minneapolis: Fortress, 2014).

105. Ray S. Anderson, *The Shape of Practical Theology: Empowering Ministry with Theological Praxis* (Downers Grove: IVP Academic, 2001), 30.

106. Mark J. Cartledge, 'The Use of Scripture in Practical Theology: A Study of Academic Practice', *Practical Theology* 6, no. 3 (January 2013): 276, https://doi.org/10.1179/1756073X13Z.00000000017.

not at all."[107] By contrast, Osmer's use of christological concepts to structure theological reflection fitted well within my evangelical context.[108] He
describes the different phases of his model as a "participation in Christ's
priestly, royal, and prophetic mediation of salvation," to which he later
adds that "Jesus is the embodiment of God's royal rule in the form of a
servant."[109] It would be difficult as an evangelical Christian to answer the
questions associated with practical theology, "What then should we do?"
and "How then should we live?", without reflecting upon the person of
the Lord Jesus Christ.[110] Osmer's model facilitates that reflection.

Osmer describes his initial Priestly Listening task (or more formally
the descriptive-empirical task) as being "grounded in the spirituality of
presence. It is a matter of attending to what is going on in the lives of
individuals, families and communities."[111] As Mercer notes, this is expressed as spiritual leadership where leaders are interpretative guides
who "gather information enabling them to describe their encounters in
ministry on multiple levels."[112] That attending may involve "many strategies of inquiry and methods of research."[113] Osmer views action research
as a good methodology for generating the data upon which to critically
correlate within the Sagely Wisdom phase.[114] This second, interpretative task is "open to the world" and will also involve "cross-disciplinary

107. Cartledge, 279; it seems to me that Cartledge includes Osmer when he describes a minority of writers "who do use Scripture to inform their methodology and
their theological construction."

108. For a critique of the use of Scripture in other models of practical theology, see
Cartledge, 276.

109. Osmer, *Practical Theology*, 28, 183; he adds to his final task descriptor on
p.184 that Christ is one who came not to be served but to serve, Mark 10:45.

110. Anderson attributes these questions to Don Browning, *A Fundamental
Practical Theology* (Minneapolis: Fortress, 1991) in Anderson, *The Shape of Practical
Theology*, 35; but Weber attributed them to Tolstoy in his 1922 lecture, 'Science as
Vocation' H. H. Gerth and C. Wright Mills, *From Max Weber: Essays in Sociology*, The
International Library of Sociology (Abingdon: Routledge, 1948).

111. Osmer, *Practical Theology*, 34.

112. Joyce Ann Mercer, 'Review of *Practical Theology: An Introduction* by Richard
R. Osmer: Grand Rapids: Eerdmans, 2008', *Theology Today* 67, no. 2 (July 2010): 236,
https://doi.org/10.1177/004057361006700212.

113. Osmer, *Practical Theology*, 161; see, for instance, Leach, 'Pastoral Theology
as Attention'.

114. Osmer, *Practical Theology*, 49, 52.

dialogue."[115] Wayne Morris cites Osmer approvingly when he argues that the practical theologian should be interdisciplinary.

> Practical theology is largely characterized by its willingness to engage with a range of disciplines. Osmer, for example, emphasizes the importance of social scientific empirical research methodologies through which the practical theologian can engage in a process of really "attending" to others.[116]

Osmer argues that his model is indeed interdisciplinary and that "we must think in terms of interconnections, relationship, and systems."[117] Osmer's third phase, Prophetic Discernment, is described as interpreting Christ as the Word of God "to address particular social conditions, events, and decisions before congregations today."[118] This normative task might involve drawing on critical social theory, dialogue with philosophy, or engagement with sociology with the aim of "seeking the guidance of God amid the complexities of life."[119] Osmer describes the final, pragmatic task of servant leadership as "the task of forming and enacting strategies of action that influence events in ways that are desirable."[120] It recognizes the leadership needed to implement theologically-inspired change within a congregation or, in my case, within my academic community of tutor groups, module contents, and timetables. Practical theology's distinctive approach, Osmer argues, is just these four tasks, albeit always within a cross-disciplinary environment and carried out in different ways.[121]

SUMMARY

This chapter provided the warrant for accepting the methods used in the research project as valid and trustworthy and is the foundation for the argument developed from the research data. I defended my epistemology and choice of methods as appropriate ways of investigating the research question and providing the right kind of knowledge. Critical realism

---

115. Osmer, 162.

116. Wayne Morris, *Salvation as Praxis: A Practical Theology of Salvation for a Multi-Faith World* (London: Bloomsbury T&T Clark, 2014), 25.

117. Osmer, *Practical Theology*, 17.

118. Osmer, 135.

119. Mercer, 'Review of Practical Theology', 238.

120. Osmer, *Practical Theology*, 176.

121. Osmer, 241.

fitted both my evangelical view of Scripture and a common approach to teaching science. My choice of Norton's pedagogical action research was based on its suitability for higher education contexts and its systematic nature that made it manageable for a non-specialist. I found Osmer's model of practical theology to be a helpful structure for critical correlation and theological reflection. It was conducive to a more christocentric, missional, and teleological view of Scripture which fitted well with both my research question and evangelical context.[122] It followed naturally from Norton's action research model, and the Priestly Listening phase of Osmer's model took over the results of my thematic analysis as part of Norton's "modifying future practice" phase. In the next chapter I outline the first cycle of Norton's action research model applied to the pilot study of the DID course.

---

122. I argue for a positive role for teleology in McKitterick, 'The Role of Teleology in Practical Theology'; see also McKitterick, 'The Theological Imperative Model for Practical Theology', 17; cf. Bennett et al., *Invitation to Research in Practical Theology*, 31.

4

Pedagogical Action Research

Pedagogical action research is not just reflective practice [. . .] nor is it simply a form of curriculum development (typical of a scholarly approach to learning and teaching). It becomes real research when we open up our investigations and findings to peer scrutiny and review (informally in departmental or institutional based seminars, and formally in conferences and peer-reviewed journal papers).[1]

THIS CHAPTER MARKS the point of taking initiative, trialling ideas, and gathering initial data for evaluation in response to the research question. It describes the systematic process of framing and completing the first action research cycle. As discussed above, the appropriate form of action research chosen for my educational context was Norton's pedagogical action research model.[2] Norton advises that there is "no secret or magic formula" for this kind of study and outlines the basics of her cycle as: observing something to be improved; planning a course of action that introduces a change to your practice; carrying it out; and then evaluating the effect of the change.[3] She introduces the helpful acronym of ITDEM (Identifying a problem, Thinking how to tackle it, Doing it, Evaluating

1. Norton, 'The Case for Pedagogical Action Research in Psychology Learning and Teaching', 8.

2. Norton, *Action Research in Teaching and Learning*; Norton, 'The Case for Pedagogical Action Research in Psychology Learning and Teaching'.

3. Norton, *Action Research in Teaching and Learning*, 69.

the findings, and Modifying future practice).[4] It represents a way of doing action research and a commitment to changing a situation.[5]

FIRST CYCLE: PILOTING THE DISCOVERING INTELLIGENT DESIGN COURSE

Identifying the problem

Norton's ITDEM (Identify, Think, Do, Evaluate, Modify) approach starts with articulating the problem to be tackled. The problem identified from student conversations with me (some of which I subsequently asked them to send me in written form) became the motivation for the research project. Several students described the problem of discussing the relationship between science and Christian faith within their ministries. For example, a student youth worker reported her experience of receiving science questions in her youth group:

> In terms of youth work, they are always the questions you get asked from those who are not from a church background. They're the questions you get asked. [. . .] There have been questions in youth groups, and when none of us were able to give a properly scientific answer they've just seen faith being anti-science. Not the church so much, but "none of you have got an answer for me," and so they put that answer in their minds. They've decided that the church is anti-science because they're not getting satisfied by their answers.(29FM)

Another student explained that her awareness of the problem began at school. She said her theologically-trained philosophy and ethics teacher was "very anti-Christian and would always tell me reasons why there was no God. [. . .] He always had a better answer than me; I never really understood the science of it."[6] Similar student conversations expressed a sense of being out of their depth, or made to feel inferior by those who had scientific arguments against a belief in God, or not providing answers that satisfy young people's questions about how to reconcile what they had heard in school with what they were hearing in their church

---

4. Norton, 70.

5. Norton, 'The Case for Pedagogical Action Research in Psychology Learning and Teaching', 10.

6. 24FM in personal email communication to me.

youth group. There was an expressed need to be able to respond to people at a scientific level and to address the science-based challenges that the students had experienced. The practical problem that requires practical wisdom (that initiates a change in practice) was how should I respond to an expressed student need of struggling with questions concerning science in their ministry contexts.

First person context

In thinking about how to tackle the problem, there are many possible approaches, and action research "choices points" need to be transparent.[7] I could have emphasized a theological response within my existing teaching load or invited guest speakers for lectures or a conference and interviewed students' responses to them. Coleman states that "it is important for the researcher to develop awareness of themselves" or what she calls the inner arc of attention.[8] Why did I respond by teaching a course on intelligent design myself? The first answer is that this was a pragmatic choice based on the requirements of the professional doctorate dissertation. As well as the pragmatic choice, there was an intuitive element to the decision. I felt that this was an opportunity to develop more formally my sense that science had the potential to inspire and encourage theology students. I also felt that it was an opportunity to develop my skills and understanding of science, even though this would change my positionality from one of strength (as a theological educator) to one of vulnerability (a science educator) simply because I had not nearly as many years of experience in that field.[9] This kenotic approach enabled me to identify somewhat with those students who felt science to be intimidating.

Norton's approach requires the researcher to be reflective about the context of the research, both personally and professionally, recognizing that my background and experiences will influence my decisions.[10] My

7. Peter Reason and Hilary Bradbury, 'Concluding Reflections: Whither Action Research?', in *The SAGE Handbook of Action Research: Participative Inquiry and Practice*, ed. Peter Reason and Hilary Bradbury, 2nd ed (London: SAGE, 2008), 704.

8. Coleman, 'Action Research', 159.

9. Sonia Ospina et al., 'Taking the Action Turn: Lessons from Bringing Participation to Qualitative Research', in *The SAGE Handbook of Action Research: Participative Inquiry and Practice*, ed. Peter Reason and Hilary Bradbury, 2nd ed. (SAGE, 2008), 423.

10. Norton, *Action Research in Teaching and Learning*, 32.

own involvement with intelligent design includes participating in several UK Intelligent Design movement (ID) conferences.[11] This marked an intellectual development in that my interest shifted from theological apologetics arguments to more scientific ones.

One incident that catalysed my interest was when one of my children's school's magazine dedicated a publication to matters of science and religion. In an interview article entitled "Science and Religion: What Teachers Believe," two science and three Philosophy and Religious Studies (PRS) teachers were interviewed and gave their answers to the question "Do you feel that intelligent design should be taught in schools?"[12] The two science teachers answered differently but for the same reasons. Yes, one said, because it is "better to tackle unintelligent ideas head-on. I am sure that most science teachers could tear this to shreds in a minute or so." "No," said the other, "it is a silly non-scientific way of trying to explain a well explained theory." Later in the interview one replied, "As for the existence of god (small g), I suggest that scientists have better things to do and more exciting avenues to explore than these rather uninteresting ideas generated by ignorant people long ago." The PRS teachers all agreed that intelligent design should be taught as part of the PRS A-level curriculum because it is "a religious (and political) theory," but to teach it as part of science would be "oxymoronic" and it "should not be taught as a scientifically credible hypothesis." These attitudes were not challenged in the school magazine and were presented as the standard view. This insight into the intellectual context of my children at school generated a sense of injustice and motivated me to seek an opportunity to respond. The incident is relevant because many of the students work in a school or youth context and will encounter similar attitudes. The professional doctorate enabled me to develop my own interests and concerns within my educational practice.

Broader context

My conviction that these teachers' comments represented an injustice came from a belief that intelligent design was widely misunderstood.

11. The abbreviation ID will be used to refer to the Intelligent Design movement to which both theorists and advocates identify themselves; the term "intelligent design" will be used when referring either to the concept or the various arguments for design.

12. All quotations in this paragraph are from 'Science and Religion: What Teachers Believe', *Portsmouth Point: Belief*, December 2013, 18–21.

This view was validated by a review of two 2009 surveys commissioned by the Theos think tank (part of the British and Foreign Bible Society) and conducted by ComRes. The first was a survey of the UK population for their views on evolution and its relationship to theism. The survey results showed that "[o]pinion was often confused and contradictory."[13] For instance, although only 11 percent of UK respondents said intelligent design was "the most likely explanation, yet 51 percent say it is either definitely or probably true."[14] In the same survey, 36 percent of people favouring atheistic evolution as probably true were, at the same time, self-defined Christians, demonstrating "that a significant proportion of people who would identify themselves as Christian believe in evolution which they say makes belief in God absurd and unnecessary."[15] The survey itself was criticised for being poorly structured leading to incoherent results, but even still Baker concurs that "the British population is confused on the matter."[16]

The second survey carried out by ComRes was an in-depth study of the view of those who were mostly sceptical of Darwinian evolution. They interviewed many key leaders and opinion formers that identified themselves along a spectrum of views including young earth creationists, old earth creationists, and intelligent design theorists.[17] The survey demonstrated much common ground amongst respondents, such as the shared perspective that a theistic worldview was in conflict with the media and the educational establishment, and that this was a significant issue for the church to face. However, it also showed the tensions between those who held to these different (even if overlapping) positions along that spectrum, particularly when it came to intelligent design. Some saw intelligent design positively "as a way of explaining reality," whereas others saw it more politically as a "movement" or "strategy."[18] "Responses divided between those for whom ID offered a 'science' that they could

---

13. Caroline Lawes, *Faith and Darwin: Harmony, Conflict, or Confusion?* (London: Theos, 2009), 11.

14. Lawes, 12.

15. Lawes, 14.

16. Sylvia Baker, 'The Theos/ComRes Survey into Public Perception of Darwinism in the UK: A Recipe for Confusion', *Public Understanding of Science* 21, no. 3 (26 August 2010): 292, https://doi.org/10.1177/0963662510376707.

17. Robin Pharoah, Tamara Hale, and Becky Rowe, *Doubting Darwin: Creationism and Evolution Scepticism in Britain Today* (London: Theos, 2009).

18. Pharoah, Hale, and Rowe, 93.

accept and which challenged the evolutionist orthodoxy, and those who didn't think it did enough to recognise the role of God and the Biblical account of creation."[19] There was tension over the priority of preaching the Gospel of God compared with the task of presenting scientific evidence to undermine confidence in an atheistic account of evolution.

> ID [. . .] proved controversial, despite some of our respondents' assertion that it had the potential to unite those with differing points of view on theology or biblical interpretation. Many of our respondents considered it offered no particular help in their fight to bring an understanding of God to those with no such understanding. For others, however, evolution was of such significance, in terms of being a misunderstanding of the world, that a detailed examination of the science around it was of paramount importance. And yet others felt that the fight against evolution was only one of several key fronts in a broader battle against secularism and atheism in general. Diversity of views within a movement is common, of course, but some of these views contradict each other. One cannot promote biblical understanding, for example, if one is trying to exclude God from one's polemic.[20]

For some, intelligent design is not sufficiently Christian in that it makes no claim to be able to identify the designer because that would go beyond the scientific evidence. One creationist Christian minister is quoted saying, "At the end of the day they do not go far enough because they are not saying who the Intelligent Designer is. It could be God. It could be Allah [. . .] I do not ally myself with them in any way."[21] For others, any appeal to a transcendent designer active within nature is to push the topic outside of the purview of science, and therefore not suitable to discuss amongst scientists. A university lecturer is quoted as saying "Intelligent Design—is that just another way of someone saying he's a creationist? I think it probably is."[22]

The ComRes research also revealed a level of doubt about the importance of evolution, and it was frequently marginalized in the minds of busy church leaders. "Church ministers [. . .] often reported that their beliefs about evolution were a relatively minor concern in daily life, a

19. Pharoah, Hale, and Rowe, 93–94.
20. Pharoah, Hale, and Rowe, 115.
21. Pharoah, Hale, and Rowe, 92.
22. Pharoah, Hale, and Rowe, 93.

comparatively unimportant aspect of their work or of their identity."[23] It seemed like a minority interest for someone with specialist qualifications, but otherwise of little relevance and might detract from the core business of being a church leader.

In choosing to teach a course on intelligent design, I recognized that mine was a minority view within the evangelical community and would mean moving out of a position of strength, but my first-hand knowledge of the subject and the people involved informed my judgement to choose this course of action. This choice was made in pursuit of my value of seeing intelligent design as addressing a problem identified by students and my belief that this would be good for their ministries as current and future Christian leaders. This final consideration resonated with the values of my organization, Moorlands College, in teaching applied theology for Christian leaders.[24]

Thinking how to tackle the problem

This is the planning stage of Norton's pedagogical action research model. The issues considered in this section were the course materials, the relationship with colleagues, the pragmatics and ethics of student feedback, and how such feedback might be validated. There would need to be a pilot of the course to allow reflection and improvement. "If your pilot reveals problems with your methods, you still have time to change them."[25] My focus at this stage was on constructing a suitable course (Stenhouse's "content model").[26] I aligned with McKernan's encouragement for curriculum development to be liberated from "end-means" or "outcomes-based" thinking and instead for the educator (and student) "to exercise intellectual and moral judgment."[27] The curriculum, he argues, must be driven by moral judgements that promote the ability of students to act wisely.[28] The moral good that my research question aimed at was

23. Pharoah, Hale, and Rowe, 107.

24. Maguire, 'Methodology as Personal and Professional Integrity: Research Designing for Practitioner Doctorates', 108.

25. Cameron and Duce, *Researching Practice in Ministry and Mission*, 96.

26. Stenhouse's three alternatives are given in James McKernan, *Curriculum and Imagination: Process Theory, Pedagogy and Action Research* (London: Routledge, 2008), 24.

27. McKernan, 10.

28. McKernan, 166.

to address the concern that science is an obstacle for students seeking to share their faith with others. A good curriculum, McKernan argues, "would choose controversial subjects and seek to exhume the irrational and unjust practices found in the classroom, school and relationships therein, community and society."[29] Intelligent design is unjustly located as irrational or insubstantial within academia, and my pedagogical decisions were aimed at discovering its value in giving evangelical students confidence when discussing matters of science. McKernan encourages the educator to adopt a "neutral chairperson" attitude to teaching controversial topics and, since that was not possible in my situation, the ethical approach must emphasize integrity by being transparent about my support for intelligent design. Creswell and Creswell emphasize the need to "avoid deceiving participants,"[30] and therefore I was clear about my positive attitude towards intelligent design, whilst not assuming students shared that positive attitude.

Choosing ID teaching material

Teaching a course on intelligent design involved deliberation of the material taught and therefore of the teaching resources supporting the course.[31] Action research requires transparency in making choices,[32] and so the rationality behind the course content needs to be made clear. One possibility considered was to design the course as a response to naturalist arguments presented in schools and the media with which my students might well be familiar. Several school textbooks and revision guides were inspected along with arguments used in biology, chemistry, and physics lessons on things like the origin of life, the structure of DNA and its transcription, and the origin of stars were collated. This approach would have the advantage of being relevant and might sharpen up the sense of challenge to the evolutionary arguments presented there. The problem I felt that approach had was that it allowed the topics to be determined by others rather than being a more unified, structured response initiated by the arguments for intelligent design.

29. McKernan, 167.

30. Creswell and Creswell, *Research Design*, 150.

31. McKernan, *Curriculum and Imagination*, 21.

32. Coghlan and Brannick, *Doing Action Research in Your Own Organization*, 28.

I decided a more unified style was preferred to present intelligent design arguments (rather than as a reaction against certain issues) and several books written by ID theorists were considered. It was important to present intelligent design arguments from the perspective of those that hold to that perspective, rather than from opponents of intelligent design.[33] Certain texts were discounted because they were too specific and technical nature, such as books only dealing with human origins or astronomy.[34] Although it would have been comprehensive, edited books covering different topics through different authors were excluded because they were not uniform in their style and register, and also because some of the arguments had moved on since some of them were published.[35] A more recent edited text was too in-depth (and too expensive) for an introductory text that students might wish to purchase.[36] Several single-author texts were written at a good level but without many images.[37] I felt it was important for the text to be as accessible and interactive as possible, making images or diagrams important.

33. David W. Bebbington, 'Response: The History of Ideas and the Study of Religion', in *Seeing Things Their Way: Intellectual History and the Return of Religion*, ed. Alister Chapman, John Coffey, and Brad S. Gregory (Notre Dame: University of Notre Dame Press, 2009), 242; for examples of books written from the perspective of opponents of intelligent design, see Forrest and Gross, *Creationism's Trojan Horse*; Leonard Susskind, *The Cosmic Landscape: String Theory and the Illusion of Intelligent Design* (London: Little Brown, 2005); Michael Shermer, *Why Darwin Matters the Case against Intelligent Design* (New York: Holt, 2006); Hafer, *The Not-so-Intelligent Designer*; Foster, Clark, and York, *Critique of Intelligent Design*.

34. Ann Gauger, Douglas Axe, and Casey Luskin, *Science and Human Origins* (Seattle: Discovery Institute Press, 2012); Guillermo Gonzalez and Jay W. Richards, *The Privileged Planet: How Our Place in the Cosmos is Designed for Discovery* (Washington: Regnery, 2004).

35. William A. Dembski, ed., *Mere Creation: Science, Faith & Intelligent Design* (Downers Grove: InterVarsity, 1998); William A. Dembski and James M. Kushiner, eds., *Signs of Intelligence: Understanding Intelligent Design* (Grand Rapids: Brazos, 2001); H. Wayne House, ed., *Intelligent Design 101: Leading Experts Explain the Key Issues* (Grand Rapids: Kregel, 2008).

36. Bruce Gordon and William A. Dembski, eds., *The Nature of Nature: Examining the Role of Naturalism in Science* (Wilmington: ISI, 2011).

37. Stephen C. Meyer, *Signature in the Cell: DNA and the Evidence for Intelligent Design* (New York: HarperOne, 2009); Stephen C. Meyer, *Darwin's Doubt: The Explosive Origin of Animal Life and the Case for Intelligent Design* (New York, NY: HarperOne, 2013); William A. Dembski, *Intelligent Design: The Bridge between Science & Theology* (Downers Grove: InterVarsity, 1999); William A. Dembski, *The Design Revolution: Answering the Toughest Questions about Intelligent Design* (Downers Grove: InterVarsity, 2004).

Two texts emerged as suitable resources. The first was *Explore Evolution*, written as a supplementary text intended for secondary school level.[38] The website supporting the book states it uses an "inquiry-based learning" style and is designed to support existing school lesson plans.[39] The book is said to help "critically analyse" and "teach both strengths and weaknesses" of the scientific theory of evolution for those US states that are required to do so. That is, the book is participating in a public debate in America about the teaching of evolution in public schools. It is an attractively laid-out and well-illustrated text specifically to provide critical insights into the US school curriculum. The authors are well qualified in their respective fields, so again it would be a reliable text to use. However, I rejected it because the book's agenda was driven by the needs of the US school sector. It was less a presentation of intelligent design and more a critical reflection on evolutionary theory as taught in the US, and I thought this something of a distraction.

The text chosen as the basis for the course was *Discovering Intelligent Design: A Journey into the Scientific Evidence*.[40] The book describes itself as part of "a comprehensive curriculum that presents both the biological and cosmological evidence in support of the scientific theory of intelligent design."[41] The authors' intention is to present the arguments of intelligent design comprehensively and clearly. It has six sections:

- Defining Intelligent Design
- Cosmology and the Solar System
- Origin of Life, Molecular Biology and DNA
- Fossils and Common Descent
- Summary Section
- Academic Freedom

Each of the sections were subdivided into various chapters. The several advantages of this text were that it was written from an intelligent

---

38. Stephen C. Meyer et al., *Explore Evolution: The Arguments for and against Neo-Darwinism* (Melbourne; London: Hill House Publishers, 2009).

39. 'Explore Evolution | Who is This For?', accessed 6 May 2019, http://www.exploreevolution.com/who_is_this_for.php.

40. Gary Kemper, Hallie Kemper, and Casey Luskin, *Discovering Intelligent Design: A Journey into the Scientific Evidence* (Seattle: Discovery Institute Press, 2013).

41. Kemper, Kemper, and Luskin, 4.

design perspective, covered a broad range of relevant topics, had a uniformity of style and academic level, was well-illustrated, and was supported by a wide range of additional materials and online resources. The textbook came with several good quality video extracts on a DVD to add multimedia content to the text.[42] It also has a supporting interactive website that follows each chapter topic.[43] There are summarizing videos, full handouts for each chapter with learning outcomes, and an online quiz to test student comprehension. Zimmerman's review notes that it is designed for those "who are not familiar with the science underlying the theory."[44] Students that were unsure of any aspects of the science taught on the course could be involved in developing and supplementing their own learning. I felt confident teaching from the *Discovering Intelligent Design* (DID) textbook as it gave the course a structure and supported students in their learning. It cohered with my view of what intelligent design is, which enabled me to teach with a sense of integrity and sincerity. A copy of the textbook was in the college library enabling students to consult the evidence for arguments from the book without having to purchase it.

Pedagogical approach

Having established the rationale for the content of the DID course, the teaching methods were considered: "What would effective teaching mean in this context?"[45] As the research question indicates, it was the introduction of the science content that constituted the change in practice, rather than innovating a new teaching format. My aim was for students to learn how the scientific evidence presented integrated with their evangelical worldview. A good outcome of the course, coherent with my

42. For more information of the video and the DVD's from which the clips were taken see 'Creating A Multimedia Experience | Discovering Intelligent Design', accessed 6 May 2019, https://discovering.design/multimedia/.

43. 'Discovering Intelligent Design', DiscoveryU, accessed 6 May 2019, http://discoveryu.thinkific.com/courses/discovering-intelligent-design.

44. Paul A. Zimmerman, 'Discovering Intelligent Design: A Journey into the Scientific Evidence by Gary Kemper, Hallie Kemper, and Casey Luskin', *Concordia Theological Quarterly* 77, no. 3–4 (2013): 364.

45. Alenoush Saroyan et al., 'The Final Step: Evaluation of Teaching', in *Rethinking Teaching in Higher Education: From a Course Design Workshop to a Faculty Development Framework*, ed. Alenoush Saroyan and Cheryl Amundsen (Sterling: Stylus, 2004), 119.

research question, would be for students to have confidence and facility in discussing scientific matters as they relate to their Christian faith. Validation of that intention would need to be through feedback from student experiences outside of the classroom. My pedagogical structure was constrained by pragmatic decisions. I decided to run the pilot course over seven consecutive weeks to fit in with the college timetable as well as giving me sufficient time to prepare the teaching material from the book. I made each session the length of a double lecture to provide a familiar format.

The main difficulty was presenting up-to-date scientific knowledge in an academically robust manner whilst remembering that the students participating in the lectures were theology undergraduates. I decided I needed to show evidence and incorporate visual imagery for the material. I made use of good quality video extracts from the DID book DVD resource, and also from several other YouTube videos that illustrated key features.[46] The lectures used image-rich PowerPoint slides to enhance the presentation of the course material.[47] I directed students to the supporting interactive website following each topic where they could find summarizing videos, handouts for each chapter, and an online quiz to test comprehension.[48] A pedagogical imperative was the active involvement of participants: "there must be the possibility for the participant to be engaged and not simply remain a passive receiver of information."[49] This included feedback from previous lectures, peer-discussions, short tasks and frequent opportunities to bring questions about the topics presented. Having a relatively small class size supported this aspect of interactivity, and there was a good, relaxed sense of involvement from the students.

When discussing Darwinian evolution, Stolberg and Teece suggest encouraging students to be critical and suggest that the teacher is "explicit about the aims and objectives of any exercise so that your students

46. The DVD videos were from 'Creating A Multimedia Experience | Discovering Intelligent Design'.

47. I agree with McKernan who argues that "[t]o my mind, the curriculum needs to be seen as a continuous educational experience: a process, rather than a product. That is, as an educative experience, rather than a behavior, or outcome of that experience." McKernan, *Curriculum and Imagination*, 6.

48. 'Discovering Intelligent Design'.

49. Cheryl Amundsen, Laura Winer, and Terry Gandell, 'Designing Teaching for Student Learning', in *Rethinking Teaching in Higher Education: From a Course Design Workshop to a Faculty Development Framework*, ed. Alenoush Saroyan and Cheryl Amundsen (Sterling: Stylus, 2004), 73.

are aware of the circumstances in which they are being asked for their opinions and share the basis for their thinking."[50] The aim of teaching science within a theological context is to prevent "simply compartmentalizing" the two disciplines and instead enable them to synthesize their knowledge.[51] They suggest that students should be "encouraged to compare and contrast the alternate, theoretical approaches available to Darwin and his contemporaries," including intelligent design.[52] This was in keeping with the approach I adopted. I also remained aware throughout the course that the scientific views presented might be contrary to "students' spontaneous assumptions" and authority sources.[53] Stolberg and Teece point to the need to create space and time to reflect if students are to change their perspective on a topic. "Your role is, therefore, to enable students to construct their own coherent explanation as to why they accept or reject, retain or dismiss a particular viewpoint."[54] They helpfully point to the difference between teaching historical evidence for a narrative hypothesis and experimentation and repeatable observation, and the way that students with different religious perspectives often prefer one or the other.[55] As discussed above, there was no attempt to be neutral about teaching intelligent design, avoiding any hint of deception.[56]

Ethical considerations

In terms of what Guillemin and Gillam call "procedural ethics," the research ethics for the project was submitted as a module in itself and was approved by Chester's ethics panel.[57] I took part in extensive consultations with my research supervisors about my specific proposals and received helpful guidance, especially since the professional contexts were similar,

50. Tonie Stolberg and Geoff Teece, *Teaching Religion and Science: Effective Pedagogy and Practical Approaches for RE Teachers* (Abingdon: Routledge, 2011), 71.

51. Stolberg and Teece, 72–74.

52. Stolberg and Teece, 75.

53. Stolberg and Teece, 59.

54. Stolberg and Teece, 58.

55. Stolberg and Teece, 60.

56. Jack R. Fraenkel, Norman E. Wallen, and Helen H. Hyun, *How to Design and Evaluate Research in Education*, 8th ed. (New York: McGraw-Hill, 2012), 63.

57. Marilys Guillemin and Lynn Gillam, 'Ethics, Reflexivity, and "Ethically Important Moments" in Research', *Qualitative Inquiry* 10, no. 2 (April 2004): 263, https://doi.org/10.1177/1077800403262360.

as both are Bible colleges.[58] The first imperative was that the research was done in a safe and secure environment to ensure that the participants' interests were protected.[59]

The pilot course was conducted in a normal classroom context that students were familiar with and during normal hours of the college time-table. I stressed at the beginning and at its conclusion that all feedback was voluntary, and that participation would not influence students' normal studies. All participants were informed of the nature of the course in documentation written in clear language.[60] Those willing to consider being participants received a formal letter of invitation outlining the doctoral programme, the purpose of the research, and inviting them to contribute to my research. Students understood that the course was part of my professional doctoral program and gave written consent to being asked for feedback from it. Students were "fully informed" in that they had the information needed "to make a decision about whether or not to participate."[61] A consent form was completed by all participants before the face-to-face discussion.[62] It confirmed that they had read and understood the participant information sheet, and had been given op-portunity to ask questions.[63] It also confirmed that they understood their participation to be voluntary and that they were free to withdraw at any time without consequence. Henning et al. emphasize the importance of protecting students' confidentiality.[64] This was limited in that all those who took part knew each other to be in the same classroom, so it was their individual responses given in feedback and face-to-face discussions

58. Oliver, *The Student's Guide to Research Ethics*, 44.

59. Martyn Denscombe, *The Good Research Guide: For Small-Scale Social Research Projects*, 4th ed., Open UP Study Skills (Maidenhead: Open University Press, 2010), 331.

60. Bryman, *Social Research Methods*, 138–40.

61. Oliver, *The Student's Guide to Research Ethics*, 28.

62. For the basis of lawful possession of data, see 'Guide to the Gen-eral Data Protection Regulation (GDPR)' (London: Information Commis-sioner's Office, 2018), 14, https://www.gov.uk/government/publications/guide-to-the-general-data-protection-regulation.

63. Judith Bell, *Doing Your Research Project: A Guide For First-Time Researchers*, 6th ed. (Maidenhead: Open University Press, 2014), 47.

64. John E. Henning, Jody M. Stone, and James L. Kelly, *Using Action Research to Improve Instruction: An Interactive Guide for Teachers* (Abingdon: Routledge, 2009), 11.

that would be anonymized if used in the dissertation.[65] Any reference to their experiences of using intelligent design arguments in their ministries would be anonymized.

Using Guillemin and Gillam's term "ethics in practice," the main issue was the relationship between myself and participants.[66] I recognized the inevitability of the power structure of teaching the topic to students as lecturer: "[p]ower and knowledge are inextricably intertwined."[67] However, I considered this pedagogical approach to be justified as it replicated the students' normal experience of being in a theology lecture with me. Students would feel they were being taught in a familiar context and manner. There is a good atmosphere in the classroom and interaction is always encouraged. This same pedagogical atmosphere would encourage students to challenge and question what was being taught about science as they would about theology. There was no exclusion of perspective, and my role as the teacher was to facilitate and help articulate any questions that students found difficulty in formulating. The effect of teaching the DID course was that it raised consciousness of issues concerning Darwinian arguments empowering students to take part in scientific debates, rather than feeling excluded from or unable to contribute to them.[68] Power in this pedagogical sense, Gaventa and Cornwall argue, enables action, in this case enabling the participation of those that previously felt excluded.[69]

In the face-to-face discussions, students would also be in a familiar environment, namely my office at college. Their chair was situated next to the door which contained a transparent glass panel. This practical action is part of McKernan's first principle of respect for persons, in this case the student participant.[70] The discussions were open and enabled the students to reflect on any aspect of the course and the experience of learning that they wanted. My role as the course teacher was changed to

65. Coghlan and Brannick, *Doing Action Research in Your Own Organization*, 77.

66. Guillemin and Gillam, 'Ethics, Reflexivity, and "Ethically Important Moments" in Research', 265.

67. John Gaventa and Andrea Cornwall, 'Power and Knowledge', in *The SAGE Handbook of Action Research: Participative Inquiry and Practice*, ed. Peter Reason and Hilary Bradbury, 2nd ed (London: SAGE, 2008), 172.

68. Gaventa and Cornwall, 174.

69. Gaventa and Cornwall, 176.

70. McKernan, *Curriculum and Imagination*, 162.

that of facilitating (McKernan talks of "chairing") discussion to ensure that the student's voice is heard and able to contribute to the research.[71]

Doing it

The pilot course was run over the first term in one of the main lecture rooms on the college campus for seven weeks on Friday afternoons when there were no other lectures timetabled. The topics covered were entitled Introduction to ID, Cosmic Design, Complexity of Life I, Complexity of Life II, Common Descent, Fossils and Skeletons, and Humans and Strategy. The lectures had a common look and feel to the chosen textbook as the same hummingbird design was used in PowerPoints and handouts. This had the effect of unifying the content delivered with the supporting online resources.

I announced my intention to run the course and put up a sign-up sheet for students to indicate interest. Twenty-five students indicated their intention to attend the lectures. Of these, eleven continued to attend to the end of the course, all of them being present for at least six out of the seven lectures. Most of the rest dropped out after only one or two lectures. This indicated that the course appealed only to certain students: reasons for that could have been the time commitment involved (see for example 24FM's comment below), or the nature or presentation style of the content.

Gathering feedback

Feedback about the course was obtained initially through an online survey (the first time I had done so) and I then invited participants to discuss it with me individually. Those willing to take part received an email with the link to "Reflection on the 'Discovering Intelligent Design' Course" on the online survey site Survey Monkey. Of the eleven participants who completed at least six out of seven sessions of the course, seven chose to complete the online survey, and all of these agreed to discuss it individually as well.

- On a Likert scale from "not at all" to "extremely," all seven participants responded either "very much" or "extremely" for "Relevance

71. McKernan, 162.

of course," "Accessibility of taught content," "Ability of course teacher," and "Quality of handouts and PowerPoint."[72]

- On the same scale, four out of seven expressed the view that Darwinism and Naturalism, Cosmos and Big Bang, Complexity of Life,
  DNA, Fossils and Common Descent, and Human Origins as "extremely" relevant. One respondent chose "slightly" for the relevance
  of Fossils and Common Descent.

- Four out of seven respondents indicated "very much" or "extremely"
  to the statement that intelligent design was important to "help prevent people you know leaving the church."

- Again, four out of seven indicated "very much" or "extremely" to
  the question about the value of the course in helping "to share your
  faith."

This feedback, although not definitive, gave early indication that the
idea of running of course on this topic was relevant to their needs and
interests. As the first time I had used this medium, however, its value was
limited because the questions were not well-formed.

Face-to-face discussions

Participating students were invited to discuss their impressions of the
course in my office. The purpose was to give space and time to hear their
perspectives on the course and to learn to what extent, if at all, it had
contributed to their confidence and ability to share their faith. In addition, I asked for critical reflections for how it could be improved. The
discussions (what Norton calls "unstructured interviews") were about
twenty minutes, with one lasting about half an hour.[73] They began with
open questions about how participants felt about the course.

The relevance of the course to the participants was affirmed through
narratives about people whose loss of faith was attributable to Darwinian ideas. Some expressed the value of intelligent design as a solution
to the problem of only having two alternatives, namely Darwinism or
creationism.

---

72. For a discussion on the use of Likert scales, see Fraenkel, Wallen, and Hyun,
How to Design and Evaluate Research in Education, 126–27.

73. Norton, *Action Research in Teaching and Learning*, 100.

My Manager at work was a Christian in his youth and childhood but when he was older he was not convinced and said that science was more logical and had more proof. (23FM)

She wanted to know how the world and everything in it came to be. The [church leaders] didn't believe creation was real but the only other answer she was given was Darwinism so she felt forced to believe that it was the answer and because it was such a contradiction to the faith she left the church. (23FM)

I know friends that have been told from a young age in Sunday school that God created the heavens and the earth in seven days and that this was something not to be questioned because it displayed "a lack of faith." However, when they got to uni they found that Darwinism seemed to provide an answer for those questions and seemed to be most likely. This threw doubt over creationism and therefore eventually in his eyes it discredited the rest of the Bible. (27MM)

A brother of mine some years ago, although he professes Christianity, appeared to have abandoned the faith altogether out of what he believed were the convincing arguments of Darwinism. He began with subtle scepticism before gradually progressing into a complete denial. (28MM)

We had an atheist [Religious Studies] teacher at school and he challenged Christians on this topic causing many to walk away from faith because they didn't have answers. (24FM)

The value of the DID course for participants was supported by their views that science and faith are frequently presented as topics of concern in their ministries. This confirmed my motivation at the start of the research project, namely hearing of similar stories of students in their placements.

Evolution tends to be the biggest topic of debate which science tends to win because no one defends Christianity at school. (25MM)

This topic is always a huge stumbling block for people from Alpha to conversations in the pub. Dawkins and the secular worldview are always thrown at us. (27MM)

While discussing the topic of science and faith with a Christian, I was able to introduce them to the area of science that is the ID perspective. After hearing about how this would have helped them when they were struggling with this issue years ago as a teenager, it has encouraged me to read more and to further inform myself on this subject so that I may have fruitful conversations with other people who may be in that situation today. (28MM)

There were several accounts of participants having used intelligent design arguments they had learned from the course in sharing their faith with others. These accounts validated the premise of the research project that teaching intelligent design was useful in giving confidence and ability to participants in sharing their faith with others.

I actually used intelligent design in a discussion with friends down the pub last week and even the ones who did biology A-Level seemed to be in agreement. We talked extensively about the basics of creation and also the Christian faith and the saviour Jesus. (25MM)

I've found giving atheist scientists a view that contradicts Dawkins and supports a biblical worldview invaluable in my apologetics in a film club I run at church. (27MM)

This area always comes up with one guy in particular. He is not yet a Christian but is very opening minded, has been to numerous Alpha/Christianity Explored courses and has started attending our Sunday services pretty regularly. His world view on creation/evolution comes primarily from Darwinist documentaries he watches on TV. I am able to respond to these objections along the lines of the ID course. (24FM)

Other feedback included an appreciation for the format of the course and the way I presented it. "This represented everything I came to Moorlands for! Loved it!" (27MM). Critical reflections on the course were invited, and students gave suggestions for how it could be improved. For a couple of students, the time chosen for the delivery of the course was difficult for them as they had placement commitments immediately after the lectures which caused a bit of time pressure for them. Another said that they had come in specially for the lectures. "Ability to attend [. . .] it meant coming to Moorlands on an additional day," (24FM). Another thought that the lecture format could have been augmented with practical activities.

It might be useful to add a practical element to the course. For example, having an opportunity to debate the topics and a critique of arguments used in order to give even more confidence whilst using material. (22MM)

In a similar vein, one participant suggested preparing sample sheets "to have answers ready for potential conversations." (23FM).

Evaluating the pilot course

I found delivering the pilot DID course encouraging and fulfilling. The most difficult aspect for me was the preparation of the materials in time amidst a normal busy term. The students demonstrated significant interest in the topic and appreciation for the effort in presenting it. The course was perceived as relevant, and the students indicated early on that it had influenced the way they interacted with those to whom they ministered. This last point was significant because a motivation for this project was to see if intelligent design arguments would be effective in accordance with Moorlands College's mission statement of equipping the students to impact the church and the world.[74]

Delivery of course

I was not able to be completely aware of the change in dynamics from being a theology lecturer to a science lecturer, and I needed to remain "open to disconfirming evidence—perhaps seeking it out through interviews."[75] My reflective journal notes did not highlight any concerns with the way that the course was delivered in terms of any changed relationship with the students. Student questions were relevant, asked in a relaxed manner, and answered with honesty including a willingness to admit where I did not know the answer and a commitment to find out what I could. The emphasis was on learning rather than persuading. I felt my positionality as lecturer was largely unchanged.[76]

In terms of "role duality," I felt enabled both by the participants and by the college organization, in that it created no tensions or confusion between my researcher and lecturer roles as colleagues expressed interest

74. 'Our Values—Moorlands College'.

75. Coghlan and Brannick, *Doing Action Research in Your Own Organization*, 62.

76. Jean McNiff, *Writing up Your Action Research Project* (Abingdon: Routledge, 2016), 25.

and support in my work.[77] There is also an institutional incentive for such support in such research as it adds to the expertise of the college in an area that it seeks to develop.[78] It was a positive experience and one that will encourage more research within the organization in the future.

Student feedback

My role as insider-researcher was most apparent when asking for feedback online (which was, at the time, an innovative method for lecture feedback) and during the face-to-face discussions, which were held in my office. The student participant would have recognized the difference in my role as researcher in the recording device on the table, and in the way the discussion was framed as participating in research, rather than, say, as a tutorial. Compared to a normal student tutorial, the power relationship between participant and researcher was more horizontal in that the student had more influence and control of what was said, and as researcher I was mainly facilitating the discussion and making notes.[79] As the researcher it was important to show that I was "someone who can be trusted and always checking with others for any misunderstanding."[80] Evidence that students did not feel under pressure to participate (and especially to respond positively) is seen in that four out of the eleven that completed the course chose not to participate either in the online feedback or the face-to-face discussions.

Response of participants

The responses from the online feedback forms and from the face-to-face discussions indicated that the subject of intelligent design was relevant and important for evangelism, and that the course was supportive of students sharing their faith. Some expressed the view that they were already confident about sharing their faith with non-Christians generally; it was confidence in responding specifically to opposition and scepticism coming from a Darwinian worldview where the course had helped. Authority figures such as schoolteachers had presented them, or those they knew,

77. Coghlan and Brannick, *Doing Action Research in Your Own Organization*, 64.
78. Coghlan and Brannick, 72.
79. McKernan, *Curriculum and Imagination*, 162.
80. Coghlan and Brannick, *Doing Action Research in Your Own Organization*, 78.

with difficulties for reconciling their faith with science. The DID course had raised their consciousness of another way of thinking about it and had enabled conversations with those whom otherwise they had found it difficult to share their faith. These comments gave an early indication that the course was meeting the research project's aim of contributing to students' confidence and ability to share their faith.

The issue of the timing of the course was an important point for reflection. As mentioned earlier, the choice for timetabling it as I did was a pragmatic one, seeking to find a space in the college timetable and ensuring that I had time to develop the course as I went along. The discussion with participant 24FM (and others) about it being difficult to attend the lectures suggested that this should be reconsidered, especially as the course was largely prepared and so I did not need an interval between each topic as before. I reflected on whether I had chosen a Friday afternoon more to meet my needs of keeping my preparation achievable than for the sake of participants' accessibility. There was similarly no longer any specific need to maintain the seven-week structure, and therefore I would need to arrive at a decision when best to run the next course for different reasons.

One aspect of the participants' responses that caught my attention was their emphasis on young people. A common focus of their concern was for those in schools or in youth groups, and the narratives they shared were largely concerned with events at a young age, either millennials like themselves or those in gen-Z generation. Those whose faith was challenged, or who lost their Christian faith, mainly related to the younger generations. This might simply be because of the nature of their ministries (mainly with young people at churches) but it might also have indicated that this topic had more resonance for a younger generation. I had not anticipated this age being the focus of their response, but it indicated an area of research to be undertaken before I entered the main delivery of the course. This had implications for my more purposive sample of interviewees and the questions asked in the main qualitative research.

Modifying future practice

Following Norton's approach, this section considers what I felt was going on, how my research ideas are being changed by what I observed and what I think might be missing.[81] The first modification of future practice was focusing questions towards younger generations to see if this topic was especially significant for them.[82] It would add a generational lens for my research. This would be reflected upon as part of identifying the problem for the next cycle.

Another important change of future practice came from an awareness of being an insider-researcher and the concern that I might be unduly influencing participants.[83] Although I did not perceive it, and had taken steps to avoid it, I became aware through reflecting upon my role of potential pressure on students to contribute and respond in a way that favoured my research.

> Potential participants must feel free to refuse to participate, and they must be free to stop participating any time they choose. Enabling this choice can be a challenging issue. Previous research has clearly demonstrated that people will act in conflict with their desires in the presence of an authority figure. Because teachers are important authority figures for students and parents, asking your students to participate in an action research study may not really offer them much of a choice. Their desire to please you could cause them to hide their true feelings.[84]

Likewise, Norton voices a word of caution about the likely relationship between students and lecturers in research situations.

> We might be so convinced of the benefits to our students that we overpower them with justification and make it very difficult for them to refuse. Even when we assure students that if they

---

81. Norton, *Action Research in Teaching and Learning*, 116.

82. For definitions and a good introduction to the relationships between millennials and gen-Z, see Penny Rue, 'Make Way, Millennials, Here Comes Gen Z', *About Campus: Enriching the Student Learning Experience* 23, no. 3 (August 2018): 5–12, https://doi.org/10.1177/1086482218804251; Michael Dimock, 'Defining Generations: Where Millennials End and Generation Z Begins', Pew Research Center, 17 January 2019, https://www.pewresearch.org/fact-tank/2019/01/17/where-millennials-end-and-generation-z-begins/; Hannah Ramlo, 'Beyond Millennials . . . ', PeoriaMagazines.com, August 2017, https://www.peoriamagazines.com/as/2017/jul-aug/beyond-millennials.

83. For a discussion of how interviewees might play more than one role, see Sue Garton and Fiona Copland, '"I like This Interview; I Get Cakes and Cats!": The Effect of Prior Relationships on Interview Talk', *Qualitative Research* 10, no. 5 (October 2010): 533–51, https://doi.org/10.1177/1468794110375231.

84. Henning, Stone, and Kelly, *Using Action Research to Improve Instruction*, 13.

do not want to take part in our research, this will in no way affect the teaching or the quality of the learning they experience, nevertheless there are other social penalties.[85]

I felt that there was good evidence that students had felt free to withhold their participation (evidenced by the fact that not everyone chose to contribute). There were no grades involved, students would not be examined on their contribution or comprehension, and the course was framed as "added value" to their student experience. There were also many unsolicited and spontaneous offers of thanks and expressions of appreciation for the course. However, in discussion with my supervisors, and noting the cautions quoted above, I was advised to consider a format for the course where that element could be minimized. This concern shaped the design of the next action research cycle and helped to develop the focus of the question from one specifically looking at students studying full time at the college to evangelical students more generally.

The feedback from the pilot study about the time commitment involved was reflected upon and recognized as an opportunity for improvement. Instead of seven weeks of two-hour talks, I decided to run the main course on two Saturdays, one week apart (see below for rationale). This would slightly reduce the contact hours but would make attendance more accessible. Running the course this way would make more demands on me as course leader, but I felt it would make for a more immersive experience. Participants could discuss and reflection on the course materials with one another over coffee breaks and lunch.

SUMMARY

This chapter marked the beginning of taking action and evaluating outcomes in response to the research question through piloting the DID course. The first cycle of Norton's pedagogical action research provided initial student feedback indicating that the research project was going in the right direction for answering its question of the extent to which students who attended the DID course had a greater sense of confidence and ability to share their faith with those who tended to use science as a reason not to engage with their evangelistic efforts in ministry contexts. It also raised ethical issues about positionality and pragmatic questions about how to run the main DID course. The second pedagogical action

---

85. Norton, *Action Research in Teaching and Learning*, 182.

research cycle would address the positionality concerns and enable me to understand more fully how participants interpreted their experience of learning intelligent design arguments.

5

Saturday School

The ultimate outcome is for the professional to become a "wise practitioner."[1]

SECOND CYCLE: SATURDAY SCHOOL DISCOVERING INTELLIGENT DESIGN COURSE

This chapter contains the second cycle of Norton's pedagogical action research and is in many ways the heart of the research project. It demonstrates the benefit of my learning from the pilot course and the changes made as a result and provides the participants' interview data. It begins the process of systematically interpreting their experience of attending the course and the influence it had on them in answer to the research question of the extent to which teaching intelligent design to evangelical students contributes to their confidence and ability to share their faith. This chapter describes the pedagogical basis for the DID course and includes analysis of a quantitative survey and thematic analysis of the qualitative interview data.

Identifying the problem and thinking how to tackle the problem

I have combined the first two phases of Norton's ITDEM approach (identifying the problem, thinking how to tackle it) for clarity on the issues addressed: course structure, positionality, and generational issues.

---

1. Maxwell, 'Philosophy and Practice—Why Does This Matter?', 13.

The problem identified for this action research cycle was the same as for the pilot course, namely my encounters with students who found relating science with their Christian faith problematic when ministering to those who either use science as a reason not to believe or find it difficult to see how Christianity can be relevant to someone with a secular scientific worldview.[2] The three modifications identified by the first action research cycle were the time commitment associated with a seven-week course, positionality issues of students potentially being under a sense of obligation or pressure from me as tutor and researcher to give encouraging or overly positive responses, and the face-to-face discussions' focus on the problem being associated with a younger generation. These modifications provided opportunities of redesigning the research methods and questions for gathering and analysing the feedback.

Finding a time in the college timetable that suited everyone was difficult, and on reflection with one of my colleagues at college we developed an alternative concept, namely a weekend course. This would overcome the problem of timetable restrictions and meet the needs of those who found it difficult to commit to a long programme. Our marketing manager suggested reframing the course as a "Saturday School" event, something that would enable broader participation, and this immediately presented itself as a means of addressing the concern of student pressure. Running the course for part-time students who had no assessment pressures and with whom I had no personal relationship would maximize the principle of respect for autonomy and adequately respond to the earlier concerns of ensuring interviewees' responses were not influenced by my role as course leader.[3]

To minimize the risk of influence yet further I decided to run the course at a local church, rather than at the college. This involved extensive discussion with church leaders to ensure the research was done transparently, met the church's needs, and would be delivered accessibly.[4] The

2. The term "secular" in this context is taken to mean something like the denial of the transcendent. For an excellent discussion of the term, see Charles Taylor, 'The Polysemy of the Secular', *Social Research* 76, no. 4 (2009): 1146; and José Casanova, 'Rethinking Secularization: A Global Comparative Perspective', *The Hedgehog Review* 8, no. 1–2 (Spring & Summer 2006): 7–22.

3. John Fulton and Carol Costley, 'Ethics', in *Methodologies for Practice Research: Approaches for Professional Doctorates*, ed. Carol Costley and John Fulton (London: SAGE, 2019), 81.

4. I have not named the church congregation to maintain confidentiality (their youth leader was a participant).

church approached was evangelical, and the college had received several full-time students from them over the years. There was a good level of trust between us, and I remain grateful to their willingness and generosity in hosting the event. The church promoted the event, and I was not involved in either inviting or selecting those who participated.

Nones

The focus on younger generations in the pilot discussions led me to study the identification and relevance of nones to the issue of science and Christian faith. Several studies have shown a fall in levels of affiliation to church for millennials (born between 1984 and 2002)[5] associated with the "rise of the nones." The Pew Forum defines nones as those who do not affiliate with any religious belief system.[6] The term nones does not simply equate to atheism: "[t]wo-third of them say they believe in God (68 percent)."[7] The Pew Forum research showed that the percentage of those religiously unaffiliated in the US is almost 20 percent of the total population, but this rises to a third of those under the age of 30. The growth in those identifying themselves as nones is "largely driven by generational replacement, the gradual supplanting of older generations by newer ones."[8] This rise is correlated with a similarly increased rate of dropping out of church for those of the same age. "The massive cultural shift from Christian to non-religious Britain has come about largely because of children ceasing to follow the religious commitments of their parents."[9] It is not that they were raised in a religiously disinterested environment. "The overwhelming majority [almost three-quarters] of the

---

5. These are the years used by Barna. Pew Research prefers a range from 1981–1996; see Michael Dimock, 'Where Millennials End and Generation Z Begins | Pew Research Center', accessed 4 May 2019, https://www.pewresearch.org/fact-tank/2019/01/17/where-millennials-end-and-generation-z-begins/.

6. Luis Lugo, '"Nones" on the Rise: One-in-Five Adults Have No Religious Affiliation' (Washington: Pew Research Center, 9 October 2012), http://www.pewforum.org/Unaffiliated/nones-on-the-rise.aspx.

7. '"Nones" on the Rise | Pew Research Center', Pew Research Center: Religion & Public Life, 9 October 2012, https://www.pewforum.org/2012/10/09/nones-on-the-rise/.

8. Lugo, '"Nones" on the Rise', 10.

9. Linda Woodhead, 'The Rise of "No Religion" in Britain: The Emergence of a New Cultural Majority', *Journal of the British Academy* 4 (2016): 249.

nones were brought up in a religious tradition."[10] Theories suggested to account for this decline in religious affiliation (and it is largely associated with a decline in Protestant evangelicalism, rather than other Christian or other faith traditions) included a political backlash to conservative religious views, particularly sexuality, or delay in getting married, or a general decline in social capital.[11]

The Barna Group conducted research for the Faith That Lasts Project on a similar topic and brought together the results of eight national studies including almost 1,300 interviews with young adults "who were regular churchgoers [. . .] during their teen years and explored their reasons for disconnection from church life after age 15."[12] The significant result was that 59 percent of all Christians interviewed have dropped out of attending church having once been active in their church involvement. Although both Pew Research and Barna studied young adults in the US, other comparable studies show that the millennial generation in Europe share similar perspectives, with particularly strong cultural connections from the US to the UK.[13] A recent study in the UK commissioned by the Bible Society and partnered with Barna Group showed that 62 percent of millennials had either a minimal or no relationship with the Bible and an additional 8 percent indicating that it was either broken or ending.[14]

A 2018 Pew Research Center European study showed that of those identifying as "religiously unaffiliated" a majority "were baptized, and many of them also say they were raised as Christians."[15] Although the UK had the smallest percentage where that was the case, the decline in those identifying as Christian was matched by the increase in those identifying themselves as nones, and at a rate that was similar to the US, namely 6 percent.[16] The main reasons given for why nones lose their Christian identity in Europe were that they "gradually drifted away" after they

10. Lugo, "'Nones' on the Rise', 16.

11. Lugo, 29–31.

12. 'Six Reasons Young Christians Leave Church', Barna Group, 2011, https://www.barna.com/research/six-reasons-young-christians-leave-church/.

13. See for example Richard Wolf et al., 'Millennials: Work, Life and Satisfaction' (Munich: Allianz, 16 November 2017).

14. 'Digital Millennials and the Bible: Produced in Partnership with Barna Group' (Swindon: Bible Society, 2018), 7.

15. 'Being Christian in Western Europe' (Washington: Pew Research Center, 29 May 2018), 40.

16. 'Being Christian in Western Europe', 83.

"stopped believing in the teachings of their childhood religion."[17] The Pew research showed that 31 percent of all UK respondents completely or mostly agreed with the statement "Science makes religion unnecessary in my life"[18] whereas that number increased to 67 percent for religiously unaffiliated millennials.[19] The Bible Society's research showed that the most common description nones used for the Bible was 'myth,' 36 percent, with 25 percent describing it as irrelevant and untrustworthy.[20]

Kinnaman's book *You Lost Me: Why Young Christians Are Leaving Church, And Rethinking Faith* summarized Barna's earlier work and anticipated some of the later findings mentioned above.[21] Kinnaman's purpose in writing was "to provoke new thinking and new action in the critical process of the spiritual development of the next generation."[22] He identified six frustrations, or "disconnections," that those from the millennial generation have with their experience of Christianity: they perceive it to be overprotective, shallow, anti-science, repressive, exclusive, and doubtless.[23] Their culture is "discontinuously different" to previous generations: it is more fluid, diverse, complex and uncertain than ever before.[24] Kinnaman calls those millennials who have "physically and emotionally disconnected" from church "exiles," and describes them as struggling to cope with competing narratives.[25] "Nomads" are those who still consider themselves to be Christian but think that going to church is optional, whereas those he terms "prodigals" are those who have lost their faith and no longer think of themselves as Christians. This last category is typically associated with the nones. About a fifth of them say that Christian beliefs do not make sense to them anymore, and their spiritual needs are not met by Christianity.[26]

17. 'Being Christian in Western Europe', 87.

18. 'Being Christian in Western Europe', 130.

19. 'Being Christian in Western Europe', 46; the age range of the Pew Research extended up to aged 40, about 5 years more than most of the Barna research when discussing millennials.

20. 'Digital Millennials and the Bible', 8.

21. David Kinnaman, *You Lost Me: Why Young Christians Are Leaving Church . . . and Rethinking Faith* (Grand Rapids: BakerBooks, 2011).

22. Kinnaman, 14–15.

23. Kinnaman, 92–93.

24. Kinnaman, 38.

25. Kinnaman, 139.

26. 'Three Spiritual Journeys of Millennials', Barna Group, accessed 3 May 2019,

Of the six sources of disconnection that he identifies, the ones that resonated most with my research question were those that suggested the church was shallow, anti-scientific, and doubtless. Young people were said to have a shallow knowledge of Christianity because the church tends not to relate their faith with experience or discipleship. Their faith is more akin to "moralistic therapeutic deism than to historic Christianity."[27] The church is seen as anti-science, and almost a fifth thought it anti-intellectual.[28] Kinnaman thinks the church needs a much more open discussion. "We must do a better job challenging and training all young Christians—not just the science geeks—to think clearly, honestly, and comprehensively about matters of science."[29] Akin to the problem of being 'shallow,' he argues that young people are "not given good intellectual tools with which to interact with science."[30] He suggests that one of the main reasons for this might be that Christian leaders themselves lack the experience or expertise necessary. Kinnaman claims that churches "have ceded the realm of knowledge to academics and institutions of higher education."[31] The need for church leaders to be able to engage deeply with issues of culture is critical. "To the extent that we in the Christian community insist that young adults should just accept our 'right' answers we perpetuate a needless schism between science and faith."[32]

Kinnaman's arguments were supported by a later Barna Group study, 'Making Space for Millennials' where those born between 1984 and 2002 were researched to find out "how can we create transformational space for and with millennials?"[33] Although it did not feature in the main body of the discussion, what stood out from my reading of that report was the response to the statement "The church seems to reject much of what science tells us about the world." Overall, 63 percent of all millennials agreed "a lot" or "somewhat" to that statement, but this rose

https://www.barna.com/research/three-spiritual-journeys-of-millennials/.

27. Kinnaman, *You Lost Me*, 115; the phrase "moralistic therapeutic deism" is from Christian Smith, *Souls in Transition: The Religious and Spiritual Lives of Emerging Adults* (Oxford: Oxford University Press, 2009), 165.

28. Kinnaman, 136.

29. Kinnaman, 142.

30. Kinnaman, 145.

31. Kinnaman, 127.

32. Kinnaman, 135.

33. 'Making Space for Millennials: A Blueprint for Your Culture, Ministry, Leadership and Facilities' (Ventura: Barna Group, 2014), 6.

to 87 percent of 'prodigals' (the nones category), or 86 percent of those claiming they had "no faith."[34] Of those millennials who were "practicing Christians" (those going to church more than once a month), 43 percent also shared that same sense that the church rejects much of what science says about the world, although the reasons for this position might be different from the nones. Madge and Hemming's 2017 study of nones who still found religion important to some extent note that, while family is important, science is the "top ranked" influencing factor of their religious identity, along with the "increasing out datedness and irrelevance of the church."[35] These insights confirmed the importance of focusing on the younger generations in my research. I modified my interview guide to provide opportunity for respondents to comment directly upon it.

Doing it

The main DID course was held in the church's hall on 24 February and 3 March 2018. The new Saturday School event was arranged using Eventbrite with the assistance of the college's marketing manager to develop the format as a brand that could be used for different courses in the future. The event was advertised on the college website and in the church where it was held. There was a fee charged (£15 or £10 concession) which covered costs; the church leaders generously did not charge a fee for the use of the room. The layout of the room was organized around multiple tables for groups of five or six people to take notes. This layout was suggested by the church leaders as they had run conferences successfully this way before in the room. The content was delivered as before using PowerPoints and video clips to illustrate the concepts. There was a book stall of several relevant intelligent design texts, and there was a constant supply of coffee and other refreshments for participants to use throughout the day.

The first day's content was as follows:

- Introducing Intelligent Design: Not as a conflict framed as "science versus faith" but interpretation of evidence driven by different worldviews. Definitions of intelligent design; abduction; inference

34. 'Making Space for Millennials', 98.

35. Nicola Madge and Peter J. Hemming, 'Young British Religious "Nones": Findings from the Youth On Religion Study', *Journal of Youth Studies* 20, no. 7 (9 August 2017): 883, 886, https://doi.org/10.1080/13676261.2016.1273518.

to the best explanation. "Specified complexity," "design filter." Intelligent design and methodological naturalism. Typology of materialism ("seven tenets of materialism").

- Cosmic Design: Historical-philosophical views of design. Kalam and "eternal universe" arguments. Big Bang and "spontaneous universe." Fine tuning, cosmological constants, and stellar origins.

- Complexity of Life: Abiogenesis and critique of chemical evolution; origin of information in DNA; fundamental doctrine of biology; complexity in the cell; genetic mutations and natural selection; protein folding; and irreducible complexity.

The second Saturday's content was:

- Tree of Life: Darwin and survival of the fittest; Lamarkianism, Mendelian genetics and Neo-Darwinism; critique of dysteleology and vestigial organisms; "junk" DNA; phylogenetic, molecular and morphological trees, convergent evolution, homology. Ontogeny, Peppered moth, Lack's finches.

- Fossils: Artefact hypothesis; Cambrian explosion; other fossil events; gradualism and punctuated equilibrium; evolutionary development and hox genes.

- Human Evolution: Hominin classification, australopithecines, homo erectus, Neanderthals, homo habilis. Ida; Piltdown; Nebraska man. Cretan footprints, human exceptionalism.

The sessions contained opportunities to discuss issues within these groups and over coffee and lunch breaks. Both days included several scheduled opportunities for question and answers and there was an extended time for questions at the end of the second day.

Moorlands College's marketing manager helped me navigate the recent GDPR rules on gathering data.[36] Eventbrite provided contact details for all participants, but there was no expectation that attending the course required or implied participating in my research. Therefore, it was not permitted to use the Eventbrite data to contact participants to invite them to take part in interviews. This was to comply with the data protection policy not to use enrolment data for any other purpose.[37] A separate sign-up sheet asking for details if they were "willing to be contacted

36. 'Guide to the General Data Protection Regulation (GDPR)'.
37. Fulton and Costley, 'Ethics', 83.

to support your research project" was used on the day so that the data collected was specifically for that purpose.

Information gathered

I indicated at the start of the presentation that the course was part of my research project. Of the fifty-three attending the Saturday School Discovering Intelligent Design course (four or five did not attend the second Saturday), forty-seven gave their names and email addresses on a separate form indicating that they were willing to be contacted concerning my research. I was delighted with the response and had more opportunities for gaining feedback than I could easily cope with, so I chose to include a focus group as well as interviews. This would enable more participation and be useful as triangulation for the responses.[38] Those who indicated their willingness to participate in the research were contacted and asked to complete Tenneson, Bundrick and Stanford's questionnaire identifying their preferred science and theology paradigm(s) and to take part either in a semi-structured interview or a focus group.[39] All data was securely held on a password-protected single computer with cloud-based backup (apart from the paper questionnaires in a locked office at my college). Twenty-eight participants responded to the email invitation to participate in the research (eight female and twenty male, a ratio that was representative of the course participants as a whole) and completed the questionnaire.

Semi-structured interviews and focus group

Semi-structured interviews "provide insights into the thinking of participants."[40] I wanted to know participants' attitudes towards what they had learned, and the extent to which (if at all) the course had affected their confidence and ability to share their faith with others. Their responses provided the data for thematic analysis.

---

38. Michael Quinn Patton, *Qualitative Research & Evaluation Methods: Integrating Theory and Practice*, 4th ed. (Thousand Oaks: SAGE, 2015), 478–79.

39. Tenneson, Bundrick, and Stanford, 'A New Survey Instrument and its Findings for Relating Science and Theology'.

40. Henning, Stone, and Kelly, *Using Action Research to Improve Instruction*, 94.

> To carry out an interview would be to take a second-order ap-
> proach, which aims to understand the issue from the perspec-
> tive of the student and not mine as the teacher-researcher. This
> type of methodology [. . .] sits very comfortably within the
> action research framework.[41]

Bryman states that it is the research question that indicates who should be identified as relevant for being interviewed. "Research questions are likely to provide guidelines as to what categories of people (or whatever the unit of analysis is) need to be the focus of attention and therefore sampled."[42] The purposeful selection of those for interview was based on their generation, a theme that came from the pilot course.[43] "The goal of purposive sampling is to sample cases/participants in a strategic way, so that those sampled are relevant to the research questions that are being posed."[44] Bryman indicates when more probabilistic sampling should be carried out, namely the need for generalization or the lack of clarity about which category of person should be interviewed.[45] Neither of these criteria applied in this project as the purpose was to consider how a particular category of person might respond to a particular form of teaching. As Paton argues, "[w]hat would be 'bias' in statistical sampling, and therefore a weakness, becomes intended focus in qualitative sampling, and therefore a strength."[46] There might be implications for groups other than evangelical Christians, but that was beyond the purpose of the research, and Bryman argues that purposeful sampling is always done with the "research goals in mind."[47] Students from the pilot course had indicated that intelligent design and the teaching of Darwinism were especially relevant to younger generations as a cause of their contemporaries, or those they ministered to, losing their faith or finding it challenged, so I decided to prioritize those from the younger generations for interviews.

41. Norton, *Action Research in Teaching and Learning*, 74.

42. Bryman, *Social Research Methods*, 416.

43. Fraenkel, Wallen, and Hyun, *How to Design and Evaluate Research in Education*, 100.

44. Bryman, *Social Research Methods*, 418.

45. Bryman, 416.

46. Michael Quinn Patton, 'Sampling, Qualitative (Purposive)', in *The Blackwell Encyclopedia of Sociology*, ed. George Ritzer (Oxford: Blackwell, 2007), 4006.

47. Bryman, *Social Research Methods*, 418.

Morse argues that the skills needed to be a good interviewer include establishing trust, focusing on relevant information, and neither leading the participant nor interrupting answers.[48] They also include locating what she calls "excellent" participants. They should be suitably "reflective, willing and able to speak articulately about the experience."[49] In my case the participants excelled in these areas. They were selected from those who had attended both days of the DID course and had indicated their willingness to take part in the research. Twenty-eight respondents initially indicated that they were willing to be interviewed, and fifteen of those were able to make the available dates. Eight were selected for interviews and the remaining seven were chosen to take part in a focus group.[50] This sample size seemed appropriate to the scale of the study,[51] was a manageable workload, and was in keeping with the paradigm given by Norton.[52]

Ethics

I had not met any of the interview or focus group participants prior to them enrolling on the DID course, and this clarified my positionality; I was the presenter and researcher. In terms of the organization (the church from which the majority of participants came from) I was an outsider to both the congregation and leadership structures. However, I identified as an evangelical Christian in the manner in which the course was run: it began with a prayer both Saturdays, was located in the church hall, and was clearly supported by the church leadership. This is best understood as an "external insider," according to Fulton and Costley's version of Banks' typology applied to practice-based researchers, because I was sympathetic to the evangelical Christian values of the participants even though I am not a member of the congregation to which they belong.[53]

48. Janice M. Morse, 'Sampling in Grounded Theory', in *The SAGE Handbook of Grounded Theory*, ed. Antony Bryant and Kathy Charmaz (London: SAGE, 2007), 230.

49. Morse, 231.

50. Creswell and Creswell, *Research Design*, 263.

51. Konstantina Vasileiou et al., 'Characterising and Justifying Sample Size Sufficiency in Interview-Based Studies: Systematic Analysis of Qualitative Health Research over a 15-Year Period', *BMC Medical Research Methodology* 18, no. 1 (December 2018): 16, https://doi.org/10.1186/s12874-018-0594-7.

52. Norton, *Action Research in Teaching and Learning*, 98, 117.

53. Fulton and Costley, 'Ethics', 85; compare the original terms in James A. Banks, 'The Lives and Values of Researchers: Implications for Educating Citizens in a

All but one of the interviews, and the focus group, were held in a ground floor room in the office building belonging to the church where the course had taken place (the final interview was held in the lounge of the participant with other family members present in the house). This ensured a familiar environment for participants, giving them a feeling of being on "home turf," and flattening the power dynamics so that I would be perceived more as a sympathetic visitor to their organization.[54] This was seen in the open and willing manner that interviewees and focus group members shared and responded to questions. I felt privileged to listen to such articulate and perceptive participants.

Semi-structured interview questions

The interview questions, or "guide," were prepared to help answer the research question of the extent to which teaching intelligent design contributes to the confidence and ability of students to share their faith, and they drew from the experience of the pilot course.[55] The face-to-face student discussions had demonstrated the importance of asking open, non-leading questions.[56] It had also pointed to the areas of concern where specific questions could draw out more detailed responses in the semi-structured interviews. The advice received from Ganiel on how to improve interview questions is gratefully acknowledged.[57] There were eight main questions asked in each interview with optional supplementary questions to draw out more details in the answers if needed.

1. What made you decide to take the course on Discovering Intelligent Design (DID)?

2. How influential is Darwinism and a material worldview in our culture and in young people's lives?

3. Where does that influence come from? [If prompt is needed, say TV, school, social media]

Multicultural Society', *Educational Researcher* 27, no. 7 (1998): 8.

54. Fulton and Costley, 'Ethics', 87.

55. Henning, Stone, and Kelly, *Using Action Research to Improve Instruction*, 96.

56. Creswell and Creswell, *Research Design*, 263.

57. Gladys Ganiel in email correspondence concerning semi-structured interview questions.

4. Do you think this is a more or less significant issue for the millennial generation 1984 to 1998 (aged about nineteen to thirty-three) or the Gen Z (1999 to 2015) which is eighteen or younger.

5. If so, why? Can you think of a particular example?

6. David Kinnaman (author of a book entitled *You Lost Me: Why Young Christians Are Leaving Church . . . and Rethinking Faith*) says that one of the factors that discourage young people from staying at church is an anti-scientific attitude. Is this something you've found?

7. Can you give me an example?

8. What do you think the value of a course like the DID course is for Christians of a millennial or gen-Z age?

9. Do you think the strictly scientific approach of the DID course is significantly more useful in equipping Christians to engage with non-Christians than, say, a biblical or theological reflection on matters of science and faith?

10. One of the aims of giving the course was to see if it would have an impact in the way you were able to share your faith with non-Christians. Do you think you are now better able to share your faith with non-Christians?

11. If so, could you give me an example of how you have shared your faith?

12. Is there anything else you want to say that I haven't covered?

This guide was followed in each interview and there was freedom to follow up answers with more probing questions or to obtain clarification of a point.[58] Keeping close to the topics of the question throughout the interviews ensured the answers given were all relevant, but participant were also encouraged to expand on answers if it seemed appropriate: "the interviewer is prepared to [. . .] let the interviewee develop ideas and speak more widely on the issues raised by the researcher."[59]

The introductory question was made less useful as there was a tendency to supply possible options (were they interested in science, did they have a scientific background in the family . . . ?) which had the effect of changing the nature of the question from "why were you at this time

---

58. Norton, *Action Research in Teaching and Learning*, 99.
59. Denscombe, *The Good Research Guide*, 175.

interested in this course?" to "why are you the kind of person that would come to a course like this?" This was an error caused by trying to make the opening question more straightforward but at the cost of losing relevant contextual details.

Data emerging or constructing?

The interviews and focus group were recorded using a digital data recorder on to a memory card and the sound files were transferred to my computer. They were each transcribed on to a Word document, a process that was time-consuming but enabled me to become immersed in the data.[60] I followed Kember's suggestions for the interview process.

> Interviews are normally tape-recorded. If detailed analysis (rather than just impression) is required, transcripts have to be produced. The transcripts are normally analysed by searching for responses or themes that commonly occur. Quotations from the transcripts can be used to illuminate or illustrate findings set out in reports and papers.[61]

Data were "sorted, categorized, and reduced to a few manageable themes" inductively.[62] As noted in my research journal, the identification of possible categories, and grouping them into themes, was one of the most creative and productive activities associated with the action research process.

As the transcription process and categorizing began, the epistemology of data and concepts emerging from the interviews became apparent.[63] The interviewer contributes to the data generated through constructive interaction between researcher and participant.[64] Alemu et al. argue that "through active engagements during the interview process, ideas are raised, discussed and knowledge is mutually constructed. According to this view, the researcher and the participants co-construct

---

60. Norton, *Action Research in Teaching and Learning*, 118.

61. Kember, *Action Learning and Action Research*, 40.

62. Henning, Stone, and Kelly, *Using Action Research to Improve Instruction*, 102.

63. Victoria Clarke and Virginia Braun, 'Thematic Analysis', in *Encyclopedia of Quality of Life and Well-Being Research*, ed. Alex C. Michalos (New York: Springer, 2014), 6627.

64. Irving Seidman, *Interviewing as Qualitative Research: A Guide for Researchers in Education and the Social Sciences*, 3rd ed. (New York: Teachers College Press, 2006), 23.

data, in a process known as data generation."[65] Instances of such generation of data were recognized in the dialogue with participants. In the first interview, 1MX was asked about the value of the DID course and answered by describing its social value in a creative and surprising way.

> 1MX: . . . I was going to follow up by saying: the questioning would hopefully lead to a seeking, and that seeking hopefully leading to God. This then opens the door to better, stronger moral values. That's one of the things that this millennial generation is going to very quickly lose. You just see the negative effects of that. People are not getting married any more. There's a lot of drinking, drugs. People not taking life as seriously as they should. I think the course will lead to more questioning and searching.

> Alistair: I like that: taking life seriously. All the way through your answers, I've often located this course as a matter of truth, which I think is really important. But actually you're saying that truth is a means to an end, and in this case the end is around life, morality and purpose.

> 1MX: Yes, absolutely. Morality, purpose, truth, and what is truth.

Participant 1MX generated the category of "taking life seriously," and in response the point was sharpened by suggesting the notion of truth as "a means to an end," a suggestion that I had not thought of before, but that 1MX was keen to endorse as a way of expressing his intention. This was less an observation of beliefs and more a co-operative activity. The interviews were open to new ideas being generated.[66] As the interviewer I tried to reflect what I had heard to check comprehension, but inevitably by putting things into my own words there was an element of crystalizing ideas that often received an affirmation by the interviewee, as in 1MX's "yes, absolutely." The category of "purpose" was created from this interaction and is an example of the way they seek to represent the participant's views from their own perspective.[67] It was noted in my journal that articulating these concepts was difficult for participants, and that this

65. Getaneh Alemu et al., 'The Use of a Constructivist Grounded Theory Method to Explore the Role of Socially-Constructed Metadata (Web 2.0) Approaches', *Qualitative and Quantitative Methods in Libraries*, no. 4 (2015): 523.

66. Jennifer M. Poole and Oliver Mauthner, 'Interviews', in *The SAGE Encyclopedia of Action Research*, ed. David Coghlan and Mary Brydon-Miller (London: SAGE, 2014), 465.

67. Norton, *Action Research in Teaching and Learning*, 116.

summarizing technique facilitated the participants to use expressions they would not otherwise have formulated themselves. As Coleman points out, at this point the boundary between first person and second person action research is less clear, but the discussion enabled us both to grow towards a better understanding of the experience, and to articulate it with greater precision.[68]

Evaluating the findings

In this section I noted how I felt the course went, how it furthered my research question, and how my ideas developed.[69] I evaluated the findings from the science-theology paradigm questionnaires and used an inductive form of thematic analysis as a method for analysing the semi-structured interview data.[70]

First person reflection

Reflecting upon the mood of the course at the time, I made the following journal note:

> The venue was excellent and there was a great atmosphere with enough scepticism in the room to keep it interesting but enough support to keep it warm. There were about fifty people there each day, although one or two didn't make it past lunchtime, but there was a real sense of interest and a high level of concentration throughout.[71]

The scepticism was seen in the form of an early challenge to a point made in the first topic. Sufficient space was given to hear the question fully and then a partial answer given at the time, followed by an indication that a fuller answer to the question would be given in a later topic that morning. The questioner was invited to respond again then, or to do so after lunch if his point had not been fully addressed. My intention was to show that challenges were valid, welcomed, and would be answered to the best of my ability. This also demonstrated that the nature of the

68. Coleman, 'Action Research', 161.

69. Norton, *Action Research in Teaching and Learning*, 116.

70. Virginia Braun and Victoria Clarke, *Successful Qualitative Research: A Practical Guide for Beginners* (London: SAGE, 2013), 177.

71. My own reflections on the Discovering Intelligent Design Saturday School.

course was concerning evidence, and that it was right and good to dispute interpretations of data. It had the effect of reinforcing the perception that the topic was contentious, and it probably helped delegates concentrate more. Other questions were asked without tension but all of them were valued and contributed to the learning environment.

The level of enthusiasm and commitment that participants showed over the two Saturdays was impressive. In my own critical reflection on it, I noted a few ways that the course might be developed in the future in my reflections on the day:

> I think, as my own sense of how it went, probably what it needed was another voice to break up the effort of listening to a single voice all day. It was certainly a challenging thing to deliver, but probably a bit tiring to concentrate on listening, and I think I should use a few more techniques to break up the day. I did use a few video clips from some of the Illustra media movies which helped, but probably another contributor would be a good idea in future. On the other hand, I had so many compliments and encouragements about the two days that I really think it has struck a chord for many people. A number of people asked if I would consider doing it again, and of course I would, so I'll have to get it into a format that is easily transplantable into another context. I think that a reduced version cutting it down to one day would be a helpful first step.[72]

Science-theology paradigm questionnaire

Part of the approach adopted for this project was to survey those willing to be interviewed or part of a focus group. The survey identified which science and theology paradigm(s) participants most identified with.[73] Although some definitions of mixed-methods imply a "time-consuming and expensive" process,[74] the idea of drawing from a quantitative method fits Norton's more inclusive form of action research: "I believe

72. My own reflections on the Discovering Intelligent Design Saturday School.

73. Maxwell argues that "the use of numbers is a legitimate and valuable strategy for qualitative researchers when it is used as a complement to an overall process orientation to the research"; Joseph A. Maxwell, 'Using Numbers in Qualitative Research', *Qualitative Inquiry* 16, no. 6 (July 2010): 480, https://doi.org/10.1177/1077800410364740.

74. Fraenkel, Wallen, and Hyun, *How to Design and Evaluate Research in Education*, 558.

that a multi-methodological approach is best suited to the ultimate goal of pedagogical action research."[75] Dick describes his approach as "eclectic, borrowed from any version that suits. Like many other action researchers, I supplement action research with methods and processes from elsewhere."[76] Reason and Bradbury likewise encourage a more inclusive methodology: "[w]e want you to delight in and celebrate the sheer exuberance and diversity that is available to you and be creative in how you use and develop it."[77] The benefit I saw from using this quantitative tool as part of my action research was to validate my knowledge claim that those selected for interview and the focus group were evangelicals, and to lend support to the view that teaching intelligent design, far from encouraging a conflict narrative between science and theology, promotes a more integrative paradigm.

"Wherever possible in carrying out your pedagogical action research study," Norton argues, "it is a good idea to use instruments that are already published."[78] The survey tool, designed by Tenneson, Bundrick and Stanford, provides a standard for describing participants' "science-faith paradigms" (also termed "science-theology paradigms").[79] The paradigms were discussed in chapter 2 relating them to intelligent design. Their five paradigms are:

1.   Conflict: Science over Theology

2.   Conflict: Theology over Science

3.   Compartmentalism

4.   Complementarism

5.   Concordism

The total number of respondents (including those who were invited to participate in an interview but were unable to) was twenty-eight, or almost 60 percent of those who attended both days of the course. Of those

75. Norton, *Action Research in Teaching and Learning*, 115; she gives an example that is analogous to my use of quantitative data in her Appendix C, 228–229.

76. Bob Dick, 'What Can Grounded Theorists and Action Researchers Learn from Each Other?', in *The SAGE Handbook of Grounded Theory*, ed. Antony Bryant and Kathy Charmaz (London: SAGE, 2007), 401.

77. Reason and Bradbury, 'Introduction', 7.

78. Norton, *Action Research in Teaching and Learning*, 155.

79. Tenneson, Bundrick, and Stanford, 'A New Survey Instrument and its Findings for Relating Science and Theology'.

twenty-eight, three showed no identifiable paradigm, thirteen used only one paradigm, and twelve used two simultaneous paradigms. Tenneson et al. surveyed five different communities to provide a way of comparing the different levels of responses. The surveyed groups were:

- University Science faculty at a range of US universities
- Assemblies of God (AG) pastors, educators, and students at a science and faith conference
- Students at a Christian university in a Southern US state
- Protestant and Pentecostal pastors, educators and students at a science and faith conference
- Faculty and students at AG colleges and universities

The Saturday School DID course participants seem to correlate with the pattern of responses given by Protestant and Pentecostal pastors, educators and students (survey of 350 was carried out in 2014) and the AG pastors, educators and students (survey of 117 carried out in 2011).[80] Both groups were a variety of ages and were attendees of Christian science and faith conferences. Like the AG pastors, educators and students, these reported high to maximal levels of religious commitment, and this matched the levels of Christian commitment expressed by the DID course participants well. A comparison between the different groups who only used one paradigm is shown in Figure 1 below. This data provided strong support for the view that those participating in my research were evangelical Christians.[81]

80. Tenneson, Bundrick, and Stanford, 210–13.

81. For the correlation of high personal religious affiliation with evangelicalism compared with other categories, see Tenneson, Bundrick, and Stanford, 'Faith and Science Integration: Surveys and Findings', 331.

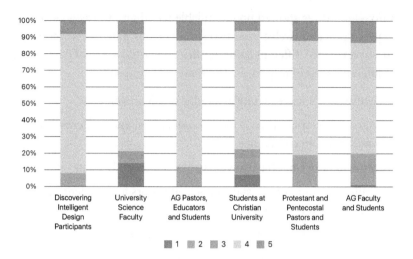

Figure 1. Comparison of respondents using one science-theology paradigm

The Complementarism paradigm (paradigm four) was the most frequent category for those using only one paradigm, and this was true across different educational environments. The data from DID course participants correlated closely with the AG pastors, educators and students and the Protestant and Pentecostal pastors and students. The interesting feature was the level of conflict that DID course participants showed between science and theology. Not only did they not exhibit Conflict: Science over Theology (paradigm one), but they also showed the lowest level of Conflict: Theology over Science (paradigm two). The survey undermines the belief that intelligent design arguments are either god of the gaps arguments or essentially scriptural arguments that oppose science. DID course respondents integrated their understanding of science and theology "to a high degree."[82]

Figure 2 below shows the data for those who used two science-theology paradigms. The main paradigms combined are the integrative paradigms 4 and 5 (Complementarism and Concordism). This contrasts with the dividing paradigms seen in the Science faculty of universities 1 and 3 (Conflict: Science over Theology and Compartmentalism). The DID, AG pastors, educators and students, and Protestant and Pentecostal pastors and students surveys all only contained what Tenneson et al. call

82. Tenneson, Bundrick, and Stanford, 343.

"integrative paradigms."[83] The DID course participants were the most likely to expect science and theology to be compatible and in concordance with each other.

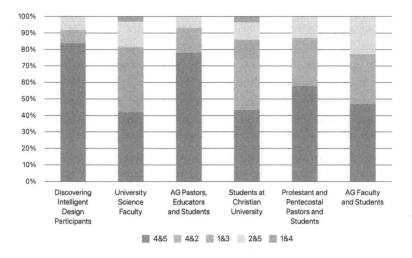

Figure 2. Comparison of respondents using two science-theology paradigms

Summary of the Tenneson, Bundrick and Stanford survey

Respondents having attended the DID course show a highly integrative view of science and theology, even compared to those that Tenneson et al. surveyed who had attended conferences on science and faith. Intelligent design arguments tend to reinforce the expectation that the disciplines of science and theology should integrate rather than conflict. This contrasts with the paradigm more associated with creation science arguments (Conflict: Theology over Science) that emphasizes conflict between the disciplines. It also contrasts with those science faculty members surveyed by Tenneson et al. who described their religious affiliation as none and were the only ones to employ "either the Conflict: Science over Theology paradigm or the Compartmentalism paradigm."[84]

The comparison with the findings of Ecklund et al. regarding scientists both in the US and in the UK is instructive. Ecklund et al. showed

83. Tenneson, Bundrick, and Stanford, 342.

84. Tenneson, Bundrick, and Stanford, 'A New Survey Instrument and its Findings for Relating Science and Theology', 209.

that UK scientists from a range of elite academic and industrial institutions are almost the inverse of the DID course participants: only 12 percent would see science and religion in some sort of collaboration, whereas 82 percent believe they are either in conflict (and on the side of science) or independent of each other. Of the eight regions or countries surveyed, the UK had the highest percentage of scientists who believed science and religion were in conflict, 35 percent, and all saw themselves on the side of science.[85] Although Ecklund et al. are at pains to show that their study demonstrates there is no intrinsic conflict between science and religion (because 12 percent of UK scientists do believe that science and religion can be in collaboration), these statistics demonstrate that significantly different worldviews are operating between those scientists surveyed by Ecklund and the participants of the DID course. As the thematic analysis shall show, participants have good reason to think that their perception of the relationship between science and theology is incongruent with the academy, and it is the scientific academy that is most likely to frame that relationship as being in conflict or incompatible, not DID course participants.

THEMATIC ANALYSIS

I followed Norton's suggestion of using thematic analysis to interpret the qualitative semi-structured interview transcripts.[86] Thematic analysis is defined by Braun and Clarke as a qualitative research method that is independent of the means of obtaining the data.[87] Its flexibility makes it suitable for the inductive approach used for the interview data.[88] It identifies patterns across the sources of data and is relatively straightforward to learn.[89] It was considered appropriate for my purposes because although thematic analysis might "gloss over differences amongst those who participate,"[90] I was not looking to identify distinctions between the interviewees but rather to identify common themes amongst them.[91] The

---

85. Ecklund et al., 'Religion among Scientists in International Context', 6.

86. Norton, *Action Research in Teaching and Learning*, 117–23.

87. Braun and Clarke, *Successful Qualitative Research*, 178.

88. Braun and Clarke, 180.

89. Bryman, *Social Research Methods*, 13.

90. Gaventa and Cornwall, 'Power and Knowledge', 180.

91. Braun and Clarke, *Successful Qualitative Research*, 180.

aim was to present an analytic narrative of the interviews relating it to the research question.[92] I followed Norton's recommendation of using software packages to assist the action researcher for this kind of analysis,[93] which Kember suggests is "worth using if there is a large amount of data in electronic form with multiple variables and constructs."[94]

Immersion

Immersing myself in the transcripts themselves through the transcription process (Norton's first phase) led to the generation of general themes: Intelligent Design, Darwinism, Christian Faith, Groups, Location, and the Discovering Intelligent Design course.[95] These were summative and functioned more as container concepts for specific categories. The second stage of generating categories was approached question by question as I sought a more general impression of the effect of the course on participants. Deciding the best way to express the data was problematic for lack of general rules, although Norton warns of risks in looking for themes related to the questions.[96]

> There is no one (ideal) way to do this; researchers rely on their own analytic judgment about what is meaningful and important for answering the research question.[97]

The source of data for the analysis was the semi-structured interviews with participants of the DID course and their questionnaire responses. It seemed sensible to use the interview guide as a structure for analysis and to find thematic "meaning patterned across the dataset."[98] I decided the best arrangement of data was the relationship between the question responses and the frequency of categories.[99] The benefit of us-

92. Clarke and Braun, 'Thematic Analysis', 6627.

93. Norton, *Action Research in Teaching and Learning*, 128.

94. Kember, *Action Learning and Action Research*, 40.

95. Norton, *Action Research in Teaching and Learning*, 118.

96. Norton, 118.

97. Clarke and Braun, 'Thematic Analysis', 6627.

98. Clarke and Braun, 6627.

99. Alternatives included the idea of analysing the answers according to generational concerns, but the results of that analysis did not prove to be significant in that the frequency of categories was not especially sensitive to generation.

ing computer software was its ability to manage the data to analyse it in different ways.[100]

Categories generated

A full list of all the categories generated are given below. They fell into the six unequal themes identified at first and represent the following number of references in the transcripts:

- Intelligent Design (Apologetics, Enabling Debate, Confidence, Creationism, Encouraging Faith, Relief, Evangelism, Conversation Starter, Not So Useful, True Science, Challenging Falsehood, Unscientific, Worldview, Purpose, Teleology); 216 references.

- Darwinism (Aggression, Evolution Science Argument, Loss of Christian Faith, Promoted in Media, Religious Defeater, Social Consequences, Taught as "Fact," Worldview Myth, Evolution as a belief); 166 references.

- Christian Faith (Bad Associations, Bible, Church, Perceived as Anti-Scientific, Source of Morality, Thinking about Science and Faith, Critical Thinking); 113 references.

- Groups (Boomers, Colleagues, Family, Friends, Gen-X, Gen-Z, Men, Millennial); 81 references.

- Location (Bible College, Home, School, Social Media, University, Workplace); 80 references.

- Discovering Intelligent Design Course (Science); 52 references.

Deleting and merging categories into themes

Norton's third and fourth stages reduce the number of categories either by removing those that have limited significance to the content or by combining similar concepts into broader themes. Reflecting on the categories least frequently identified in interviews suggested their lesser importance, but even then it was a matter of judgement as to their significance

---

100. Jennifer Rowley, 'Data Analysis', in *The SAGE Encyclopedia of Action Research*, ed. David Coghlan and Mary Brydon-Miller (London: SAGE, 2014), 240.

to the analysis.[101] Discernment was needed in judging whether a category represented an important counter voice or was of peripheral concern to the core themes of the data. Some categories were readily merged into broader themes.[102] Two categories that merged easily were the references to Church and Perceived as Anti-Scientific because it was church that was the focus of concern when the latter category was being discussed, and independent references to church did not add to the narrative. Similarly, the separate categories of Millennials and Gen-Z were better represented by the theme of Young People as none of the respondents was precise in using the more specific terms for the different age groups, but all shared a common concern for the theme that younger generations in the church were at special risk of losing their faith and those not in the church were especially likely to adopt a Darwinian worldview. The category of Conversation Starter merged into the broader theme of Evangelism.

The categories identified at this stage as significant were as follows:

1. Thinking About Science and Faith

2. Church Perceived as Anti-Scientific

3. School

4. Taught as Fact

5. Social Consequences

6. Worldview Myth

7. Young People

8. Loss of Christian Faith

9. Evangelism

10. Challenging Falsehood

11. Enabling Debate

12. True Science

13. Discovering Intelligent Design Course

---

101. Norton, *Action Research in Teaching and Learning*, 119–20.

102. Norton, 120.

Linking themes and presenting a narrative analysis

The final stages of thematic analysis are to link themes together and present evidence for doing so. This followed extensive re-reading of the data ensuring that the themes were a good reflection of the content. Linking themes identifies "the most important features of the coded data relevant to the research question."[103] It is more than a summary of the content; it is an analytic narrative that gives "a coherent and convincing account of what the data tells you."[104] Rowley argues that analysis should bring out key themes and that the narrative should be "comprehensive and transparent so that readers can read it for themselves and make their own interpretations."[105] Braun and Clarke argue for a "good balance between analytic commentary and data extracts."[106] The aim, as Norton puts it, "is to present an analytical narrative that makes some sort of reasoned case in response to your original research question."[107] The research question investigates the extent to which a course like DID helps evangelicals share their faith by giving confidence and abilities, and the thematic analysis identifies the way in which the participants' responses contribute to that question. The themes that were identified through the linking process are presented below.

The Church Does Not Encourage Engagement Between Science and Faith

This theme links the categories of Thinking About Science and Faith, Church, and Perceived as Anti-Scientific. Respondents stated that they came on the DID course to meet a felt need to understand science from a Christian perspective, something that they felt was lacking within their churches. There was a need to think about the relationship between science and faith specifically from the science perspective. This was not simply the gaining of knowledge for its own sake but was instead to develop the participants' ability to engage others, especially those who are not Christians. Lack of scientific understanding was perceived as either

103. Clarke and Braun, 'Thematic Analysis', 6627.
104. Norton, *Action Research in Teaching and Learning*, 121.
105. Rowley, 'Data Analysis', 242.
106. Braun and Clarke, *Successful Qualitative Research*, 304.
107. Norton, *Action Research in Teaching and Learning*, 122.

a missed opportunity, a disadvantage, or an obstacle to maintaining a dialogue with people, something that put the Christian on the defensive or meant simply missing out on a common topic of conversation within society. An important feature in the transcripts was that church was perceived as being opposed to science or "anti-scientific," or at least not a welcoming place for that kind of discussion.

The research participants thought that evangelicals were not being equipped to think about their faith in relation to science within their churches, and that this created a perception of being hostile to science. A quotation that sums up the value of the DID course for participants is from Austin Farrer:

> Though argument does not create conviction, the lack of it destroys belief. What seems to be proved may not be embraced; but what no one shows the ability to defend is quickly abandoned. Rational argument does not create belief, but it maintains a climate in which belief may flourish.[108]

The DID course, set as it was within a church and supported by the church leaders, addressed these concerns by looking at scientific evidence and defending the scientific rationality of believing in a transcendent designer.

Unquestioning Certitude of Darwinism in School

The interviews brought out a clear sense that school was a source of the problem that the DID course addressed. The themes of School and Taught as Fact linked naturally together, although the theme of school should be thought of as including university. Darwinism is taught in school as a sufficient (materialist) explanation for life without the need to appeal to God. Participants thought of themselves as being out of step with school teaching and the worldview associated with it. Participants felt that the DID course provided an alternative perspective and a counter voice to the certitude of school teaching about the fact of evolution. It entered that discussion with scientific evidence, rather than starting from the perspective of Christian faith. Identifying the source of the widespread

108. Austin Farrer, 'Grete Clerk,' in Jocelyn Gibb, comp., *Light on C.S. Lewis* (New York: Harcourt and Brace, 1965), 26; cited in McGrath, 'New Atheism—New Apologetics: The Use of Science in Recent Christian Apologetic Writings', 5.

problem of Darwinian belief was an important step in giving participants a sense of confidence to respond.

Young People Vulnerable to Losing Christian Faith

Associated with the problem of school teaching, participants were concerned about the effect that this teaching had on the younger generations either in school or having recently attended it. The DID course was described as useful in responding to a perceived loss of religious affiliation by young people, and this led to my linking the themes of Young People with Loss of Christian Faith. The theme of Young People Vulnerable to Losing Christian Faith brought out important insights for my research question. Giving young people scientific evidence that supported a theistic worldview gave them confidence and helped them to avoid a sense of ridicule or feeling foolish within the educational establishment or amongst friendship groups. Empowering a marginalized group is very much at the heart of action research, especially within an academic context.[109] The research identified that the DID course was useful in addressing a key vulnerability of Christian young people through education, and I took this as validation for the premise of my research project, namely that teaching intelligent design might have a positive impact in giving evangelicals confidence in sharing their faith in an environment that showed antipathy towards a theistic worldview.

Recognizing Darwinian Consequences

The Worldview Myth associated with the materialist version of Darwinian teaching had concerning Social Consequences expressed by several respondents that suggested linking these two themes together.[110] Partici-

109. Joseph Cunningham, 'Academic Discourse', in *The SAGE Encyclopedia of Action Research*, ed. David Coghlan and Mary Brydon-Miller (London: SAGE, 2014), 1; cf. Tabetha Adkins, 'Critical Pedagogy', in *The SAGE Encyclopedia of Action Research*, ed. David Coghlan and Mary Brydon-Miller (London: SAGE, 2014), 212.

110. For a theological discussion about using "myth" in this way, see Moye who writes: "[M]yth, perhaps more clearly than any other type of fiction, as a mode of understanding distinct from logical or discursive understanding, illustrates how a narrative construction embodies a way of conceptualizing and representing reality, including the reality of the past." Richard H. Moye, 'In the Beginning: Myth and History in Genesis and Exodus', *Journal of Biblical Literature* 109, no. 4 (1990): 578, https://doi.org/10.2307/3267364; for a discussion about contemporary usage of the

pants thought that Darwinism had an ethic associated with it and that evolutionary science was a powerful lens to view the world through and principle to live by. They expressed concerns about the moral implications of living that way. The significant finding of the research is that the DID course did not locate itself within a conflict of theology against science, but rather within worldview conflicts. It is metanarratives that are in opposition, rather than science and theology.

Enabling Conversational Evangelism

The research question investigated how teaching science to evangelicals might affect the way they engaged in evangelism. Would it, for instance, give them a greater sense of confidence to share their faith with non-Christians? Respondents gave several examples where what they learned on the course helped them to have conversations with people they otherwise would have found it difficult to engage with. They reported that the subject of intelligent design helped to initiate conversations by providing a common point of interest. These responses led me to link the Evangelism and Conversation Starter categories to my broader theme of Enabling Conversational Evangelism. They validated my research question that teaching intelligent design would enable evangelicals to share their faith with more confidence. The content of this sharing changed from more biblically-based content to a conversation about scientific observations of nature, but it was perceived by respondents as a positive first step in forming relationships with people who are low down on the Engel Scale (no or some awareness of God) with the intention of leading them ultimately to put their faith in the Christian Gospel.[111] It enabled

---

term, see Robert A. Segal, 'Myth', in *The Blackwell Companion to the Study of Religion*, ed. Robert A. Segal, Blackwell Companions to Religion (Oxford: Blackwell, 2006), 352–54; William R. Herzog, *Parables as Subversive Speech: Jesus as Pedagogue of the Oppressed* (Louisville: Westminster; John Knox, 1994), 47; and Dallas Willard, 'The Bible, the University, and the God Who Hides', in *The Bible and the University*, ed. David Lyle Jeffrey and C. Stephen Evans, vol. 8 (Milton Keynes: Paternoster, 2007), 18–19; cf. Wright's use of the term "true myth" (referring to the New Testament) in Wright, *NTPG*, 471.

111. James F. Engel and Wilbert Norton, *What's Gone Wrong with the Harvest? A Communication Strategy for the Church and World Evangelism* (Grand Rapids: Zondervan, 1975); for an updated diagram and discussion from the Evangelical Alliance, see 'What is the Engel Scale?', Evangelical Alliance, accessed 18 September 2020, https://www.eauk.org/what-is-the-engel-scale.

participants to generate interest and initiate conversation with those who showed little interest in the Gospel.

Responding to the Challenge of Darwinism

Participants felt a responsibility to defend their Christian worldview in a public forum where evolution is Taught as Fact and felt empowered to do so. Responses tended to take an evidentialist apologetic approach.[112] Participants shared how the DID course had not only given them a means to initiate a conversation but also enabled them to join in a discussion with those advocating a secular or Darwinian worldview. This was a direct response to the central question of the research project.

Participants articulated a sense of pressure they felt from a hegemonic worldview that drew strength from a foundation of scientific "facts" and left them feeling marginalized. They described how they now felt better equipped to respond to the various claims and assertions made. They showed a sense of frustration with that worldview communicated especially in schools and felt that this dominance should be challenged. The nature of the challenge envisaged was of reasoned argument over scientific evidence, and the DID course had empowered them to enter the debate. The value of the DID course was perceived as providing a way of challenging the Darwinian worldview with scientific evidence thereby resisting the power and authority of the dominant secular worldview of the school environment. The goal of challenging the perception of Darwinism as fact was to legitimate the possibility of a different (Christian) worldview for young people based on what some termed True Science. The categories of Challenging Falsehood, True Science, and Enabling Debate were linked, therefore, into the broader theme of Responding to the Challenge of Darwinism.

Triangulation

The thematic analysis above provided evidence for the main themes as being:

---

112. Kenneth D. Boa and Robert M. Bowman, *Faith Has its Reasons: Integrative Approaches to Defending the Christian Faith.*, 2nd ed. (Downers Grove: InterVarsity, 2005), 237.

1. The Church Does Not Encourage Engagement Between Science and Faith

2. Unquestioning Certitude of Darwinism in School

3. Young People Vulnerable to Losing Christian Faith

4. Recognizing Darwinian Consequences

5. Enabling Conversational Evangelism

6. Responding to the Challenge of Darwinism

I undertook a more deductive approach in analysing the transcripts of the focus group to provide evidence that the themes are a valid interpretation of participants' understanding of the effect that the DID course had on them. It is common, Hathcoat and Nicholas argue, for action researchers to demonstrate the validity of interpretations by using a different data source to cross-reference, or triangulate, observations.[113] Creswell argues that the triangulation of data "strengthens reliability" of the interpretations made.[114] Fraenkel et al. describe this validity enhancement as "cross-checking sources of information."[115] Braun and Clarke give a nuanced discussion of its use in both realist and interpretivist contexts and argue that it is useful in both.[116] Helskog discusses the relationship of action research with empirical science and compares the need for both to justify their results.[117] Triangulation provides evidence that the methods of analysis used, namely interviews and the focus group, had a consistency about them.[118] Mertler argues that it enhances the rigor of the action research process,[119] and Maguire sees it as demonstrating the trustworthiness of the data.

> At the end of the day it is about using *reliable* methods, *reliable* as in trustworthiness of all aspects of the research including the researcher, to gather the data that will make the evidence of

113. Hathcoat and Nicholas, 'Epistemology', 305.

114. Creswell and Creswell, *Research Design*, 290.

115. Fraenkel, Wallen, and Hyun, *How to Design and Evaluate Research in Education*, 426.

116. Braun and Clarke, *Successful Qualitative Research*, 323–24.

117. Helskog, 'Justifying Action Research', 15.

118. For a discussion connecting triangulation with realism, see Goldman, 'Truth and Realism', 235–36.

119. Craig A. Mertler, *Action Research: Improving Schools and Empowering Educators*, 3rd ed. (Thousand Oaks: SAGE, 2012), 28.

most value to the intention of, and to the stakeholders in, the research; and the quality of data is strengthened by cross-referencing the results from each of the different data sources. This is commonly referred to in the social sciences as triangulation.[120]

Indicative evidence from the focus group analysis that supports the themes identified in the semi-structured interviews is given below.

The Church Does Not Encourage Engagement Between Science and Faith

Participant 11MB expressed a frustration that his home group "didn't want to talk about it. They're firm Christians, nothing to talk about." There was a lack of curiosity and no sense of urgency expressed about the relationship of science and faith. 10FB agreed, saying that young people are "not given any impression from school in education that actually the two could interlink and support one another." (10FB)

Unquestioning Certitude of Darwinism in School

There was a consensus that schools presented Darwinism as fact, and 9MB was bullish about challenging that notion: "I think they've had it very easy for a good number of years. Everybody just says, 'Oh, I believe in evolution,' but nobody argues the question." (9MB)

Young People Vulnerable to Losing Christian Faith

Participants in the focus group all had children or grandchildren and were enthusiastic about the benefits of the DID course to respond to their real concerns over them losing their Christian faith. 11MB shared that he thought "it is radically different to anything they've been taught. The whole concept of God has been missed out, particularly for younger people in their education." (11MB)

---

120. Maguire, 'Methodology as Personal and Professional Integrity: Research Designing for Practitioner Doctorates', 103.

Recognizing Darwinian Consequences

This theme was less evident in the focus group because it spent more time discussing the benefit of the course, rather than the problem it addressed. However the consequences of being ignorant of scientific alternatives, and the need for young people to be able to integrate their faith with the rest of their education, pointed towards a broader worldview concern, even if the concepts were not put in those terms.

Enabling Conversational Evangelism

This important theme was consistently stated by almost all the participants. The benefit of learning about intelligent design, 15MX said, was that it was "a way of getting people in for the first time." 11MB emphasized that the DID course "gives people that confidence when you're talking to many friends, particularly teachers even, who've no idea. They've no intention of believing in a God." This provided a validation for the knowledge claim that the DID contributed to evangelicals' confidence and ability in sharing their faith.

Responding to the Challenge of Darwinism

Intelligent design was anthropomorphized as a champion and framed in pugilistic terms: 14FB felt a sense of "relief to hear it spoken about intelligently in a way that can stand up to opposition." The value of the course was in giving the content for argument as well as the opportunity for discussion.

The evidence from the focus group triangulated the argument that the themes identified in the semi-structured interview were a valid and rigorous reflection of the interview data.

SUMMARY

In this second action research cycle I have described the processes of gathering the information needed to respond to the research question. In addition to the more quantitative data above, the semi-structured interviews were transcribed and analysed using thematic analysis. At this point it would be normal to summarize the results of the thematic analysis and then propose changes to modify future practice implied by that summary. This stage of thematic analysis, Clark and Braun say, would involve situating this analytical narrative "within the relevant field of scholarship, in a way that convinces the reader of the validity of their interpretations."[121] However, as I argued in chapter 3, it was important for me to structure the critical reflection of these findings within a model of practical theology.

The argument at this point is that the cycles of action research have supported a positive response to the research question that teaching intelligent design does enable and give confidence to evangelical students in sharing their faith with those holding to a more materialistic worldview. However, the thematic analysis, pedagogical action research, and professional doctorate are located within my practice as an evangelical theologian and any action produced by my research project should also be the product of theological reflection. Modified future practice must be theologically informed as well as correlated with other disciplines.[122] I chose to structure my theological reflection according to Osmer's model of practical theology and have placed the summary of the thematic analysis within his first phase. In the next chapter I describe the first two phases of Osmer's mode, namely the Priestly Listening and Sagely Wisdom phases where I summarize the thematic analysis and then critically correlate it with insights from the social sciences.

121. Clarke and Braun, 'Thematic Analysis', 6627.

122. Osmer describes it as a "revised correlation" model Drawing from Tracy and Browning; see Osmer, *Practical Theology*, 166.

6

Osmer's Practical Theology

Practical theology, while emerging from the inner life of the church in its mission to the world, has its praxis in the interaction of God's mission to the world.[1]

THIS CHAPTER DESCRIBES THE process of practical theology undertaken as a continuation of the two cycles of pedagogical action research to reach a theologically-informed change of practice. It marks a shift of emphasis in the research project as it adds an explicitly theological dimension to the reflective process appropriate for a professional practical theology doctorate. For reasons outlined in pages 48–54, I chose Osmer's model of practical theology to organize my reflections on the research findings and to provide a theological basis for any modified future practice. The reflection became more dialogical and interdisciplinary. It facilitated a deeper understanding of the results of the action research cycles through critical correlation and enabled me to frame my actions and reflections within a scriptural, and indeed christological structure that cohered with my evangelical theological context.[2] The research project's theological analysis enabled theologically-laden revised praxis, or what Osmer calls "servant leadership."[3]

1. Anderson, *The Shape of Practical Theology*, 32.
2. Osmer, *Practical Theology*, 11.
3. Yvonna S. Lincoln and Egon G. Guba, 'Paradigmatic Controversies, Contradictions, and Emerging Confluences', in *The SAGE Handbook of Qualitative Research*,

As the agent of change, my values, beliefs and my *teloi* all contributed towards the changes I sought to make in benefitting the students whose concerns first began this process, and whose interview responses directed it. It was not primarily a goal of self-enhancement, although without doubt my professional skills were developed through this systematic process of inquiry and reflection. Rather, the goal was action in the service of the good of the student community through intellectual transformation.[4] The criteria of validation of this stage of the research were congruity with the interview data, quality of interdisciplinary reflection (through critical correlation) and integration with the Christian tradition, which in my context meant primarily with Scripture.

PRIESTLY LISTENING

Osmer describes the act of Priestly Listening as attending to different voices, in this case the voices of my interviewees.[5] The themes drawn out from the thematic analysis constitute the core interpreted data of the research project "from the participant's point of view."[6] Participants had a dynamic engagement with the DID course. Their sense of excitement and motivation came through clearly in their enthusiastic responses. They were able to share their experiences and the effects of attending the DID course, and the thematic analysis enabled me to draw out concepts from these accounts in a rigorous and sustained way. Denscombe argues that the "development of these concepts is the main purpose of the analysis because the concepts provide some new understanding of the data and constitute the foundations for any theory or general conclusions to emerge from the research."[7] This formal, disciplined attending is what Osmer calls priestly listening, modelled on Christ's priestly ministry, producing a deeper understanding of what is going on.[8] A summary of that priestly listening, the analytic story from the thematic analysis, is given below.

---

ed. N. K. Denzin and Yvonna S. Lincoln, 3rd ed. (Thousand Oaks: SAGE, 2005), 167.

4. Lincoln and Guba, 166.

5. Osmer, *Practical Theology*, 37.

6. Norton, *Action Research in Teaching and Learning*, 128.

7. Denscombe, *The Good Research Guide*, 286–87.

8. Osmer, *Practical Theology*, 38–39.

The focus of interest for participants was the course content and its implications for church, society, young people, evangelism, apologetics and understanding worldviews. Participants articulated the problem of a dominant secular worldview and realized their own opportunity and ability to take part in challenging that dominance. They felt empowered to challenge with evidence what institutions had presented as fact, and they had seen the effects of their new knowledge in opening doors to meaningful conversations with people that they had felt were unreachable. It gave them confidence to participate in scientific conversations, and they felt more willing to challenge scientific assertions that undermined their Christian worldview. Most felt the church contributed to the problem by reinforcing the division between science and faith and not challenging the secular worldview in schools and in society more broadly. Participating in the course enabled them to debate with others at the right level, the worldview level, avoiding the risk of reinforcing a science-versus-faith perception. This increased ability to communicate made them feel less marginalized by those who held a Darwinian worldview. There was a sense of hope that the social consequences associated with Darwinism were not inevitable, and that young people especially could be shown a worldview where their existence was meaningful and not attributable to chance. Participants saw the strategy of sharing insights from intelligent design theory as an important stage in the process of evangelizing those whose scientific worldview made them less receptive to the Gospel.

The two concepts of worldview and hegemony constituted the main "problem" of the thematic analysis. The concept of participant empowerment focused on their sense of transformation and liberation, enabling greater communication. "Empowerment" and "enabling" represented a sense of "solution" or dénouement to the research problem. The overall "analytic story" is that the DID course raised critical awareness of worldview conflict, framed the conflict in terms of power and authority of institutions advocating a certain kind of evolutionary discourse, empowered participants with confidence that the hegemony of scientism is neither inevitable nor necessary, equipped participants to respond within a scientific register, and enabled them to communicate better with those holding a more secular worldview.[9]

---

9. Clarke and Braun, 'Thematic Analysis', 6627; emphasis removed.

SAGELY WISDOM

The Priestly Listening stage of Osmer's model gives way to the reflective task of interpretation, or Sagely Wisdom.[10] I have chosen the method of critical correlation where the main concepts attended to in the Priestly Listening phase are reflected on from the perspective of different disciplines to understand the issues more deeply.[11] Osmer argues that this interpretative phase requires wisdom to navigate the themes that come through from the Priestly Listening task. He uses the metaphor of "the art of steering," drawn from his reflection on Proverbs 1:5 "let the wise listen and add to their learning, and let the discerning get guidance." Wisdom is associated with an openness to the world, reflection on human experience, and virtuous action.[12]

> Drawing on theories of the arts and sciences to interpret the relevant particulars of episodes, situations, and contexts takes wise judgement and moral sense, as well as a solid grasp of the theories being used.[13]

This second phase of Osmer's model emphasizes the role of Jesus the sage who "seeks to disclose God's royal rule, which is breaking into the present through his ministry."[14] His wisdom, as we shall see below, is often disruptive. In a telling passage, Osmer quotes Paul's first letter to the Corinthians:

> For it is written:
>   "I will destroy the wisdom of the wise;
>
>   the intelligence of the intelligent I will frustrate."

---

10. Osmer, *Practical Theology*, 79.

11. Osmer, 164–67; Watkins uses the term "conceptual conversation"; Clare Watkins, *Disclosing Church: An Ecclesiology Learned from Conversations in Practice* (Abingdon: Routledge, 2020), 29; Pattison uses the similar concept of "critical conversation" in Stephen Pattison, 'Some Straw for the Bricks: A Basic Introduction to Theological Reflection', *Contact* 99, no. 1 (1 February 1989): 4–5, https://doi.org/10.10 80/13520806.1989.11759678.

12. Osmer, *Practical Theology*, 93; Anderson defines practical theology as a form of practical wisdom; Anderson, *The Shape of Practical Theology*, 33.

13. Osmer, *Practical Theology*, 85.

14. Osmer, 97.

Where is the wise person? Where is the teacher of the law?
Where is the philosopher of this age? Has not God made foolish
the wisdom of the world?
1 Corinthians 1:19–20

Wisdom has the capacity, Osmer argues, to reverse and subvert,
"pointing to the counterorder of God's royal rule."[15] I chose to critically
correlate the main sagely insights from the problem of worldview and
hegemony and from the solution of empowerment and enabling, namely:
Darwinism as fact, symbolic universe, Darwinian consequences, critical
consciousness, science as politics, muted group theory, teleology, democracy of science, and conversational evangelism. This interdisciplinary approach is in keeping with practical theology that has, as Miller-McLemore
says, "a steadfast interest in concepts that overstep any one discipline"
and that involve "a movement and conversation across areas of expertise
and knowledge."[16]

Darwinism as fact

An important theme identified in the analysis was the unquestioning
certitude of Darwinism. Darwinism is commonly presented as fact. The
idea of a fact is something that is a "given," a datum that contributes to
theories, and something that any theory must accommodate.[17] Theories
can be contested, and the relative strength of arguments can be compared
to discern their merits, whereas facts are incontestable. Debates about
Darwinism are often framed as a debate between science and religion,
usually understood as a choice between fact and faith. Darwinists are
rightly suspicious of those who would choose faith rather than facts.

The participants' perception of Darwinian evolution being taught as
fact is widely reflected in the literature. Coyne argues that "evolution is
far more than a scientific theory: it is a scientific fact."[18] Dawkins claims

15. Osmer, 100.

16. Bonnie J. Miller-McLemore, 'Introduction: The Contributions of Practical
Theology', in *The Wiley-Blackwell Companion to Practical Theology*, ed. Bonnie J.
Miller-McLemore, Wiley-Blackwell Companions to Religion (Chichester: Wiley-
Blackwell, 2012), 17.

17. Audrey B. Champagne, 'Facts, Concepts, Principles, and Theories in Science,
Assessment of: An Overview', in *Encyclopedia of Science Education*, ed. Richard Gunstone (Dordrecht: Springer, 2015), 427.

18. Jerry A. Coyne, *Why Evolution is True* (Oxford: Oxford University Press, 2009),

it "is a fact. Beyond reasonable doubt, beyond serious doubt, beyond sane, informed, intelligent doubt, beyond doubt evolution is a fact."[19] He elsewhere argues that, when it comes to evolution, scientists should no longer use the Oxford English Dictionary definition of the word "theory" (sense 1) to mean "a hypothesis that has been confirmed or established by observation or experiment."

> The party line among scientists arguing for evolution is to pro-
> mote Sense 1, and I have followed it until today. But now I want
> to depart from the party line. I now think that trying to clear
> up this terminological point about the meaning of "theory" is a
> losing battle. We should stop using "theory" altogether for the
> case of evolution and insist, instead, that evolution is a *fact*.[20]

In a press release concerning the teaching of evolution to eleven year-olds, the head of the Royal Society of Chemistry emphasised that "[a]bove all, we should no longer talk of the theory of evolution, as though it is 'just an idea'; so well established is it, that it now warrants the designation of an immutable scientific law, and should be taught as such."[21]

Jean and Lu analysed the use of "factual" language in what they call the "fact of evolution" discourse. Its use is "systematic and agreement-based," and its goal is "to counter antievolutionism by associating the term 'fact' with evolution, thereby making evolution appear more certain to the public."[22] Jean and Lu refer to those using the terminology of fact for such purposes "discourse advocates." The "fact of evolution" discourse is contested within the wider scientific community because the use of such popular vernacular promotes misunderstanding.

242.

19. Richard Dawkins, *The Greatest Show on Earth: The Evidence for Evolution* (London: Black Swan, 2010), 9.

20. Richard Dawkins, 'Is it a Theory? Is it a Law? No, it's a Fact', Richard Dawkins Foundation, 30 November 2015, https://www.richarddawkins.net/2015/11/is-it-a-theory-is-it-a-law-no-its-a-fact/; emphasis original.

21. The press release is available through this website: Richard Pike, '"Teach Children Evolution as Fact Not Theory" Says UK Chemistry Chief', Royal Society of Chemistry, 25 April 2006, https://www.rsc.org/AboutUs/News/PressReleases/2006/Evolution.asp.

22. Jason Jean and Yixi Lu, 'Evolution as a Fact? A Discourse Analysis', *Social Studies of Science* 48, no. 4 (August 2018): 616, https://doi.org/10.1177/0306312718785773.

> Associating the term "fact" with evolution is [. . .] a means to attack antievolutionist claims and arguments, despite the negative consequences of a minority scientific terminology, ignoring established scientific consensuses, and creating a morass of contradictory and confusing explanations for how evolution is a fact.[23]

There is internal disagreement between advocates as to whether evolution is both a theory and a fact, or no longer a theory and only a fact. Coyne believes that "[a] theory becomes a fact (or a 'truth') when so much evidence has accumulated in its favor,"[24] whereas a National Academy of Sciences 2008 report states that evolution is "both" a theory and a fact.[25] In an earlier publication in 1998 it had claimed that "theories do not turn into facts through the accumulation of evidence. Rather, theories are the end points of science."[26] It is significant to note that other scientific disciplines do not use this "fact" terminology for their theories.[27] Despite this lack of agreement even amongst advocates, there is no desire to harmonize terminology because that would introduce criticism within the discourse. "Criticism is anathema to the public scientists who advocate for the discourse, as it would only serve to undermine their professional goals."[28] This results, Jean and Lu argue, in a "criticism-free zone" where any terminology is accepted without challenge if it is used "to conclude that evolution is a fact."[29]

Symbolic universe of materialism

Participants recognized the difficulty in challenging this "fact of evolution" discourse from within a social environment where Darwinism is presupposed. Things taken for granted, Bourdieu argues, are "socially

---

23. Jean and Lu, 618.

24. Coyne, *Why Evolution is True*, 16.

25. 'Evolution Resources from the National Academies', 11, accessed 10 June 2019, http://www.nas.edu/evolution/TheoryOrFact.html.

26. National Academy of Sciences *Science and Creationism: A View from the National Academy of Sciences*, 2nd ed. (Washington: National Academies, 1999), 2; cited in 'Evolution Resources from the National Academies', 628.

27. For the few exceptions, see Jean and Lu, 'Evolution as a Fact?', 626.

28. Jean and Lu, 621.

29. Jean and Lu, 626.

produced in and by a collective work of construction of social reality."[30] This Darwinian "taken-for-grantedness" is sustained by the constructed narrative of common descent from abiogenesis to the abundance of life forms experienced today. "Darwinism tells us that, like all species, human beings arose from the working of blind, purposeless forces over eons of time. As far as we can determine, the same forces that gave rise to ferns, mushrooms, lizards, and squirrels also produced us."[31] This narrative is part of what Berger and Luckman call the conceptual machinery of "universe-maintenance,"[32] and its success is "related to the power possessed by those who operate them."[33] Dreher, building on Berger and Luckman's arguments, notes that it is not the words themselves, or the ideas themselves, that maintain the symbolic universe but rather the power of those who legitimate them.

> The abstract theories which sustain symbolic universes are validated more by social support than by empirical evidence. Theories function because they work, and they work because they are said to work and therefore they are convincing. They function because they have become standard in the form of knowledge taken for granted in a particular society.[34]

Evolution discourse serves to maintain the symbolic universe of materialism where academic legitimators define reality. Referring to scientists as "specialist élites," Berger and Luckman associate the production of materialist conceptual machineries with the secularisation of society (understood in this instance as the emancipation of science "from religious institutions and norms").[35]

> Modern science is an extreme step in this development, and in the secularization and sophistication of universe-maintenance. Science not only completes the removal of the sacred from

30. Pierre Bourdieu and Loïc J. D. Wacquant, *An Invitation to Reflexive Sociology* (Chicago: University of Chicago Press, 1992), 239; emphasis removed.

31. Coyne, *Why Evolution is True*, 245.

32. Peter L. Berger and Thomas Luckmann, *The Social Construction of Reality: A Treatise in the Sociology of Knowledge* (London: Penguin, 1966), 123.

33. Berger and Luckmann, 126.

34. Jochen Dreher, 'The Social Construction of Power: Reflections Beyond Berger/ Luckmann and Bourdieu', *Cultural Sociology* 10, no. 1 (March 2016): 60, https://doi.org/10.1177/1749975515615623.

35. Casanova, 'Rethinking Secularization: A Global Comparative Perspective', 7.

the world of everyday life, but removes universe-maintaining knowledge as such from that world.[36]

Cultural elites in positions of power use evolution discourse to established a secular symbolic universe or worldview with Darwinism as its metanarrative and with the notion of evolution as fact as its authorized language.[37] McGrath describes the ideology of Darwinism as being "beyond meaningful scientific investigation, precisely because it is a creedal statement, not a scientific viewpoint."[38] Berger and Luckman argue that contemporary society cannot be understood without considering its sociology of knowledge, and that without this insight "the 'lay' member of society no longer knows how his universe is to be conceptually maintained, although, of course, he still knows who the specialists of universe-maintenance are presumed to be."[39]

Consequences of Darwinian worldview

Moreland describes the Darwinian worldview as an expression of scientific naturalism (although the term generally used in this discussion will be "materialism"). It asserts that what can be known must be known by scientific means, and anything that exists must be some combination of matter and energy only.[40] It is a worldview "from which purpose, design, and transcendence are eliminated."[41] This reductionist worldview is called scientism because only science is said to provide "genuine knowledge of reality."[42] Three quotations illustrate the influence of this worldview. Firstly, Nagel notes that "reductive materialism is widely assumed to be the only serious possibility."[43] Secondly, in an interview

36. Berger and Luckmann, *The Social Construction of Reality*, 130.

37. The phrase is attributed to Bourdieu in Dreher, 'The Social Construction of Power', 58.

38. Alister E. McGrath, *Darwinism and the Divine: Evolutionary Thought and Natural Theology* (Chichester: Wiley-Blackwell, 2011), 33.

39. Berger and Luckmann, *The Social Construction of Reality*, 130.

40. J.P. Moreland, *Kingdom Triangle: Recover the Christian Mind, Renovate the Soul, Restore the Spirit's Power* (Grand Rapids: Zondervan, 2007), 40.

41. McGrath, *Darwinism and the Divine*, 33.

42. J.P. Moreland, *Scientism and Secularism: Learning to Respond to a Dangerous Ideology* (Wheaton: Crossway, 2018), 26; for an example of scientism, see Pinker, 'Science is Not Your Enemy'.

43. Nagel, *Mind and Cosmos*, 4.

Bellah explained that his sociological study of religion was motivated by wanting to know "what the universe is and where we are in it."

> The meta-narrative that is really the only one intelligible to all well-educated people everywhere in the world is the meta-narrative of evolution, which is in turn embedded in a narrative of cosmological development since 13.7 billion years ago in the Big Bang.[44]

Finally, Churchland claims:

> [T]he important point about the standard evolutionary story is that the human species and all of its features are the wholly physical outcome of a purely physical process. [. . .] If this is the correct account of our origins, then there seems neither need, nor room, to fit any nonphysical substances or properties into our theoretical account of ourselves. We are creatures of matter. And we should learn to live with that fact.[45]

These quotations illustrate why participants recognized the consequences of a Darwinian worldview to be antithetical to their evangelical Christian faith. They could not accept as fact the claim that human existence is without purpose, that there is no God, that they are uneducated, and that they should get used to it.[46]

"Critical consciousness"

The DID course was a pedagogical event that brought about critical awareness of and greater confidence with scientific concepts. It changed the perception of participants from feeling marginalized because of a lack of scientific knowledge to a recognition, or conscientization, of being excluded because of an unwillingness to accept a materialist worldview that

---

44. Cited in Heather Horn, 'Where Does Religion Come From?: A Conversation with Robert Bellah, Author of a New Book about Faith's Place in Evolution', *The Atlantic*, 17 August 2011, https://www.theatlantic.com/entertainment/archive/2011/08/where-does-religion-come-from/243723/.

45. Paul M. Churchland, *Matter and Consciousness: A Contemporary Introduction to the Philosophy of Mind*, Rev. ed (Cambridge, Mass: MIT Press, 1988), 35; cited in J.P. Moreland, 'Theistic Evolution, Christian Knowledge and Culture's Plausibility Structure', *Journal of Biblical and Theological Studies* 2, no. 1 (2017): 16.

46. Plantinga describes the naturalist worldview as a "quasi-religion" that is in "profound conflict" with the worldview of intelligent design; see Plantinga, *Where the Conflict Really Lies*, 311.

excludes God.[47] The term "conscientization" is drawn from Freire's *Pedagogy of the Oppressed*.[48] He defines *conscientização* as "critical consciousness" of oppressive sectarianism and associates it with "a truly liberating education."[49] Of the two kinds of oppressive sectarians he typologizes, it is the "rightist" that most resembles the authoritarianism seen in the culture of science. For rightist sectarians, the past is "something given and immutable."[50] They close themselves into "circles of certainty," and "suffer from an absence of doubt,"[51] (an accusation that is sometimes directed towards evangelicals).[52] Freire describes those oppressed as having "internalized the image of the oppressor,"[53] accepting the authority structures as being rightfully imposed. Elsewhere he describes oppressors as "[t]hose who propagate the superstructure's myths."[54] The solution is for people to "critically recognize its causes, so that through transforming action they can create a new situation."[55] This is achieved by "education for freedom."[56]

There are obvious difficulties with this critical correlation with Freire's approach. Firstly, labelling some as oppressors and others as oppressed is a divisive strategy that does not easily embody the kingdom value of "love your enemy" (Matthew 5:44). A more theological reflection on the problems of overcoming oppression is Volf's *Exclusion and Embrace*.[57] We must, he argues, prevent the dehumanization of those in positions of power, and oppose any legitimizing of revolutionary violence. Secondly, the form of teaching used for the DID course, to some extent, resembles the "bank" pedagogy that Freire criticizes as oppressive in that

47. Alvin Plantinga, 'Games Scientists Play', in *The Believing Primate: Scientific, Philosophical, and Theological Reflections on the Origin of Religion*, ed. Michael J. Murray and Jeffrey Schloss (New York: Oxford University Press, 2009), 149.

48. Paulo Freire, *Pedagogy of the Oppressed*, trans. Myra Bergman Ramos (London: Penguin, 1970).

49. Freire, 9.

50. Freire, 12.

51. Freire, 13; the latter quotation is cited as from Marcio Alves.

52. Kinnaman, *You Lost Me*; see his chapter 10 entitled 'Doubtless'.

53. Freire, *Pedagogy of the Oppressed*, 21.

54. Paulo Freire, 'Conscientisation', *CrossCurrents* 24, no. 1 (1974): 27.

55. Freire, *Pedagogy of the Oppressed*, 21.

56. Freire, 'Conscientisation', 28.

57. Miroslav Volf, *Exclusion and Embrace: A Theological Exploration of Identity, Otherness, and Reconciliation* (Nashville: Abingdon, 1996).

it remains in the gift of the teacher to give it rather than being explored together with the student.[58] "A conscientising—and therefore liberating—education is not that transfer of neatly wrapped knowledge."[59] As a response to this critique, online resources accompanying the course, and the provision of a small book stall, were ways of empowering learners for further study, something many participants took advantage of and expressed appreciation for. I invited them to reflect on their learning experience through surveys and interviews, which enabled interviewer and interviewee to learn together.

Intelligent design as foxes

My use of Freire's work framed the intelligent design argument in political terms. The hegemony of Darwinism in schools and universities is secure because intelligent design is not able to challenge it. In 2006, Lord Adonis, the Parliamentary Under-Secretary of State for the Department for Education and Skills, stated that:

> Intelligent design is not a recognised scientific theory; therefore, it is not included in the science curriculum. [. . .] Intelligent design can be explored in religious education as part of developing an understanding of different beliefs.[60]

As Chapp argues, this expression of "scientism" is "the inevitable metaphysical consequence of modem science's penchant for hegemony in academic discourse."[61]

Fuller has framed this tension over who gets to decide what counts as science in terms of Vilfredo Pareto's metaphor of lions and foxes. The establishment lions see the way things are at present as reliable (similar to Freire's rightist sectarians) and do not want to give the foxes any credence,

58. Freire, *Pedagogy of the Oppressed*, 45; see also the critique in Herzog, *Parables as Subversive Speech*, 19, 22.

59. Freire, 'Conscientisation', 27.

60. 'Lords Hansard Text for 18 Dec 200618 Dec 2006 (Pt 0006)', accessed 17 June 2019, https://publications.parliament.uk/pa/ld200607/ldhansrd/text/61218w0006.htm.

61. Larry Chapp, 'Is Nature Enough? Meaning and Truth in the Age of Science—By John F. Haught', *Modern Theology* 23, no. 4 (October 2007): 644, https://doi.org/10.1111/j.1468–0025.2007.00420.x.

whereas foxes see the lions as inhibiting a "better future."[62] Both groups are about winning not so much the argument as the game.

> In philosophical slang, the post-truth condition is all about *going meta*. You try to win not simply by playing by the rules but also by controlling what the rules are. The lions try to win by keeping the rules as they are and the fox tries by changing them. [. . .] In a post-truth game, the aim is to defeat your opponent in the full knowledge that the rules of the game might change.[63]

Intelligent design is seen by many as the foxes that seek to call out the weakness of the lion, and to flip the rules as soon as possible. An example of this view was Judge Jones' opinion that "ID aspires to change the ground rules of science to make room for religion."[64] The main leonine strategy for excluding theological foxes has been the "equal but separate" strategy, whereby science is defined epistemically as methodological naturalism and associated with public knowledge, fact, objectivity, reason, and truth.[65] Harris, for example, claims that "[s]cience, in the broadest sense, includes all reasonable claims to knowledge about ourselves and the world."[66] Theology would then be defined epistemologically as subjective belief, associated with personal meaning, opinion, preference, and emotion.[67] By dividing these two subjects into separate "magisteria," theology is excluded from making truth claims about science.[68] This strategy leaves religious faith occupying the private sphere only.[69] Krauss

62. Steve Fuller, *Post-Truth: Knowledge as a Power Game*, Anthem's Key Issues in Modern Sociology (New York: Anthem, 2018), 2.

63. Fuller, 3; emphasis original.

64. John E. Jones III, 'Kitzmiller v. Dover Area Sch. Dist. Opinion, 400 F. Supp. 2d 707, 719 (M.D. Pa. 2005)', American Civil Liberties Union, accessed 17 June 2019, https://www.aclu.org/legal-document/kitzmiller-v-dover-memorandum-opinion.

65. See, for instance, the discussion in Plantinga, 'Games Scientists Play', 152; and Trigg, *Rationality and Religion*, 70.

66. Sam Harris, 'Science Must Destroy Religion', in *What is Your Dangerous Idea?*, ed. John Brockman (New York: Harper Perennial, 2007), 149.

67. Billingsley, 'Teaching and Learning about Epistemic Insight', 62.

68. Taylor gives a similar description of how the concept of the "secular" left religion outside of public truth claims; see Taylor, 'The Polysemy of the Secular'; the term "magisteria" comes from Gould, 'Nonoverlapping Magisteria'.

69. For a helpful diagram, see Paul G. Hiebert, *Transforming Worldviews: An Anthropological Understanding of How People Change* (Grand Rapids: Baker Academic, 2008), 144; for an extended discussion on the fact/value divide see Moreland, *Scientism and Secularism*, 45.

encourages his reader to be "informed by fact, not by revelation";[70] he, like Harris, associates reason with science and religion with naïve fideism.

Willard thinks this separation of religion from fact and knowledge pushes it into the "merely" political sphere. "What is political, as now understood, does not require knowledge, but only advocacy. Its only issue is how to 'win' for 'your side.'"[71] Most critical references to those holding an intelligent design view describe them as "ID advocates" to maintain that impression. Others are more careful to distinguish between those whose aim is to introduce religion into science lessons in schools and those whose aim is to do better science.

> Although of course there are religious sentiments behind intelligent design, from what we have read, most intelligent design theorists take a different approach. They do not take any sacred narrative as their theoretical starting point and then attempt to support the narrative. Instead, they seem to take the deficiencies of evolutionary theory (as they see them) as the starting point and then attempt to present a more convincing hypothesis. We will call this group of scientific ID proponents the *ID theorists*. ID theorists, who can be found in several relevant academic positions at respectable institutions, claim that their theory is agnostic with respect to the nature of its designer and also with respect to how this designer fits, or does not fit, with traditional religious narratives.[72]

This distinction between advocates and theorists pushes back on the typology of lions and foxes and suggests that the intelligent design challenge to the materialist worldview's hegemony is more restorationist than revolutionary. It does not seek to change the rules, but rather to uphold the best traditions of academia and public discourse, as well as such scientific methodology as the inference to the best explanation.[73]

70. Lawrence M. Krauss, *A Universe from Nothing: Why There is Something Rather than Nothing* (New York: Free Press, 2012), 175.

71. Dallas Willard, *Personal Religion, Public Reality?: Towards a Knowledge of Faith* (London: Hodder & Stoughton, 2009), 27.

72. Bryan R. Warnick and C. David Fooce, 'Does Teaching Creationism Facilitate Student Autonomy?', *Theory and Research in Education* 5, no. 3 (2007): 374, https://doi.org/10.1177/1477878507081761; emphasis original.

73. For a good introduction, see Peter Lipton, 'Inference to the Best Explanation', in *A Companion to the Philosophy of Science*, ed. William H. Newton-Smith, Blackwell Companions to Philosophy 18 (Malden: Blackwell, 2000), 184–93; alternatively see Peter Lipton, *Inference to the Best Explanation*, 2nd ed., International Library of

My experience of meeting many of the main intelligent design theorists informed my perspective that just framing the conflict politically was too simplistic. Intelligent design theorists are not seeking to flip the game or change the rules simply to win. Curtis is wrong to say that "ID appears to be a clear attack on secular public reason."[74] Far from wanting to privatize knowledge and belief, intelligent design theorists seek debate in the public square with their opponents.[75] They highlight their mainstream academic credentials. They hold doctorates in relevant subjects from prestigious academic institutions.[76] They actively research in relevant scientific fields and publish peer-reviewed articles in relevant journals.[77] Intelligent design theorists locate themselves within the academic tradition and see themselves as arguing from within the scientific community.

Intelligent design theorists are seen as foxes by the lions (or, to change the metaphor, as a Trojan Horse about to let the enemy into the citadel of science).[78] Intelligent design theorists resist these labels and appeal to the history of science as something not at all inimical to the concept of design but rather compatible, complementary and even in concordance with it. The DID course demonstrated that the real challenge to Darwinism is not from religious believers: the challenge is from within the scientific community itself.[79] A recent dissenting voice is the Yale computer scientist Gelernter who, although not fully convinced of intelligent design itself, agrees with its critique of Darwin:

Philosophy (Abingdon: Routledge, 2004).

74. Finbarr Curtis, 'The Secularity of Intelligent Design', *The Hedgehog Review* 13, no. 2 (2011): 71.

75. Johnson, *The Wedge of Truth*, 16.

76. See the list of over 1000 PhD scientists that have put their name on a list of dissenters; 'Scientists—Dissent from Darwin', accessed 18 June 2019, https://dissent-fromdarwin.org/scientists/.

77. This was asserted even before the Dover trial; see Francis J. Beckwith, 'Public Education, Religious Establishment, and the Challenge of Intelligent Design', *Notre Dame Journal of Law, Ethics & Public Policy* 17, no. 2 (2003): 518.

78. Forrest and Gross, *Creationism's Trojan Horse*.

79. Noble, Professor Emeritus of Anatomy and Genetics at Oxford University, writes "In this article, I will show that all the central assumptions of the Modern Synthesis (often also called Neo-Darwinism) have been disproved." Denis Noble, 'Physiology is Rocking the Foundations of Evolutionary Biology', *Experimental Physiology* 98, no. 8 (August 2013): 1235, https://doi.org/10.1113/expphysiol.2012.071134.

An intelligent designer might seem more necessary than ever now that we understand so much cellular biology, and the impossibly long odds facing any attempt to design proteins by chance, or assemble the regulatory mechanisms that control the life cycle of a cell.[80]

Participants recognized that the issue of origins is by no means a settled scientific conclusion, despite all leonine impressions. The conflict is within science and between theist and materialist worldviews.[81] Gelernter argues that attacks on intelligent design theorists show "the extent to which Darwinism is no longer just a scientific theory but the basis of a worldview, and an emergency replacement religion for the many troubled souls who need one."[82]

Intelligent design challenges the hegemony of those who maintain the border between magisteria.[83] In this regard intelligent design brings a sword, not peace (Matthew 10:34) as it challenges evolution's "hegemony as the central organizing principle of biology."[84] It challenges the oxymoronic language of atheists such as Searle's comment that "[i]f the supernatural existed, it too would have to be natural,"[85] or of theistic evolutionists such as Ayala's "design without a designer"[86] or "indeterminate teleology."[87] Participants understood Darwinism to be what Gelernter calls "a plain case of the emperor's new clothes."[88] The Darwinists' claim to be the scientific consensus was recognized as a rhetorical move required "only when scientific authorities feel that they are under threat

---

80. Gelernter, 'Giving up Darwin', 109.

81. Plantinga argues the real conflict is between science and what he calls naturalism; Plantinga, *Where the Conflict Really Lies*, 309–16.

82. Gelernter, 'Giving up Darwin', 105.

83. For an excellent summary, see Johnson, *The Wedge of Truth*, 95–102.

84. Coyne, *Faith versus Fact*, 15.

85. John Searle, *Mind, Language, and Society* (New York: BasicBooks, 1998), 35; cited in Johnson, *The Wedge of Truth*, 165.

86. Francisco J. Ayala, 'Darwin's Greatest Discovery: Design without Designer', *Proceedings of the National Academy of Sciences* 104, no. Supplement 1 (15 May 2007): 8572, https://doi.org/10.1073/pnas.0701072104.

87. Ayala confuses teleology with efficient causation. Francisco J. Ayala, 'Reduction, Emergence, Naturalism, Dualism, Teleology: A Précis', in *Back to Darwin: A Richer Account of Evolution*, ed. John B. Cobb (Grand Rapids: William B. Eerdmans, 2008), 86.

88. Gelernter, 'Giving up Darwin', 104.

in a way that cannot be dismissed by the usual peer-review process."[89] Participants were motivated to reintroduce the concept of design, such as Dembski's design filter,[90] or Behe's irreducible complexity,[91] into scientific discourse. Freire argues that the "oppressed must see examples of the vulnerability of the oppressor so that a contrary conviction can begin to grow within them."[92] The DID course brought into the open the internal disputes over "established scientific theory."[93] Intelligent design challenges both atheist and theist adherents to methodological naturalism and their belief in the sufficiency of the modern Darwinian synthesis to account for life.[94] Participants responded that the plausibility structures of the dominant worldview had been challenged, and that they were more encouraged to participate in debate as a result.

Muted group theory

Participants expressed that they (and especially young people they knew) often felt, or were made to feel, inferior or marginalized for their evangelical Christian faith. This occurred at school or university, amongst colleagues at work, or even amongst friends in the pub. The sense of marginalization was expressed as "you can't mention religion in school" (2MX), or having colleagues who "really do know their stuff around general sciences [and are] very difficult to counter argue without having at least a basic foundation in sciences" (1MX). Freire's notion of conscientization, discussed above, is associated with "developing the 'voice' of the oppressed and claiming and legitimating that voice in larger arenas."[95]

Muted Group Theory (MGT) captures something of the sense of marginalization heard in the interviews. The main idea of MGT is that

89. Fuller, *Post-Truth*, 49.

90. Dembski, *Intelligent Design*, 134.

91. Behe, *Darwin's Black Box*, 42.

92. Freire, *Pedagogy of the Oppressed*, 38.

93. Robert Long, 'Religious Education in Schools (England)', Briefing Paper, House of Commons Library (London: House of Commons Library, 7 July 2016), 23, researchbriefings.files.parliament.uk/documents/CBP-7167/CBP-7167.pdf.

94. For an excellent overview of the rise of naturalism, see Bruce Gordon, 'The Rise of Naturalism', in *The Nature of Nature: Examining the Role of Naturalism in Science*, ed. Bruce Gordon and William A. Dembski (Wilmington: ISI, 2011), 25–26.

95. Greenwood, 'An Analysis of the Theory/Concept Entries in the *SAGE Encyclopedia of Action Research*', 211.

"[l]anguage serves its creators better than those in other groups who have to learn to use the language as best they can."[96] Barkman outlines MGT's three "tenets" as: the dominant group creates and defines terms; the sub-dominant (muted) group's expressions are less acceptable or less respected; and the sub-dominant group feels obliged "to use the dominant mode of communication."[97] Often used within feminist studies (and Barkman uses it to discuss the muting effect prison has on those released), these tenets also describe the sense of marginalization experienced by evangelical Christians in the face of Darwinian claims to authority about origins. Christians engaging in scientific discussion about origins must navigate (to use Osmer's term) between equivocating definitions of evolution, the theodicean problems of mutations and extinctions, whilst maintaining the semantic domain of imminence rather than transcendence. Their natural voice of creation, creator and purpose is unacceptable as scientific concepts, and so they give a muted response when required to use evolutionary terminology.[98] The lack of respect towards the subdominant evangelical Christians is seen in the way that conservative groups are assumed to be dogmatic and, indeed, "simple-minded."[99] The dominant group's lack of self-awareness is highlighted by MGT.[100] Participants said the DID course empowered those who saw themselves as being in the subdominant group by enabling them to use the dominant group's language and terminology more confidently, which in turn made them feel less muted.

96. Richard L. West and Lynn H. Turner, *Introducing Communication Theory: Analysis and Application*, 6th ed. (New York: McGraw-Hill Education, 2018), 494.

97. Linda Lee Smith Barkman, 'Muted Group Theory: A Tool for Hearing Marginalized Voices', *Priscilla Papers* 32, no. 4 (Autumn 2018): 3.

98. A similar point is made by Gaventa and Cornwall when they argue that "where previously excluded actors [. . .] enter the policy process, they may be required to mimic the language and knowledge of the powerful, in order to begin to be heard." Gaventa and Cornwall, 'Power and Knowledge', 174.

99. Lucian Gideon Conway et al., 'Are Conservatives Really More Simple-Minded than Liberals? The Domain Specificity of Complex Thinking: Ideology and Complexity', *Political Psychology* 37, no. 6 (December 2016): 777–98, https://doi.org/10.1111/pops.12304.

100. For an outstanding example of myopic scientism see Solomon Schimmel, *The Tenacity of Unreasonable Beliefs: Fundamentalism and the Fear of Truth* (Oxford: Oxford University Press, 2008), 185–87.

Teleology and children

The main arena in which participants reported marginalization taking place was school. Excluding the teaching or discussion of intelligent design in science classes at school is an expression of power from the dominant group, denying the marginalized sub-dominant group a voice. A 2012 UK parliamentary petition entitled "Teach Evolution, Not Creationism" labelled intelligent design as a fundamentalist view and sought to prevent it from being taught in publicly funded schools including "faith schools, religious Academies and religious Free Schools," whilst at the same time seeking to make mandatory the teaching of evolution in primary schools.[101]

The pedagogical problem with this approach is that children are instinctively teleological. The discipline of cognitive science of religion has shown that "we are primed to see purpose in so many things, and it may seem too dismissive to see religious beliefs as accidental in this way."[102] The instinct to see purpose in nature is intuitive. Grayling believes that "we are all born atheists,"[103] but that turns out not to be true. Kelemen's early work in both America and the UK demonstrated that preschoolers were "intuitive theists" having "a general bias to treat objects and behaviors as existing for a purpose [. . .] and are also broadly inclined to view natural phenomena as intentionally created, albeit by a nonhuman agent."[104] She and co-writer DiYanni find that young children tend to "ascribe purpose to nature" independently of their religious backgrounds. To account for this, Kelemen suggests that "children's teleofunctional intuitions might reflect an indefeasible, innate, cognitive bias"; in other words, they are

101. 'Archived Petition: Teach Evolution, Not Creationism', Petitions—UK Government and Parliament, accessed 24 April 2019, https://petition.parliament.uk/archived/petitions/1617.

102. Justin L. Barrett and Roger Trigg, 'Cognitive and Evolutionary Studies of Religion', in *The Roots of Religion: Exploring the Cognitive Science of Religion*, ed. Roger Trigg and Justin L. Barrett, Ashgate Science and Religion Series (Farnham: Ashgate, 2014), 9.

103. A.C. Grayling, 'The God Argument', Text, Radio National, 26 March 2013, https://www.abc.net.au/radionational/programs/latenightlive/the-god-argument-ac-grayling/4594806.

104. Deborah Kelemen, 'Are Children "Intuitive Theists"?: Reasoning About Purpose and Design in Nature', *Psychological Science* 15, no. 5 (1 May 2004): 295, https://doi.org/10.1111/j.0956–7976.2004.00672.x; the word "albeit" in this context is meaningless.

born that way.[105] Throughout her work Kelemen's own cognitive bias is evident. The natural tendency she observes in children to attribute purpose to objects in nature is considered a "misconception," a "problem," and "scientifically inaccurate."[106] Given that this instinct impedes children from a proper understanding of natural selection, Kelemen et al. propose:

> to begin comprehensively familiarizing children with counterintuitive scientific explanations [. . .] relatively early, during ages at which alternative commonsense explanatory frameworks are still relatively fragmentary.[107]

Kelemen seeks to break what she describes as these fragile intuitions by introducing picture storybooks teaching "the basic population-based logic of natural selection" to young children in what she calls an "intervention."[108] The language she uses of intervention, cognitive bias, misconception, incompetence and even "promiscuous teleology"[109] reveals her ideology that the innate intuitions of children are a cause for psychological concern and require institutional intervention. The dominant group is defining innate teleology in children as problematic because it does not concur with their materialist worldview. It illustrates again why theists express concern over the negative impact of materialism in science lessons.[110]

105. Deborah Kelemen and Cara DiYanni, 'Intuitions About Origins: Purpose and Intelligent Design in Children's Reasoning About Nature', *Journal of Cognition and Development* 6, no. 1 (1 February 2005): 7, https://doi.org/10.1207/s15327647jcd0601_2.

106. Deborah Kelemen et al., 'Young Children Can Be Taught Basic Natural Selection Using a Picture-Storybook Intervention', *Psychological Science* 25, no. 4 (April 2014): 894, https://doi.org/10.1177/0956797613516009.

107. Kelemen et al., 894.

108. Kelemen et al., 900.

109. Kelemen and DiYanni, 'Intuitions About Origins: Purpose and Intelligent Design in Children's Reasoning About Nature', 4.

110. More recent studies suggest that understanding natural selection and acceptance of evolution is not significantly related. See M. Elizabeth Barnes et al., 'Teleological Reasoning, Not Acceptance of Evolution, Impacts Students' Ability to Learn Natural Selection', *Evolution: Education and Outreach* 10, no. 1 (December 2017): 10, https://doi.org/10.1186/s12052-017-0070-6.

Democratic common science

The DID course supported the intuition that the natural world shows abundant evidence of real, not just apparent, design.[111] It helped participants who were not in the dominant group to recognize the conflict of worldviews and ideologies that influence society at different levels, and it gave them the language and evidence to resist and change that social dominance. It empowered those who saw themselves as marginalized from science discourse and reinforced their intuitions of purpose and their common-sense perceptions of the improbabilities of evolution. As Nagel puts it, it supports "the untutored reaction of incredulity to the reductionist neo-Darwinian account of the origin and evolution of life."[112] After considering the evidence from Kelemen and DiYanni, Bering concludes that "thinking like an evolutionist is hard work because, ironically, our psychological development—and, in particular, our theory of mind—strongly favors the purposeful-design framework."[113] Intelligent design thinking coheres with our natural self-understanding.

Axe argues that the practice and insights of science are not restricted to elites but are a democratic part of normal life.[114] "Basic science is an integral part of how we live."[115] This includes the everyday habits of making observations, reflecting on them and spotting patterns that might explain how things work. "Without doubt, this is science. I have called it *common science* to emphasize the connection to common sense."[116] Medewar argues along the same lines. In identifying the cause for a faulty lamp, he writes, the lay-person goes through a number of tests to see if it is the fuse, the bulb, the socket or the switch. This "hypothetico-deductive" approach, he writes, "differs only in degree of difficulty from that which a scientist employs in studying more difficult and more important problems."[117] Axe argues that common science (he also calls it

111. The reference is to Dawkins' famous definition of biology as being "the study of complicated things that give the appearance of having been designed for a purpose." Richard Dawkins, *The Blind Watchmaker* (London: Longman, 1986), 1.

112. Nagel, *Mind and Cosmos*, 6.

113. Jesse Bering, *The God Instinct: The Psychology of Souls, Destiny, and the Meaning of Life* (London: Nicholas Brealey Pub, 2011), 59.

114. For Lewin's similar view, see Bargal, 'Lewin, Kurt', 502.

115. Douglas Axe, *Undeniable: How Biology Confirms Our Intuition That Life is Designed* (New York: HarperOne, 2016), 60.

116. Axe, 60.

117. Peter Medawar, *The Limits of Science* (Oxford: Oxford University Press, 1984),

"open science") is democratic. It "dispels the elitist myth" and "brings an end to authoritarian science by emphasizing the scientific value of public opinion."[118] He makes clear the implication of making the ideas of professional scientists accountable to the public:

> Embracing open science empowers people who will never earn PhDs to become full participants in the scientific debates that matter to them. Instead of merely following expert debates, nonexperts should expect important issues that touch their lives to be framed in terms of common science. Once they are, everyone becomes qualified to *enter* the debate.[119]

Enabling conversational evangelism

Axe's argument resonated with the participants' comments reflecting on their experience of attending the DID course. Consistent with Freire's aim of empowering the oppressed, the DID course gave participants greater critical awareness to contribute to scientific debates.[120] Participants also expressed confidence and ability in having conversations about their faith or about matters of ultimate importance.

Evangelical Christians are often characterized as conversionist, and communicating the Gospel is a priority.[121] Encouraged to make the most of every opportunity (Ephesians 5:16), evangelicals seek conversations that lead, directly or indirectly, those who are not Christians to believe in, and submit their lives to, the resurrected Lord Jesus Christ (Romans 10:9).[122] The main application from attending the DID course for participants was initiating or developing relationships with non-Christians with a view to their conversion. Participants reported that the DID course was "a very good way of opening the door and approaching the subject with people" (1MX). Participant 3MM said he had the confidence to express that he had a different worldview: "That's what led to more conversation,

---

17.

118. Axe, *Undeniable*, 62.

119. Axe, 63; emphasis original.

120. Freire, *Pedagogy of the Oppressed*, 52–53.

121. Bebbington, *Evangelicalism in Modern Britain*, 2–3; for a critique of Bebbington's quadrilateral see Harris, 'Beyond Bebbington'.

122. David Bentley Hart, *Atheist Delusions: The Christian Revolution and its Fashionable Enemies* (New Haven: Yale University Press, 2009), 8.

because they wanted to understand why I didn't believe in evolution. We had a very good discussion" (3MM). Similarly, 8FX shared how she felt supported to "argue the case with them in a slightly different way now, so that's helpful" (8FX).

Participant 4FX believed that the scientific approach of the DID course gave her confidence when speaking with young people, "and that is what we need to be able to give our young people." That science was not simply materialism was the message young people needed to hear. "I think especially for young people, some of the guys that I know from the youth here, often they have issues with faith and evolution and how it all fits together" (3MM). Young people were said to have a pessimistic worldview: "they may say 'yeah you can experience some love in this life,' but actually the end of all of that thought pattern is that it doesn't matter. And so I don't matter" (7MM). Participants believed the DID course reinforced belief in transcendent meaning and purpose, and they were able to respond to the worldview of those young people who say, "well when I die, that's the end, and it doesn't really matter" (7MM).

Most young people are not taught to think worldviewishly.[123] Anderson et al. believe that young people in the West are naïve regarding the worldview they hold: they are "easily swayed and can have their faith quickly deconstructed. An unconscious, unexamined worldview can be challenged and overturned."[124] This may be true of young people holding a Christian worldview, but the young person holding a Darwinian worldview "knows" that evolution is a fact. Participants felt that the DID course had deconstructed the materialist worldview and built confidence in their theistic worldview. The course was perceived both as equipping and supporting them in evangelism.

SUMMARY

This chapter marked a shift of emphasis in the research project to reflect theologically on the findings of the research question so far and to provide a theological basis for future practice. Osmer's model of practical theology facilitated a deeper understanding of the results of the action

123. The term is from James W. Sire, *Habits of the Mind: Intellectual Life as a Christian Calling* (Downers Grove: InterVarsity, 2000), 166.

124. Tawa J. Anderson, W. Michael Clark, and David K. Naugle, *An Introduction to Christian Worldview: Pursuing God's Perspective In A Pluralistic World* (London: IVP, 2017), 38.

research cycles through critical correlation. The Sagely Wisdom phase of Osmer's model enabled me to understand the concepts that emerged from the Priestly Listening phase more deeply, to see more clearly "what is going on."[125] The process of critical correlation opened the discussion of what was going on to different interdisciplinary perspectives that situated it more politically and philosophically. The main insights were the rhetoric associated with teaching Darwinism as fact, the way in which that view is maintained as part of the symbolic universe, insights into the moral consequences of the Darwinian worldview, the way that intelligent design changed the perception of participants akin to Freire's notion of conscientization, the political representation of intelligent design as Pareto's foxes and the way intelligent design theorists resist this metaphor, the muting effect of Darwinism on those holding a theistic worldview, the counterintuitive view of Darwinists on teleology, the notion that intelligent design is a more democratic view of science, and the way it enabled participants to engage in significant conversations with people they might otherwise have found it difficult to do so. These reflective insights develop the overall argument about how students understand their learning of intelligent design and how it contributes to their ability to evangelize others.

The next phase of Osmer's model is the normative task of Prophetic Discernment that emphasizes the need to reflect on these insights theologically. This prayerful and spirit-led phase of the model provides the theological justification and motivation for subsequent acts of servant leadership.

125. Osmer, *Practical Theology*, 4.

7

Prophetic Discernment

[P]arables were not earthly stories with heavenly meanings but earthy stories with heavy meanings, weighted down by an awareness of the workings of exploitation in the world of their hearers.[1]

CAMERON AND DUCE DESCRIBE as "essential" the conversation "between the data and the Christian tradition" to "identify theological disclosures in the data."[2] This chapter articulates that disclosure, what Osmer calls Prophetic Discernment, as a *kairos* moment, a moment of clarity that provides theological imperative for faithful praxis flowing from reflection on the outcome of the research question.

NORMATIVE TASK OF PROPHETIC DISCERNMENT

Osmer describes the normative task of his practical theological model as Prophetic Discernment to answer the question "what ought to be going on?"[3] It involves theological interpretation which he defines as "the use of theological concepts to interpret episodes, situation, and contexts."[4] The biblical prophets call Israel back to faithfulness to God and remind

1. Herzog, *Parables as Subversive Speech*, 3.

2. Cameron and Duce, *Researching Practice in Ministry and Mission*, 106.

3. For a discussion about the relationship between descriptive and normative in Osmer and Cameron et al's models, see Wier, 'From the Descriptive to the Normative', 121–27.

4. Osmer, *Practical Theology*, 130.

them of his acts of salvation in the past and his promises of judgement and rescue in the future.[5] The prophetic call is to live faithfully in the present, inhabiting the ongoing story of God. This was a difficult task to achieve, and the prophets made use of literary features to hold the attention of listener or reader.[6] Osmer points to the cultural sympathy expressed by the prophet, exemplified in Jesus' tears over the "hard-heartedness of Jerusalem" (Luke 19:41–44). He argues that leadership of a prophetic nature turns away from the "protective ideologies of 'court and temple'" and instead "opens out" to theological and biblical reflection.[7]

The task of Prophetic Discernment emphasizes the public dimension of theology, its interface with the other academic disciplines, and the importance of bringing a biblical framework to practical theology. It involved me reflecting theologically on the concepts generated in the Sagely Wisdom task and considering how Scripture as divine revelation might guide and inspire my professional practice in the pragmatic task of servant leadership.[8] This reflection is influenced by my personal and theological commitments, and no claim to objectivity is made here. However, neither is it simply subjective, as the insights below are made public and are open to criticism and comparison from others. As Wright argues, "Christian theologians open themselves up to both internal and external critique."[9] Validity comes from competence in handling Scripture (2 Timothy 2:15), how faithfully I integrate the insights from the previous phase, and how faithfully this inspires servant leadership.

Wisdom theology

My first theological reflection is on the definition of science. Earlier I quoted Ratzsch's definition of it being "a deeply empirical project aimed most fundamentally at understanding and explaining the natural realm, typically in natural terms."[10] It is common for Christians to associate sci-

---

5. Clendenen writes that "the function of the prophets should be understood as something like covenant mediators or 'enforcers." E. Ray Clendenen, 'Textlinguistics and Prophecy in the Book of the Twelve', *Journal of the Evangelical Theological Society* 46, no. 3 (2003): 386.

6. Richard Patterson, 'A Literary Look at Nahum, Habakkuk, and Zephaniah', *Grace Theological Journal* 11, no. 1 (1991): 17–27.

7. Osmer, *Practical Theology*, 137, 139.

8. Watkins, *Disclosing Church*, 34.

9. Wright, *Christianity and Critical Realism*, 5.

10. Ratzsch, 'Science and Religion', 55.

ence with wisdom theology because of its focus on creation.[11] Wisdom theology reflects on creation, rather than nature, and infers patterns of behaviour that are conducive to living under the blessing of the creator.[12] The first principle of wisdom theology is the "fear of the Lord" (Proverbs 1:7; 2:5; etc.), and this principle offers a prophetic view of science as studying creation with a reverent fear of God. Intelligent design fits more readily with wisdom theology than does methodological naturalism because of its inference to a wise mind at work.[13]

Biblical wisdom implies learning to live within natural boundaries, living in a way that fits the world as it is.[14] It is political insofar as the archetypal wisdom text, Proverbs, is framed as passing on wisdom for wise leadership. It speaks into polarized contexts, helping the learner to identify the righteous and the lawless, the good and the evil, the wise and the foolish. The wisdom writers often use the technique of personification with Lady Wisdom lifting her voice to those willing to hear.[15] At the place of judgement she invites people to consider their ways.

> Does not wisdom call out?
> Does not understanding raise her voice?
> At the highest point along the way,
> where the paths meet, she takes her stand;
> beside the gate leading into the city,
> at the entrance, she cries aloud:
> To you, O people, I call out;
> I raise my voice to all humanity.
> You who are simple, gain prudence;
> you who are foolish, set your hearts on it.
> Proverbs 8:1

11. Several articles discuss the relationship between wisdom and evolutionary biology in Celia Deane-Drummond, ed., *The Evolution of Human Wisdom* (Lanham: Lexington, 2017).

12. For a good review of wisdom and creation, see C. Hassell Bullock, 'Wisdom, the "Amen" of Torah', *Journal of the Evangelical Theological Society* 52, no. 1 (2009): 5–10.

13. Torrance argues for "methodological agnosticism" in Andrew B. Torrance, 'Should a Christian Adopt Methodological Naturalism?', *Zygon*, How to Do Religion and Science?, 52, no. 3 (September 2017): 718, https://doi.org/10.1111/zygo.12363.

14. For an overview see Raymond C. Van Leeuwen, 'Liminality and Worldview in Proverbs 1–9', *Semeia* 50 (1990): 116.

15. Claire Mathews McGinnis, 'The Old Testament', in *The Blackwell Companion to Catholicism*, ed. James J. Buckley, Frederick Christian Bauerschmidt, and Trent Pomplun (Oxford: Blackwell, 2007), 19, https://doi.org/10.1111/b.9781405112246.2007.00002.x.

Intelligent design functions as a public challenge to those holding to a materialist worldview and is a source of intrigue to those who have not considered the connection between science and God. Treier argues that theological education "should be about the acquisition of wisdom."[16] This passage of wisdom calling out in the public square is closely followed by a theological reflection of wisdom's role in creation (Proverbs 8:22–31).[17] The theological implications of teaching intelligent design as wisdom are clear, namely that materialism is identified as foolish (Psalm 14:1; 53:1) and the question of God is a properly scientific enquiry.[18] Some are convinced, some will want to hear more, while others reject it as incomprehensible.[19]

The task of Prophetic Discernment is to interpret the cultural context theologically and create a "conversation space" between "the data and the Christian tradition."[20] The prophet, Brueggemann argues, aims "to disrupt, destabilise, and invite to alternative perceptions of reality."[21] My experience of teaching the DID course, then, was that it had the prophetic characteristics of speaking wisdom into a conflicted cultural context, yet restrains from preaching or using biblical exegesis. Teaching intelligent design as wisdom was my first prophetically discerned reflection.

---

16. Daniel J. Treier, 'Theology as the Acquisition of Wisdom: Reorienting Theological Education', *Christian Education Journal* 3NS, no. 1 (1999): 139; see also Graham Tomlin, 'The Telos of Theological Education', *Theological Education* 51, no. 2 (2018): 113–25.

17. Paul R. House, 'Creation in Old Testament Theology', *The Southern Baptist Journal of Theology* 5, no. 3 (2001): 14–15.

18. Dawkins agrees: "Either he exists or he doesn't. It is a scientific question." Dawkins, *The God Delusion*, 70.

19. The allusion here is to Acts 17:32–34 and the reaction of the Areopagites to Paul's creation argument.

20. Cameron and Duce, *Researching Practice in Ministry and Mission*, 106; for a discussion of the term "conversation space" see Ralph Norman, 'Theological Foundations of Action Research for Learning and Teaching', *Discourse: Learning and Teaching in Philosophical and Religious Studies* 8, no. 1 (2008): 5, https://doi.org/10.5840/discourse20088112.

21. Walter Brueggemann, *Theology of the Old Testament: Testimony, Dispute, Advocacy* (Minneapolis: Fortress, 1997), 625–26.

The parable of intelligent design

The prayerful hope during this phase of reflection is to gain unexpected insight or inspiration, to see things from a different theological perspective, and to gain confidence that this perspective has a sense of scriptural authority about it, much as a sermon is a prayerful act of bringing the Word of God into a community. Watkins describes it as the "theological moment—the 'disclosure' of theological insight."[22] Prophetic Discernment is certainly connective, imaginative, compassionate, and critical,[23] but it is also revelatory. In practical theology this moment of insight is sometimes called a *kairos* moment and is discerned by prophets for their specific contexts.[24] A moment of clarity, or disclosure, that I experienced during my theological reflection was in discerning the teaching of intelligent design as being like a parable.[25] This insight had a revelatory quality to it and constituted, at least from my perspective, a *kairos* moment.[26] It integrated themes of wisdom, creation, and revelation, as well as other insights from the Sagely Wisdom phase as Freire's criticality.

Parables deal with the everyday world of crops and treasure, fields and sheep, servants and masters. They "meld normal reality with an illuminating image and open hearers to God's future."[27] Parables invite a response from their hearers, making it difficult to remain neutral.[28] They

22. Watkins, *Disclosing Church*, 30.

23. These terms are all from Zoë Bennett, *Using the Bible in Practical Theology: Historical and Contemporary Perspectives* (Farnham: Ashgate, 2013), 102.

24. John De Gruchy, '*Kairos* Moments and Prophetic Witness: Towards a Prophetic Ecclesiology', *HTS Teologiese Studies / Theological Studies* 72, no. 4 (31 May 2016): 3, https://doi.org/10.4102/hts.v72i4.3414.

25. For similar approaches in drawing analogies with parables see Craig L. Blomberg, 'The Miracles as Parables', in *The Miracles of Jesus*, ed. David Wenham and Craig L. Blomberg (Eugene: Wipf and Stock, 2003), 327–59; and Eduard Schweizer, *Jesus, the Parable of God: What Do We Really Know about Jesus?*, Princeton Theological Monograph Series 37 (Eugene: Pickwick, 1994), 32.

26. For another example of its use, see Elizabeth Conde-Frazier, 'Participatory Action Research', in *The Wiley-Blackwell Companion to Practical Theology*, ed. Bonnie J. Miller-McLemore (Chichester: Wiley-Blackwell, 2012), 239–40, https://doi.org/10.1002/9781444345742.ch22.

27. John M. McDermott, 'Jesus: Parable or Sacrament of God? An Ecumenical Discussion on Analogy and Freedom with E. Schweizer, K. Barth, and R. Bultmann', *Gregorianum* 78, no. 3 (1997): 479.

28. Simon J. Kistemaker, 'Jesus as Story Teller: Literary Perspectives on the Parables', *The Master's Seminary Journal* 16, no. 1 (2005): 52.

are rich in imagery and often contain ambiguity. Dodd famously defined a parable in this way:

> At its simplest the parable is a metaphor or simile drawn from nature or common life, arresting the hearer by its vividness or strangeness, and leaving the mind in sufficient doubt about its precise application to tease it into active thought.[29]

A parable is not the Gospel, but it plays an important role within the Gospel narratives. Parables are used to confront "the reigning systems of oppression that dominated Palestine in the time of Jesus,"[30] and comfort those who are marginalized. "Jesus' parables function as narratives of alternative wisdom or stories of disorientation. [. . . They] interrogate and find wanting much conventional wisdom."[31] Those who find themselves at the periphery of society are welcomed in (the lost sheep, Matthew 18:12–14; the sheep and the goats, Matthew 25:31–46), whereas those in positions of authority find themselves diminished or excluded (the Levi and Priest, Luke 10:30–37; the pharisee of Luke 18:9–14).[32] The parables are for the crowds and those in authority in the everyday context of life (Luke 20:19). The non-religious content of parables was emphasized by Notley:

> [T]here are no synagogues or rabbis, no mention of the temple in Jerusalem [. . .] they are literary instruments meant to communicate theological ideas or sublime notions by way of examples drawn from everyday life.[33]

29. C. H. Dodd, *The Parables of the Kingdom* (New York: Scribner, 1961), 5.

30. Herzog, *Parables as Subversive Speech*, 7.

31. Matthew S. Rindge, 'Luke's Artistic Parables: Narratives of Subversion, Imagination, and Transformation', *Interpretation: A Journal of Bible and Theology* 68, no. 4 (October 2014): 405, https://doi.org/10.1177/0020964314540406.

32. Herzog, following Freire, would add the Master of Matthew 25:14–30 to this list. See Herzog, *Parables as Subversive Speech*, 158–59; for a critique of Herzog's non-allegorical reading of the parables, see Ben Chenoweth, 'The Vulnerability of the Literalist: A Critique of William R. Herzog II's Interpretation of the Parable of the Talents', *Pacifica* 21 (2008): 175–91.

33. R. Steven Notley, 'Reading Gospel Parables as Jewish Literature', *Journal for the Study of the New Testament* 41, no. 1 (28 August 2018): 33, https://doi.org/10.1177/0142064X18788960; although the use of 'house' in Matthew 7:24 might well imply the temple. See N. T. Wright, 'Jerusalem in the New Testament', in *Jerusalem Past and Present in the Purposes of God*, ed. P. W. L Walker, 2nd ed. (Carlisle: Paternoster, 1994), 76n13; and, of course, Luke 18:9–14 is set within the temple.

Moreover, they are not told in a synagogue context: Jesus "tells them at meals, in casual conversations, and in encounters in public."[34] There is no scriptural engagement in the parables themselves,[35] but instead they show Jesus' concern to restore the marginalized: Jesus' "table fellowship with those living on the margins of the religious community was intended to encourage, strengthen and restore them in their faith."[36]

Florence considers Jesus' methodology as living in a "parable universe": "[y]ou start living in the parable universe, and everything is a story. Everything is a segue to the realm of God."[37] The study of biology, physics or astronomy can be every bit as much a spiritual activity, a place where "religion becomes secular without loss."[38] Rindge encourages the return to using parables for "deconstructing myths" and to rehabilitate the practice of creating parables for that purpose.[39]

The theological reflection of intelligent design as parable resonates with the themes discussed in the previous chapter.[40] The DID course was not a church service, nor did it engage in biblical discussion (although some of those in attendance did ask theologically motivated questions). It offered alternative wisdom and challenged those who would find adequate a materialist explanation for life, and it pointed towards the transcendent reality of the kingdom of heaven. By presenting only scientific evidence that has profound theological implications, intelligent design functions as a parable: it divides its hearers, it challenges authority, it tends to empower the marginalized, and it invites a response. I develop this Prophetic Discernment phase by considering the parable of the sower as an analogy for teaching intelligent design.

34. Notley, 'Reading Gospel Parables as Jewish Literature', 33.

35. Rindge, 'Luke's Artistic Parables', 414.

36. Notley, 'Reading Gospel Parables as Jewish Literature', 40.

37. Anna Carter Florence, 'A Parable Universe', *Journal for Preachers* 38, no. 2 (2015): 8.

38. Amos Wilder, *Early Christian Rhetoric* (Cambridge: Harvard University Press, 1971), 73; cited in Rindge, 'Luke's Artistic Parables', 414.

39. Rindge, 415.

40. I was encouraged to develop this reflection by the work of Bennett, *Using the Bible in Practical Theology*, 134; "I have learnt that 'seeing' connections is more important than 'making' connections."

The parable of the sower

The first parable of Matthew's Gospel is that of the sower (Matthew 13:1–9). Jesus declares this to be the archetypal parable (Mark 4:13). It describes different responses to the message of the kingdom of God. Those who do not understand it have the seed snatched away from their heart by the "evil one." Some do not retain the benefit of the seed sown because of the effects of persecution, and they fall away. Others are too concerned with wealth and temporary things to allow the seed to bear fruit. Those for whom the message bears fruit are those that hear and understand (Mark's version says "accept"; Mark 4:20) the message of the kingdom (Matthew 13:9). This reflection on the parable of the sower correlates with an insight from the focus group regarding the function of the DID course, namely that it was "sowing the seed," (10FB), a necessary step towards the goal of evangelism.

Rather than focusing on the abundant crop of the good soil, Dunn argues that "the emphasis of the parable is [...] on the different kinds of unfruitful hearing" and that it provides a "window" into Jesus' use of parables.[41] Although the seed sown is quite capable of producing a rich harvest, that outcome is in the minority, and most do not receive it that way.[42] There are various reasons given for the harvest failing, showing that the issue of acceptance is not trivial or reducible to simple categories, and the overall impression is that more will reject than accept. However, that is only half of the interpretation. The parable is told to the large crowds (Matthew 13:2), and the crowds are challenged to identify with one of the soils of the parable. The parable itself does not make people insiders or outsiders, but it causes them to reveal their own position, their own state of heart. It is not a question of comprehension but of spiritual involvement. The parable makes those in the crowd aware of their reasons for accepting (or not) the invitation to grow spiritually in the kingdom of God.[43]

---

41. James D. G. Dunn, *Jesus Remembered*, vol. 1, Christianity in the Making (Grand Rapids: Eerdmans, 2003), 492.

42. Donald Peters, 'Vulnerable Promise from the Land (Mark 4:3b–8)', in *Jesus and His Parables: Interpreting the Parables of Jesus Today*, ed. V. George Shillington (Edinburgh: T&T Clark, 1997), 75–76.

43. For an overview of how Jesus' parables produce responses see Grant R. Osborne, *The Hermeneutical Spiral: A Comprehensive Introduction to Biblical Interpretation* (Downers Grove: InterVarsity, 1991), 242.

Intelligent design provokes different reactions in people. For many, the notion is derisible, believable only to ignorant or simple souls, and is dismissed before it is even considered. When referring to the message of the kingdom, Jesus attributes the unfertile path to a hardened heart with its protective birds playing the role of Satan to deprive it of any growth.[44] It is not clear which is the cause, and which is the effect: is the heart hardened because the birds steal the seed, or do birds only steal seed from hearts already hardened? The initial image is passive (Matthew 13:4): seed falls on a path and is taken by birds. In the interpretation, however, the seed is "sown" in a person's heart, is heard but not understood by that person, and is "snatched away" by the evil one (Matthew 13:19). There is more going on than passive forgetfulness. The seed is removed because the mindset is hardened to the idea and guarded by forces that screen out such thoughts before they get a chance to take root.

Parable as a paradigm for intelligent design

Jesus began to speak in parables because of the institutional decision made by the Pharisees to reject Jesus' demonstration of power (healing of a demon-possessed man) as a sign of his political authority (Son of David). Accused of being in league with Beelzebub, Jesus frames his rejection as part of the old story of evil versus good initiated by the serpent in the Garden of Eden, and those who have just rejected him are declared to be on the side of the serpent, having stored up evil in their hearts, Matthew 12:35.[45] The parable of the sower is therefore given in response to rejection by the authorities. It confronts the crowds to become aware of their own response to the message of the kingdom.

The parable, then, is a paradigm for the intelligent design argument. It is located within a secular social context where cultural authorities have (justly, to their mind) excluded God-talk within the scientific environment. There is an irony (appropriate for a parable) in identifying the cultural forces of materialism with the spiritual and personal evil powers

44. An intriguing analogy is found in Jubilees 11 where birds are described by Knowles as "demonically-inspired," leaving the earth barren and the people impoverished. Michael P. Knowles, 'Abram and the Birds in *Jubilees* 11: A Subtext for the Parable of the Sower?', *New Testament Studies* 41, no. 1 (January 1995): 145, https://doi.org/10.1017/S0028688500022992.

45. James M. Hamilton, *God's Glory in Salvation through Judgment: A Biblical Theology* (Wheaton: Crossway, 2010), 372.

of the parable. The analogy identifies bird-like materialist institutions that steal away the seed sown in a person's heart with Satan (the connection that Jesus makes in Mark 4:15). This perspective is less radical than it may sound given that the early church knew of no neutral public space but rather perceived life as constantly influenced for good or ill by spiritual beings, and often saw human actors representing or embodying evil.[46] An example of this would be Jesus rejecting Peter's rebuke as coming from Satan himself (Matthew 16:23).[47]

Apart from seed fallen on the path, the other reasons given why the seed does not flourish are persecution, worry and wealth. Intelligent design supporters have often experienced loss of academic freedoms and privileges and loss of status within an educational institution.[48] Teachers lose employment positions and are forced to relocate.[49] West warns that "scientists who express public doubts about Darwinian theory should be prepared to have their integrity challenged and their personal lives exposed."[50] Persecution is one reason why the teaching of intelligent design might be unfruitful in some people's lives, but the loss of status and public recognition are also strong influences. The weeds that choke the seed are interpreted as being the worries of this life and wealth. The social benefits of remaining within the dominant group can compromise the seed's growth. Mohler identifies the characteristic of embarrassment as a key motivator for rejecting intelligent design within the academy: "embarrassment is the gateway drug for theological accommodation and

---

46. "For Paul, the *stoicheia* were an integral part of the present evil age and used a variety of means to hold humanity in bondage and blind people to the revelation of Jesus Christ as proclaimed in the gospel." Clinton E. Arnold, 'Returning to the Domain of the Powers: *Stoicheia* as Evil Spirits in Galatians 4:3,9', *Novum Testamentum* 38, no. 1 (January 1996): 75.

47. Craig A. Evans, 'Jesus and the Spirits: What Can We Learn from the New Testament World?', *Transformation* 27, no. 3 (2010): 147.

48. Casey Luskin, 'Darwin Believers Hide Fears of Intelligent Design Behind a Wall of Denial and Ridicule', US News & World Report, accessed 28 June 2019, https://www.usnews.com/opinion/blogs/room-for-debate/2009/02/12/darwin-believers-hide-fears-of-intelligent-design-behind-a-wall-of-denial-and-ridicule; David Klinghoffer, 'NASA Versus David Coppedge: Most Reprehensible Case of Anti-Intelligent Design Persecution Yet?', Evolution News, 20 December 2016, https://evolutionnews.org/2016/12/david_coppedge/.

49. For the case of DeHart, see John G. West, *Darwin Day in America: How Our Politics and Culture Have Been Dehumanized in the Name of Science* (Wilmington: ISI, 2015), 237–38.

50. West, 241.

denial."[51] Reeves argues that it is the loss of authority of the "priestly class" of scientists that is at the root of the problem.[52] The seed is choked for those holding theistic evolutionary views because, in Moreland's view, they desire to retain credibility within the "dominant intellectual culture."[53]

The disciples ask Jesus why he is now using parables, rather than preaching directly as he did in the Sermon on the Mount. Jesus explains his use of parables by perceiving Israel as having fallen into two camps: those who have, and those who do not (Matthew 13:12). There is an echo here of the seed falling on the path (13:4): those who hear but do not understand have the seed taken from their heart by the evil one.

> "You will be ever hearing but never understanding;
> you will be ever seeing but never perceiving.
> For this people's heart has become calloused;
> they hardly hear with their ears,
> and they have closed their eyes.
> Otherwise they might see with their eyes,
> hear with their ears,
> understand with their hearts
> and turn, and I would heal them."
> Matthew 13:15

Jesus anticipates Israel hearing but not understanding, seeing but not perceiving (Isaiah 6:9), and therefore uses a parable that clarifies, in the minds of his hearers, the reason why his message is, or is not, received. Intelligent design parallels this parabolic discourse: it reveals opposition to the message of design not as coming from empirical evidence or reasoned argument but rather from worldview and authority. It functions as a parable in that it makes clear for the hearer what is really going on in accepting or rejecting it. The rocky path is institutional insistence on materialism in the academy that makes the message of intelligent design incomprehensible, and well-guarded against.[54] Materialism declares the design intuition to be false: Crick argues that "[b]iologists must constantly

51. Mohler, cited in Colin R. Reeves, 'Bringing Home the Bacon: The Interaction of Science and Scripture Today', in *Theistic Evolution: A Scientific, Philosophical, and Theological Critique*, ed. J.P. Moreland et al. (Wheaton: Crossway, 2017), 722.

52. Reeves, 728.

53. Moreland, *Kingdom Triangle*, 46.

54. Again, it is important to emphasize that the conflict is not science versus religion; see Plantinga, *Where the Conflict Really Lies*, 254.

keep in mind that what they see was not designed, but rather evolved."[55] Intelligent design as parable suggests that this bird-like vigilance to remove all design-bearing seed that falls on the path is motivated by a hard heart, not compelling evidence (Matthew 13:15).

Intelligent design and the marginalized

Most of Jesus' encounters with Pharisees are conflict narratives. The Pharisees go from questioning the message of Jesus, to challenging him, to seeking to exclude him by force.[56] They accuse him of demonic possession (Matthew 12:12), one of the strongest social taboos, and collude with the chief priests to ensure his grave is guarded to maintain control of him even in death (Matthew 27:62–66. Yet others of them warn Jesus of the danger he is in (Luke 13:31–33), and another hosts for Jesus (although even then there is still a level of conflict; Luke 7:36–39). Pharisees focus on the rule of law, seeking to enforce their will legally, but in the end they are willing to abuse their power to achieve their goal. They have significant control over the people as authority figures and they chose to rejected Jesus as the Son of David and as Israel's king. The people had asked their leaders "could this be the Son of David?" (Matthew 12:23) and the Pharisees responded with the only answer that made sense of Jesus' miraculous healing within their worldview: Jesus must have been operating with evil power, and therefore cannot be Israel's king. Jesus challenges their accusation immediately, but also points to the consequences of this authoritarian pronouncement on him: "whoever is not with me is against me" (Matthew 12:30). Having been formally rejected, Jesus appeals to the crowd directly through his parables. This democratic approach is, of course, a political decision, and it undermines the Pharisees' authority. Intelligent design, certainly at the present time, has been formally rejected by those in positions of political power and in elite cultural and academic institutions. The DID course appealed to people directly, empowering them to take their part in the conversation about science, enabling them to express their opinions and to challenge arguments they

---

55. Francis Crick, *What Mad Pursuit: A Personal View of Scientific Discovery.* (New York: Basic Books, 1988), 138, http://public.eblib.com/choice/publicfullrecord. aspx?p=903645.

56. For an overview of Pharisees, see Donald E. Cook, 'A Gospel Portrait of the Pharisees', *Review & Expositor* 84, no. 2 (1987): 221–33.

think are false. It empathizes with those whose theological intuitions are opposed or denied by those in positions of cultural authority.

The parables that Jesus told often restored the dignity of those marginalized. For instance, the prodigal son (Luke 15:11–32), the good Samaritan (Luke 10:27–35), and the beggar Lazarus (Luke 16:19–31) are all located on the margins of society but are restored with authority, or held up as a role model, or comforted and brought into God's presence. The parable of the Pharisee and the tax collector, Luke 18:9–14, is paradigmatic of this reversal of expectations and the way the marginalized are restored. The punchline of the parable is not that the culturally despised tax collector, against all expectations, is declared righteous before God (the true arbiter of justice) but that the arrogantly self-assured Pharisee is not.[57] The DID course gave those who felt belittled for their faith reasons to feel justified for their intuition that life shows abundant evidence of design. It suggested that materialists in positions of influence should question their self-confidence. Contrary to common cultural assumptions, it is not the theistic worldview that conflicts with science, but the materialist one. Plantinga describes the "deep unease, deep discord, deep conflict between naturalism and science."[58] The debate is not between science and faith, but between science and materialism. This surprising reversal is analogous to the Pharisee not being justified before God. Materialism is not justified within the very science that it seeks to uphold because materialism undermines confidence in the very concept of truth. If our minds are products of natural selection and physical forces alone then, as Darwin himself recognized, there is no reason to believe that our mental convictions "are of any value or at all trustworthy."[59] Materialism deconstructs itself and relocates itself outside of reasoned debate.[60] As Jesus said, "whoever has will be given more, and they will have an abundance. Whoever does not have, even what they have will be taken from them," (Matthew 13:12; cf. 25:29).

---

57. *Pace* Kistemaker, 'Jesus as Story Teller: Literary Perspectives on the Parables', 55; see Osborne, *The Hermeneutical Spiral*, 242–43; and Kenneth E. Bailey, *Poet & Peasant and Through Peasant Eyes: A Literary-Cultural Approach to the Parables in Luke*, Combined edition (Grand Rapids: Eerdmans, 1983), 155.

58. Plantinga, *Where the Conflict Really Lies*, 309.

59. Charles Darwin, 'Letter to William Graham', July 3rd, 1881; cited in Plantinga, 316.

60. Plantinga, 309; See also Lewis' discussion in C.S. Lewis, *Miracles: A Preliminary Study* (London: Geoffrey Bles, 1947), 24–34.

Like parables, the intelligent design argument is an invitation to change one's pattern of thought (Matthew 4:17), to renew the mind (Romans 12:2), to tear down strongholds and demolish arguments (1 Corinthians 10:4–5), and to restore a sense of fear of the Lord appropriate for wisdom.

> Instruct the wise and they will be wiser still;
> teach the righteous and they will add to their learning.
> The fear of the Lord is the beginning of wisdom,
> and knowledge of the Holy One is understanding.
> Proverbs 9:9–10

Undertaking this Prophetic Discernment on the insights gained during the Sagely Wisdom phase helped me to locate teaching the DID course within the broader, ongoing story of God as a contemporary parable. Despite the tendency to treat them as timeless truths, the parables were rooted in the Gospel narrative which is itself the decisive *kairos* moment in biblical theology. Hays states that parables locate "the story of Jesus within the unfolding story of Israel."[61] The parable of intelligent design is part of the ongoing improvisation of the story of God,[62] and part of the message of the kingdom of God for a society holding to a materialist worldview.

SUMMARY

Osmer's model of practical theology enabled me to structure my reflection on the participants' responses by critically correlating the main themes observed in their interviews with disciplines ranging from linguistics, psychology, sociology, political theory and philosophy. This process deepened my understanding of what was going on in answer to the research question of the effects of attending the DID course from the perspective of the participants. The Prophetic Discernment phase of this cycle moved my reflections from describing the effect of teaching intelligent design to its broader teleological function of supporting

---

61. Richard B. Hays, 'The Canonical Matrix of the Gospels', in *The Cambridge Companion to the Gospels*, ed. Stephen C. Barton, Cambridge Companions to Religion (Cambridge: Cambridge University Press, 2006), 54.

62. Samuel Wells, *Improvisation: The Drama of Christian Ethics* (London: SPCK, 2004).

a theistic worldview and challenging materialist authority.[63] A moment of theological disclosure was to frame it as a contemporary parable: it crystalized concerns within the participants' interviews and transformed the significance of teaching it within my own ministry in my evangelical college. The substantive change for me was from seeing teaching the DID course as a "planned problem-solving process" of a knowledge deficit in the student body,[64] to seeing it as a contribution to the Christian mission of proclaiming the kingdom of God. It is not the Gospel, of course, but like the parables its role is to challenge presuppositions and claims to authority. This reframing of what was going on gave me a sense of confidence to seek more faithful practice within an evangelical context.[65] This theologically-motivated change of practice is the good desired for the students in response to theological reflection on the research question. It is Osmer's final task of servant leadership where that faithful practice is implemented in application of the research question.

---

63. Wier, 'From the Descriptive to the Normative', 114.

64. Bargal, 'Lewin, Kurt', 502.

65. Swinton and Mowat, *Practical Theology and Qualitative Research*, 262.

8

Servant Leadership

[P]ractical, theological action always has the goal of interacting with situations and challenging practices in order that individuals and communities can be enabled to remain faithful to God and to participate faithfully in God's continuing mission to the world.[1]

Swinton and Mowat argue that combining practical theology with qualitative research can produce creative responses to complex problems. "The combination of these two disciplines provides a wonderful context for the development of fresh insights, challenging dialogue and revised and more faithful modes of practice."[2] The research question was addressed through action research and practical theology with the hope of producing beneficial revised practice. This chapter describes practical applications of the Prophetic Discernment phase for more faithful praxis.

The servant leadership phase of Osmer's model has "the task of forming and enacting strategies of action that influence events in ways that are desirable."[3] The Priestly Listening task articulated the analytic story, and the Sagely Wisdom task critically correlated the main points to deepen and complexify the understanding gained from the action research. The Prophetic Discernment task reflected theologically to give a normative direction (or what I prefer to call a theological imperative) that

1. Swinton and Mowat, 263.
2. Swinton and Mowat, 260.
3. Osmer, *Practical Theology*, 176.

motivates the pragmatic response. Osmer describes this final phase of his model as the pragmatic task but, as Lewin's famous dictum goes, "there is nothing as practical as a good theory."[4] Osmer's description of this task as "servant leadership" captures this balance: Christian praxis takes its direction as a servant from Prophetic Discernment and shows leadership in taking initiative to implement that vision in concrete actions.

The action research cycles reflected on the participants' responses that teaching a form of intelligent design to evangelical students, both inside and outside of Moorlands College, gave them confidence to share their faith with those whose worldview might otherwise make it difficult to engage with (in answer to the research question). Teaching intelligent design raised the students' awareness of the philosophical and educational structures that make discussing science difficult for them, and it gave encouragement to those who felt marginalized for their belief in God as the creator of life. It seemed to me the faithful modes of practice that flowed from my thesis went in two directions: the academic development of teaching within my educational context, and the developing of teaching intelligent design, or what might now be called faithful science, within the ministry context of the students who were the focus of my thesis. Both areas fulfil the sense of servant leadership that Osmer advocates, although they operate on different levels. Norton's focus is on developing the academic dimension of the research (especially within higher education), whereas Osmer's emphasis is on Christian ministry. My teaching context within an evangelical college enabled me to follow both these directions without confusion, but it is helpful to address them separately within this chapter.

ACADEMIC SERVANT LEADERSHIP

Norton draws from Fanghanel's description of different levels of activity within the academic context. Pedagogical action research, she argues, "has the potential to have influence at Fanghanel's (2007) three levels of academic practice: the micro, the meso and the macro."[5] The micro is the individual level, the meso is the department or subject-discipline

4. Bargal, 'Lewin, Kurt', 503.

5. Norton, *Action Research in Teaching and Learning*, 68; referring to Joëlle Fanghanel, 'Investigating University Lecturers' Pedagogical Constructs in the Working Context' (York: Higher Education Academy, 2007).

level, and the macro is the institutional or policy-making level, and I address academic servant leadership at each level.

Micro level

One of the most important results of completing this research project has been the ability to reframe my self-understanding of teaching in a higher educational context. As a teacher who researches, undertaking a professional doctorate has encouraged me to take a research approach to problems and opportunities within my academic context. It has made me a better supervisor of MA dissertations students in their various interests and methodologies. However, the specific change at the individual level that the research project produced was to locate my teaching of science within a Bible college context as part of a biblical ministry. Reframing the teaching of intelligent design as a modern parable has given me a sense of coherence about the practice of teaching science and challenged me to consider how teaching other subject areas might be brought within a theological framework.

The research project focused on student responses to my teaching them intelligent design and whether they felt enabled to use what they had learned in their ministry situations. It was insufficient for me simply to demonstrate the existence of knowledge about intelligent design: I needed to impart that knowledge in a way that would benefit students' relationship-building with others. As Jesus said to his disciples, "Now that you know these things, you will be blessed if you do them," John 13:17. As the previous chapter discussed, parables invite a response from their hearers, and teaching intelligent design as a form of parable meant reflecting on my role as teacher in terms of "information transmission" and "supporting students' learning."[6] Teaching intelligent design brought the skills I have learned as a more content-led teacher together with the need to employ a more student-centred facilitation approach. Hearing the voices of students through face-to-face discussions and semi-structured interviews of how the knowledge they had learned benefitted them in their ministry contexts demonstrated the practical value of good theory, but also pointed to areas where I could improve my facilitation skills. The servant leadership change from this section was a pedagogical commitment to integrate my more student-centred practice of teaching

6. Norton, *Action Research in Teaching and Learning*, 6.

practical theology with my more traditional teacher-centred approach to apologetics. I would seek confirmation of the effectiveness of this change of practice through regular face-to-face feedback from students. This "perspective transformation" was made possible by the action research cycles and my reflection on practice.[7] It echoed Osmer's emphasis on the importance of transformation in servant leadership.[8]

Meso level

Norton writes that "[o]ne of the goals of pedagogical action research is to have an immediate effect on practice."[9] The first meso or department-level change was introduced through collaboration with my colleague responsible for the apologetics module. Consistent with the values coming from this project, we redesigned my contribution to the module to emphasize the role of conflicting worldviews. The challenge of Darwinism had been presented and understood as a conflict between those who have religious faith, and those who believe in science. The research project had challenged the Darwinian claim to be a fact and had recognized the conflict in worldviews underlying the challenge. It is not science versus faith, or Christianity versus secularism, or even creation versus Darwinism. The research project helped me restructure the primary way of presenting the discussion about science in the apologetics module as a conflict between materialist and theist worldviews.[10] Teaching intelligent design, framed as a contemporary parable based on the Parable of the Sower, challenged the authority structures that maintained the conceptual machinery of things taken for granted (see pages 121–123).[11] Framing the teaching of intelligent design this way integrated this aspect of apologetics within a broader biblical paradigm based on the Gospels.

Norton emphasizes the importance of communicating the results of pedagogical action research, and this too can occur at various levels.[12] Staying at the meso level, I was able to share my research with colleagues

---

7. Kember, *Action Learning and Action Research*, 26–27.

8. Osmer, *Practical Theology*, 177.

9. Norton, *Action Research in Teaching and Learning*, 198.

10. Plantinga, *Where the Conflict Really Lies*, 309–10.

11. Bourdieu and Wacquant, *An Invitation to Reflexive Sociology*, 239; Dreher, 'The Social Construction of Power', 60.

12. Norton, *Action Research in Teaching and Learning*, 194.

at college after the DID course and received useful critical feedback on my methodology. I intend to present the thematic analysis and theological reflections at a future college colloquium. I presented a talk on faithful science and received helpful feedback at a youth conference held at Moorlands College entitled "3:15" (from 1 Peter 3:15, a foundational verse for apologetics). The title of the talk given for my session was "Creation vs. Science" which did not fit well with the reframing of the issue as a conflict of worldviews, but which did resonate with those who perceive that to be the state of the argument.[13] The presentation developed my parabolic approach and challenged the view that Christian faith conflicted with science by showing that many of the founding fathers of science were Christians. Arguments were presented against the materialist view of science, drawing from the study of information and consciousness, and the talk concluded that since many scientists and philosophers support a theistic worldview the conflict was not between science and the Christian faith.

The questions that the young people asked after my talk demonstrated that the content and level of my presentation influenced the audience in the desired way, which is how Osmer describes servant leadership.[14] It provided intellectual stimulation and provoked relevant and meaningful questions from the young people. The four questions asked were:

- Why is the Big Bang relevant?

- How does artificial intelligence link with the soul?

- Why would God limit our understanding of things like eternity?

- Where did God come from?

All these are worldview-type questions, indicating that the parabolic approach was understood and responded to at the level intended. Delegate feedback on the talk from both young people and their youth leaders was positive suggesting it was effective in its intention. Participants of the DID course noted the anxiety that church leaders and youth workers feel at not being able to provide a direct answer to a scientific question, resulting in the impression that the Christian faith does not have relevant knowledge in these areas.[15] As Kinnaman argues, "[w]e must

13. See, for example, Denis Alexander, *Creation or Evolution: Do We Have to Choose?* (Oxford: Monarch, 2009).

14. Osmer, *Practical Theology*, 176.

15. See especially Moreland, *Kingdom Triangle*, 121–30; also chapter 1 of Willard,

do a better job challenging and training all young Christians—not just the science geeks—to think clearly, honestly, and comprehensively about matters of science."[16] The 3:15 conference presentation encouraged me to participate in more events of a similar kind as an expression of servant leadership.

Macro level

Norton describes the macro level of academic influence as the institutional policy-making level and the place where external factors impinge on teaching practice. It is expected that the benefits to the college curriculum of researching practice through a professional doctoral program will encourage more colleagues to apply for similar opportunities. Norton encourages teaching staff to engage in research regarding the content of their courses and to pass on these skills to students.[17] An external factor that impinged directly on student ministries was the problem of worldviews within the school context, a theme also identified in the thematic analysis. Billingsley et al. identified the compartmentalized relationship between science and religious views in school to be problematic.[18] The notion of design was excluded from the teaching of science and appeals to God as a causal explanation of natural phenomena were not permitted. Science was taught as factual, whereas religious views were taught as opinions.[19] They thought it marginalized those having a Christian faith in a creator God by giving the impression that such a belief was unscientific, and that it was difficult to integrate their faith within all the school curriculum.[20]

The Prophetic Discernment of teaching intelligent design as a modern parable lends itself to challenge the kind of the authority that

---

Personal Religion, Public Reality?: Towards a Knowledge of Faith.

16. Kinnaman, *You Lost Me*, 142.

17. Norton, *Action Research in Teaching and Learning*, 14.

18. Berry Billingsley et al., 'How Students View the Boundaries Between Their Science and Religious Education Concerning the Origins of Life and the Universe', *Science Education* 100, no. 3 (May 2016): 463, https://doi.org/10.1002/sce.21213.

19. Billingsley et al., 473.

20. For suggestions of how that might happen, see Berry Billingsley, Keith Taber, and Mehdi Nassaji, 'Scientism, Creationism or Category Error? A Cross-age Survey of Secondary School Students' Perceptions of the Relationships between Science and Religion', *The Curriculum Journal*, 13 October 2020, 6, https://doi.org/10.1002/curj.83.

sustains this intellectual segregation within the school environment.[21] One response to this challenge is the recommendation by the Commission on Religious Education (CoRE) to change the structure and content of religious education in the UK.[22] The Commission's report argued for Religious Education (RE) to be restructured as teaching "Religion and Worldviews."[23] The connotation of RE as religious instruction is no longer viable, and its general decline in take up at higher levels suggests it is not viable in its current form.[24] Previous reviews had suggested religion be taught from the perspective of a believer. This view was summarized in the 2004 Qualifications and Curriculum Authority (QCA) document: religious education, it said, "encourages pupils to learn from different religions, beliefs, values and traditions while exploring their own beliefs and questions of meaning."[25] However, more recent consultations have suggested the subject needs "rejuvenating" and that the focus should be on worldviews. The CoRE report refers to teaching "religious and non-religious wordviews" as a national entitlement for all pupils in secondary education.[26] Focusing on the main six religions has been problematic in that it left other, more secular worldviews unexamined, and those who did not identify themselves as religious felt they had little to gain. The CoRE report argues that what is needed is a "deeper understanding" of worldviews, how they operate, and "the accounts they provide of the nature of reality."[27]

21. Billingsley et al., 'How Students View the Boundaries Between Their Science and Religious Education Concerning the Origins of Life and the Universe', 466.

22. 'Commission on Religious Education | A New Vision for Religious Education in Schools', Commission on Religious Education, accessed 2 December 2020, https://www.commissiononre.org.uk/.

23. 'Religion and Worldviews: The Way Forward; A National Plan for RE' (London: Commission on Religious Education, September 2018), 11, religiouseducation-council.org.uk.

24. Adam Postans, 'Not a Single Pupil Took a Religious Education GCSE at This School', Bristol Post, 1 July 2019, https://www.bristolpost.co.uk/news/local-news/not-single-pupil-took-religious-3027640.

25. For an overview of different perspectives, see Geoff Teece, 'The Aims and Purpose of Religious Education', in Learning to Teach Religious Education in the Secondary School: A Companion to School Experience, ed. L. Philip Barnes, 3rd ed., Learning to Teach Subjects in the Secondary School Series (Abingdon: Routledge, 2018), 1–14.

26. 'Religion and Worldviews', 12.

27. 'Religion and Worldviews', 6.

> Deeper academic study of the experience of those who hold both religious and non-religious worldviews suggests that the distinction between religious and non-religious worldviews is not as clear-cut as one might think.[28]

Supporting the CoRE's proposal flows well from the Prophetic Discernment phase as an expression of servant leadership in that it addresses directly the worldviews present in society, and seeks to influence policy decisions about education in schools at what Fanghanel calls the macro level.[29] It also has a subversive edge to it, suitable for a parable,[30] in that it shows genuine inclusivity of secular and explicitly humanist worldviews, yet its intention is to demonstrate their weaknesses. Poplin argues that "all worldviews begin with faith, a metaphysical belief that cannot be verified using scientific methods."[31] The Humanists UK society supports both the renaming of RE to "Religion and Worldviews" and the CoRE's recommendation of full inclusion of non-religious worldviews including humanism.[32] My support for these reforms stems from the belief that the more the atheistic worldview is examined the more its inherent weaknesses will be revealed, and the comparative strengths of the theistic worldviews will be recognized.

A recent review of the CoRE reforms by Cooling supported the teaching of worldviews "constituted by those deeply-held, unquestioned beliefs and taken-for-granted ways of behaving that often only come to the forefront of our attention when they are challenged in some way."[33] The correlation between this definition of worldviews and the themes of the Prophetic Discernment task are striking. The role that science plays within each person's worldview could be identified and compared, especially in answering questions of origins.[34] Those holding a non-religious

28. 'Religion and Worldviews', 6.

29. Fanghanel, 'Investigating University Lecturers' Pedagogical Constructs in the Working Context', 2.

30. Herzog, *Parables as Subversive Speech*, 47.

31. Mary S. Poplin, *Is Reality Secular? Testing the Assumptions of Four Global Worldviews* (Downers Grove, IL: InterVarsity, 2014), 30; emphasis removed.

32. 'Humanists UK Welcomes Recommended New Subject "Religion and Worldviews"', *Humanists UK* (blog), accessed 2 December 2020, https://humanism.org.uk/2018/09/09/humanists-uk-welcomes-landmark-commission-on-re-recommending-new-subject-religion-and-worldviews/.

33. Trevor Cooling, *Worldviews in Religious Education* (London: Theos, 2020), 28.

34. For the influence of science on the worldview of young British nones see Madge and Hemming, 'Young British Religious "Nones": Findings from the Youth On

worldview would no longer see themselves as being outside of a faith and belief structure.[35] A "compartmentalized" school environment that separated science and religious belief might, under these new proposals, encourage greater freedom for students to consider how different world-views change perspectives on life:[36] or, as Poplin puts it, "are one or more of these an adequate description of reality?"[37] Cooling highlights the "un-questioned epistemic belief that science and religion inevitably clash with each other" as an example of a problematic issue that studying personal worldviews might address.[38] The macro-level support for introducing CoRE's recommendations is a good example of Osmer's servant leader-ship within the academic sphere. It is a policy-level, strategic action that would affect positively the ministry environment of many of my students.

MINISTRY SERVANT LEADERSHIP

This section considers strategic developments in ministry servant leader-ship coming from the research project. These are another presentation of the DID course at the college, a worldview chat group, and a further de-velopment of the DID course for training students to be presenters. The concepts used to frame this discussion are the themes of empowerment and enabling that arose from the thematic analysis of the participants' interviews. By empowerment I mean a move from feeling marginalized by the universe-maintaining concepts associated with Darwinism and secularism to feeling legitimated in holding an evangelical worldview.[39] By enabling I mean facility to use intelligent design arguments to defend or promote the legitimacy and strength of an evangelical worldview.

Religion Study'.

35. Woodhead, 'The Rise of "No Religion" in Britain: The Emergence of a New Cultural Majority'.

36. Billingsley, 'Teaching and Learning about Epistemic Insight', 60.

37. Poplin, *Is Reality Secular?*, 31.

38. Cooling, *Worldviews in Religious Education*, 45; referring to Billingsley, 'Teach-ing and Learning about Epistemic Insight'.

39. Berger and Luckmann, *The Social Construction of Reality*, 130.

Presentation of the DID course at Moorlands College

The first theologically-motivated act of servant leadership in terms of ministry is to continue to run the DID course as an optional course for students. Feedback from the pilot and main DID courses was encouraging with participants sharing their stories of how it had enabled them to relate to others in fresh ways and had been the means of building relationships with those who were otherwise unreceptive to the Gospel. Removing the research element from the course will ameliorate residual power dynamics as there will be nothing asked of the students. This is an act of servant leadership in that it is extracurricular work for the sake of the benefit of college students and requires leadership to organize and present the course. I will reflect on the tension over when the course was run last time and will accommodate the pressures that some students found in the previous time chosen during the college term: it may well be best to run it again on two successive Saturdays.

Worldview chat

The second ministry servant leadership is a worldview chat group set up by one of my former students. This student had taken part in the pilot study of the DID course and, after graduating, initiated with apologetic intent an online discussion forum for those who wanted to debate topics from their different worldviews. He invited me to join and contribute to the conversation covering topics such as veganism, vitalism, sexuality, slavery, evolution, and scientism. There are normally between four and six contributors whose worldviews range from atheist to agnostic to the evangelical Christian worldview of myself and my former student. There is explicit acknowledgement that these discussions are for open dialogue with the intention to convince the others of the strength of (in my case) an evangelical Christian worldview.

This chat group is a relevant example of servant leadership in ministry for two main reasons. First, it has provided a lively forum for developing my skills at engaging with topics at the worldview level, one of the key observations from my research. The chat room contributors are intelligent and articulate and defend their worldviews with evidence and argument. The forum prevents me from making assumptions about other views and forces me to articulate my own perspective (and recognize my biases) clearly and with evidence that they find convincing. Because of the more intimate nature of online chat rooms (where you are close to a screen and able to see people's facial expressions clearly) I am also reminded of the importance of giving reasons for the hope that I have with gentleness and respect, keeping a clear conscience (1 Peter 3:15–16).

Secondly, being invited by my former student encouraged me to reflect on the value of the DID course as having borne good fruit. He had felt empowered to start the group partly because the course had helped him grow in confidence in the strength of his own evangelical worldview. He had developed an independent ministry and had empowered me to participate in his outreach project. This change in the power relationship was an example of the way education has a liberative dimension to it and does not encourage dependency of the student upon the teacher. As he quipped in an email to me, "the student becomes the master"[40] and offered to grade my contribution to the chat. A virtue associated with both action research and practical theology is emancipation and empowerment (see the discussion in pages 45–51), and I was encouraged to see this expressing itself in his ministry.

Training to lead DID courses

A theme emphasized in the interviews was the way the DID course enabled participants to use arguments in conversations and debates. This was different from having confidence in one's own worldview, and it focused on the skills of communication and understanding the scientific concepts associated with intelligent design arguments. As discussed in pages 78–79 (and noted above), the relationship between teacher and learner can lead to some dependency, whereas the goal of teaching intelligent design was to give students greater agency in their ministries, to equip them, to facilitate their critical reasoning and practical judgement, and to be enable them to be more independent.[41] My aim of teaching intelligent design was to enable students to communicate that information themselves in ways that benefitted their relationships with others. Communicating intelligent design within an inhospitable intellectual environment means equipping students to go out like sheep among wolves (Matthew 10:16). That is a different teaching context to the college and

40. Personal email correspondence, 2020.

41. See the broader discussion in Gibbs, 'Is Higher Education Inherently Good, Educative Practices Intrinsically Good and Universities Instrumentally Good?', 237.

church environment in which I taught the DID course. It suggests I need to consider the new contexts that learners might well go on to teach in. The next phase in developing the intelligent design course would be to redesign it in such a way that it enables students to teach it to others in their own local contexts.

Enabling others to teach the DID course in this way requires a process of reflection and input from those interested in participating. A new project of participatory action research would be an appropriate approach because the design of the project would need collaboration from participants to define the goals and evaluate the progress.[42] Henning et al. argue that "collaboration establishes a culture for continuous [. . .] improvement and a means for rapidly disseminating new teaching strategies."[43] Developing the course in this way would enable participants better to present information in the places of their ministry such as schools and youth groups. Participatory action research is "attentive to local context" and encourages participants to take ownership of their learning to better adapt to the learning styles, age ranges and ministry contexts.[44] In this way it is a more democratic approach to learning. The development of such a training course in teaching intelligent design will follow from the next presentation of the current DID course and would be an expression of sowing seed on good soil (Matthew 13:8).

SUMMARY

In this chapter I have outlined the application of my research project "in ways that are desirable" through the lens of Osmer's fourth task, namely servant leadership.[45] I have integrated themes of worldview, empowerment, and enabling from the Priestly Listening phase with Norton's use of Fanghanel's academic levels of application of pedagogical action research and sought to apply them as a fulfilment of the normative task of Osmer's cycle. This integration of qualitative research and practical theology was anticipated by Swinton and Mowat as producing "faithful modes of

42. Stephen Kemmis and Robin McTaggart, 'Participatory Action Research: Communicative Action and the Public Sphere', in *Strategies of Qualitative Inquiry*, ed. N. K. Denzin and Yvonna S. Lincoln (Thousand Oaks: SAGE, 2007), 320.

43. Henning, Stone, and Kelly, *Using Action Research to Improve Instruction*, 139.

44. Craig McGarvey, 'Participatory Action Research: Involving "All the Players" in Evaluation and Change', GrantCraft (Foundation Center, 2007), 2.

45. Osmer, *Practical Theology*, 176.

practice."[46] The faithful modes of practice ranged from individual changes of academic practice to the broader dissemination of my research at
conferences, ministry opportunities in a worldview chat room and developing a new course for developing teachers of intelligent design. Each
of these faithful modes of practice are expressions of servant leadership.

Although this concludes the research project it indicates avenues
of development, both as a theological lecture and Christian minister of
evangelical students who themselves are training for ministry. The concluding chapter restates the argument, reviews how the chapters of the
thesis contribute to it, and suggests its broader relevance for two other
contexts.

---

46. Swinton and Mowat, *Practical Theology and Qualitative Research*, 260.

9

Conclusions

But the seed falling on good soil refers to someone who hears the word and understands it. This is the one who produces a crop, yielding a hundred, sixty or thirty times what was sown.'
MATTHEW 13:23

SUMMARY OF THE ARGUMENT AND OVERVIEW OF THE THESIS

My research question asked, "to what extent, if at all, does teaching intelligent design to evangelical students contribute to their confidence and ability to share their faith?" I wanted to find out if learning intelligent design arguments would enhance their ability to evangelize those whose materialist worldview resisted such conversations. The action taken was to create a science course based on the book *Discovering Intelligent Design* and (after piloting it) run it as a two-day course called Saturday School for part-time evangelical students as part of an action research project. The evidence from the cycles of pedagogical action research, semi-structured interviews, and thematic analysis suggests that teaching intelligent design was effective in giving these students greater confidence and ability to share their faith and engage in debate with those they previously found it difficult to do so. A cycle of Osmer's model of practical theology framed the results of the thematic analysis within a christological reflection to

167

produce revised, theologically-laden praxis. The argument is that teaching intelligent design to evangelical students is a faithful mode of practice consistent with my professional role as a theology lecturer at an evangelical college and my role as a minister of the Gospel.[1] Like a contemporary parable of the sower, teaching intelligent design challenges the authority structures of a Darwinian worldview and empowers evangelical students to share their faith and engage in apologetic debates within their ministry contexts.

Each chapter contributed to the overall argument. The first chapter outlined the motivation for addressing this question and the professional context in which it was carried out, and chapter 2 identified intelligent design as amongst the most integrative of five paradigms of theology and science and appropriate to teach to evangelical students. I defended the decision to use Norton's pedagogical action research model and Osmer's model of practical theology in chapter 3. The first cycle of action research in chapter 4 involved piloting the DID course and considering issues of positionality and focus. The second, main cycle in chapter 5 generated, analysed, and triangulated the data from student interviews and a focus group of participants who had attended the Saturday School. The quantitative survey showed that evangelical students of intelligent design integrated their theology with science more than other comparable groups. The thematic analysis showed that:

- Participants recognized a need for churches to encourage engagement between science and theology;

- schools taught Darwinism as a sufficient materialist explanation for life, and that intelligent design provided a counter-voice;

- the Christian faith of young people was negatively affected by that school context, and learning intelligent design empowered students to resist feeling marginalized for holding a theistic worldview;

- participants were able to frame the problem as a broader social conflict of worldviews, rather than of science versus faith;

- and participants felt empowered to initiate significant conversations and debate with those holding to a more materialist worldview for the purposes of evangelism.

---

1. Jennifer Mason, *Qualitative Researching*, 2nd ed. (London: SAGE, 2002), 176.

These results validated the research question that teaching intelligent design did give confidence to evangelical students to share their faith with others, but they also required a theological reflective stage before applying them in my specific context.

The sixth chapter marked the beginning of Osmer's model of practical theology, namely the Priestly Listening phase (attending to the thematic analysis of Norton's action research). Using Osmer's model ensured and enabled a christocentric reflection and reframing of the qualitative research as faithful Christian praxis. The themes identified were critically-correlated using a transdisciplinary approach in the second sagely listening stage, providing depth and insight into the issues arising from the thematic analysis through discourse analysis, sociology and philosophy of scientific worldviews, critical consciousness and political hegemony, forces of marginalization, and anti-teleological child-psychology. The democratic, liberative nature of teaching intelligent design was framed as "common science" and, combined with greater critical awareness, it enabled more confident participation in scientific topics related to a materialist worldview.

An important stage of the thesis, chapter 7, was identifying the theological disclosure associated with my change of practice in Osmer's Prophetic Discernment phase. Teaching intelligent design was discerned as teaching a contemporary parable and an extension of Jesus' proclamation of the kingdom of God. It integrated a christological interpretation of teaching science with parabolic wisdom theology. Like the parable of the sower (Matthew 13:1–9), teaching intelligent design clarifies people's attitudes to the kingdom of God including special divine action in the material world. The argument is that, like a parable, intelligent design empowers the marginalized and challenges institutional power and a materialist worldview that excludes God's reality and necessity. Chapter 8 applies these insights as expressions of servant leadership within Norton's typology of academic leadership (micro, meso, and macro) and my own ministry contexts. My professional context was enhanced through research, my practice made more rigorous though greater depth of understanding, and I have opportunities to communicate the results within my college and contribute to broader educational policy discussions concerning argumentation and worldviews within the teaching of RE. Teaching intelligent design to evangelical students is a faithful mode of practice to adopt within a professional, theological context as an expression of proclaiming the kingdom of God and sowing seed on good soil.

IMPLICATIONS AND RECOMMENDATIONS FOR
PROFESSIONAL PRACTICE

> AR produces knowledge that cannot be generalised in the way
> normally expected of research results, and is not repeatable in
> the same manner by other people at a different time.[2]

The question of whether my research has broader relatability de-
pends upon whether extending the relevance of the study constitutes
generalizing or not. Norton argues that, to the extent that similar issues
are faced, it is reasonable to recommend similar approaches.

> The lack of generalisability is a common accusation levelled
> against action research but this is a principle associated with
> a largely quantitative method of data collection. I agree with
> Kember when he says that if our action research study finds that
> an innovation works well, it is only sensible to recommend to
> our colleagues that they try something similar, if they are facing
> a similar type of issue.[3]

I felt justified including the teaching of intelligent design as a modern parable within an apologetics module taught at Moorlands College.
Recent student feedback (obtained through the normal modular feedback methods) shows support for this decision. Similarly, it was consistent with my aim of extending the kingdom of God to run the DID
course for part-time students from the Moorlands College campus. The
implication of these decisions to extend teaching intelligent design, what
Richie and Lewis call "inferential generalisation," is that other Christian
ministry training centres might consider the value of teaching intelligent
design arguments to support their Christian students in evangelism and
apologetics.[4] The context for encouraging students to be able to reach
those whose worldviews are resistive to evangelism is that there is a significant rise in young people identifying as nones (see pages 83–87).[5] Part
of the complex reasons for this rise is a view that science is a matter of

2. Coleman, 'Action Research', 168.

3. Norton, *Action Research in Teaching and Learning*, 63; referring to Kember, *Action Learning and Action Research*, 34–35.

4. Jane Ritchie and Jane Lewis, 'Generalising from Qualitative Research', in *Qualitative Research Practice: A Guide for Social Science Students and Researchers*, ed. Jane Ritchie and Jane Lewis (London: SAGE, 2003), 267–68.

5. Lugo, '"Nones" on the Rise'.

fact, whereas religious faith is a matter of opinion, a view that also contributes to rising dropout rates of young people from church.[6] Madge and
Hemming claim that science is the "top ranked" influencing factor for
nones associated with "increasing out datedness and irrelevance of the
church."[7] My research showed that teaching intelligent design to Christian students (who are often working with young people or training for
church leadership positions) enabled them better to challenge the view
that science had made the church irrelevant and to build confidence in
their Christian faith.

This also has implications for those seeking to develop the relationship between science and religion in a school context.[8] Schools were
perceived by participants as problematic environments by compartmentalizing science and religion, making it difficult for young people to sus-
tain a Christian worldview.[9] The Oxford Argumentation in Religion and
Science project (OARS) seeks to develop interdisciplinary conversations
to develop justified claims.[10] Erduran, OARS' principal investigator, notes
the lack of evidence put forward by RE teachers in arguments compared
with the way science teachers appealed to evidence to argue for "the
correct view."[11] Intelligent design arguments provide scientific evidence
that warrants belief in a theistic worldview. Despite cultural opposition
to teaching intelligent design in schools, my research shows its capacity
to make an important contribution to the development of dialogue and
integration between the disciplines. That many people disagree is not the

6. Billingsley et al., 'How Students View the Boundaries Between Their Science and
Religious Education Concerning the Origins of Life and the Universe', 472; David Kinnaman and Mark Matlock, *Faith for Exiles: 5 Ways for a New Generation to Follow Jesus
in Digital Babylon* (Grand Rapids: Baker, 2019), 14; 'Losing My Religion: Millennials
and Faith Loss', accessed 5 December 2020, https://discipleshipresearch.com/2018/02/
losing-my-religion-millennials-and-faith-loss/; Madge and Hemming, 'Young British
Religious "Nones": Findings from the Youth On Religion Study', 886.

7. Madge and Hemming, 'Young British Religious "Nones": Findings from the
Youth On Religion Study', 883, 886.

8. Immy Holloway and Lorraine Brown, *Essentials of a Qualitative Doctorate*,
Qualitative Essentials (Walnut Creek: Left Coast, 2012), 126–27.

9. Billingsley similarly recognizes compartmentalization in schools; see Billingsley,
'Teaching and Learning about Epistemic Insight'.

10. 'OARS Education—OARS Education', accessed 4 December 2020, https://
oarseducation.com/.

11. Sibel Erduran, Liam Guilfoyle, and Wonyong Park, 'Science and Religious
Education Teachers' Views of Argumentation and its Teaching', *Research in Science
Education*, 7 November 2020, 10, 14, https://doi.org/10.1007/s11165-020-09966-2.

point. Speaking of universities (but the same could be said of schools), Nixon writes:

> [U]niversities are [. . .] spaces that acknowledge as their raison d'être the need for dissent and disagreement within an agreed framework of deliberative endeavour. Universities are places where we learn how to disagree and where disagreement forms the basis of rational discourse. Such discourse is impossible in the absence of mutual respect and the willingness to listen, which is why universities are also places of civility and civic engagement.[12]

The implication is that space could be made within science education to hear the intelligent design arguments more broadly. As Erduran argues:

> Considering the extensive and explicit reference to arguments and argumentation in RE syllabi (Oxfordshire County Council 2015) in contrast to a lack of any explicit emphasis in the science curriculum in England (DfE, 2014), there may be opportunities for enhancing curriculum content, for example by including more specific pedagogical guidelines for teachers to use argumentation as a strategy in their teaching.[13]

Incorporating intelligent design arguments into a school context would, it seems to me, constitute the kind of "novel areas at the interface of teaching science and RE" that she seeks.[14]

REFLECTION AND CRITICISM

The research project was an expression of my values and core beliefs: in addition to the criteria of validity (the trustworthiness of my data collection, the reliability of analysis, the ethics of practice, and reflexive awareness) the research project was also an expression of my desire to further the kingdom of God. If, as McNiff argues, research "is the developmental process of following through the idea, seeing how it goes, and continually

---

12. Jon Nixon, 'Resources of Hope: Truth and Reason', in *Higher Education and Hope: Institutional, Pedagogical and Personal Possibilities*, ed. Paul Gibbs and Andrew Peterson (London: Palgrave Macmillan, 2019), 10.

13. Erduran, Guilfoyle, and Park, 'Science and Religious Education Teachers' Views of Argumentation and its Teaching', 6.

14. Erduran, Guilfoyle, and Park, 6.

checking whether it is in line with what you wish to happen,"[15] then my research project concluded well. It also raised the possibility of bias because of my interest in seeing the project succeed on just those terms. I reflected on the uniformly positive feedback I received from participants, both from students that I knew well and from those I knew not at all before interviewing them. The positive responses inevitably reflected the self-selection of those who chose to attend the DID course who were then willing to be interviewed. Dick encourages a prospective response to the question of "how might it be done differently?"[16] A development of this research would be to seek feedback from those less enthusiastic about the subject (noting the difficulties in involving such people voluntarily). Similarly, it would be good to survey those students opting not to attend the DID course to identify if that were the main influence on evangelical participants having a largely concordist paradigm.

The Prophetic Discernment of framing teaching intelligent design as a contemporary parable could be critiqued as self-serving, although it was the result of prayerful reflection after critical correlation. It integrated a good deal of interdisciplinary engagement and generated new insights that strengthened my reflection (for instance, the heuristic engagement with Herzog was subsequent to my initial reflection on the subversive nature of teaching parables).[17] A feature of practical theology (cyclical models of it at least) is ongoing theological reflection, and revised contexts of ministry invite fresh theological concepts. The goal, I suppose, is for the intelligent design argument to become mainstream in academia and culture where it would lose its critical function. The journey towards that goal would involve theologically reframing the teaching of intelligent design multiple times.

This research project involved learning and employing many additional skills to my normal professional practice including taking action in response to ministry problems, collaboration with church leaders and supervisors, presenting papers, planning events, quantitative surveys, qualitative interviews and focus group, reflecting, thematizing and theorizing the results using spreadsheets and computer-aided qualitative data analysis software. It was located within the ministry of full-time students and tutees at the college, with part-time students of a short course, with

15. McNiff, 'Action Research for Professional Development', 6.

16. Bob Dick, 'Robust Processes: Action and Research (2)', vol. 41, 2002, 4, http://www.aral.com.au/DLitt/index.html.

17. Herzog, *Parables as Subversive Speech*.

my supervisors and fellow research students at Spurgeon's College, and with my colleagues at Moorlands College. And more broadly, it was located as part of my own professional development that, again, was framed as ministerial development. Its contribution to knowledge has, I hope, been demonstrated by my increased capacity to respond to the need that initiated it.[18] The doctoral program, and the thesis especially, has stretched my abilities enormously. It has been a privilege to work with such encouraging friends and colleagues throughout the process.

18. Maxwell, 'Philosophy and Practice—Why Does This Matter?', 6.

Bibliography

Adkins, Tabetha. 'Critical Pedagogy.' In *The SAGE Encyclopedia of Action Research*, edited by David Coghlan and Mary Brydon-Miller, 211–15. London: SAGE, 2014.

Alemu, Getaneh, Brett Stevens, Penny Ross, and Jane Chandler. 'The Use of a Constructivist Grounded Theory Method to Explore the Role of Socially-Constructed Metadata (Web 2.0) Approaches.' *Qualitative and Quantitative Methods in Libraries*, no. 4 (2015) 517–40.

Alexander, Denis. *Creation or Evolution: Do We Have to Choose?* Oxford: Monarch, 2009.

'American Association for the Advancement of Science (2002) | National Center for Science Education.' Accessed 27 July 2020. https://ncse.ngo/american-association-advancement-science-2002.

Amundsen, Cheryl, Laura Winer, and Terry Gandell. 'Designing Teaching for Student Learning.' In *Rethinking Teaching in Higher Education: From a Course Design Workshop to a Faculty Development Framework*, edited by Alenoush Saroyan and Cheryl Amundsen, 71–94. Sterling: Stylus, 2004.

Anderson, Ray S. *The Shape of Practical Theology: Empowering Ministry with Theological Praxis*. Downers Grove: IVP Academic, 2001.

Anderson, Tawa J., W. Michael Clark, and David K. Naugle. *An Introduction to Christian Worldview: Pursuing God's Perspective in a Pluralistic World*. London: IVP, 2017.

Archer, Margaret S., Andrew Collier, and Douglas V. Porpora. *Transcendence: Critical Realism and God. Critical Realism: Interventions*. London: Routledge, 2004.

Archer, Mike, Bradley Smith, Sue Serjeantson, and Paul Carnemolla. 'Letter—Intelligent Design Is Not Science | Australian Academy of Science', 21 October 2005. https://www.science.org.au/supporting-science/science-policy/submissions-government/letter%E2%80%94intelligent-design-not-science.

Petitions—UK Government and Parliament. 'Archived Petition: Teach Evolution, Not Creationism.' Accessed 24 April 2019. https://petition.parliament.uk/archived/petitions/1617.

Arnold, Clinton E. 'Returning to the Domain of the Powers: Stoicheia as Evil Spirits in Galatians 4:3,9.' *Novum Testamentum* 38, no. 1 (January 1996) 55–76.

Arnold, Lydia, and Lin Norton. 'Problematising Pedagogical Action Research in Formal Teaching Courses and Academic Development: A Collaborative Autoethnography.' *Educational Action Research*, 2020, 1–18. https://doi.org/10.1080/09650792.2020.1746373.

Avise, John C. *Inside the Human Genome: A Case for Non-Intelligent Design*. Oxford: Oxford University Press, 2010.

Axe, Douglas. *Undeniable: How Biology Confirms Our Intuition That Life is Designed*. New York: HarperOne, 2016.

Ayala, Francisco J. 'Darwin's Greatest Discovery: Design without Designer.' *Proceedings of the National Academy of Sciences* 104, no. Supplement 1 (15 May 2007) 8567–73. https://doi.org/10.1073/pnas.0701072104.

———. 'Reduction, Emergence, Naturalism, Dualism, Teleology: A Précis.' In *Back to Darwin: A Richer Account of Evolution*, edited by John B. Cobb, 76–89. Grand Rapids: Eerdmans, 2008.

Bailey, Kenneth E. *Poet & Peasant and Through Peasant Eyes: A Literary-Cultural Approach to the Parables in Luke*. Combined edition. Grand Rapids: Eerdmans, 1983.

Baker, Sylvia. 'The Theos/ComRes Survey into Public Perception of Darwinism in the UK: A Recipe for Confusion.' *Public Understanding of Science* 21, no. 3 (26 August 2010) 286–93. https://doi.org/10.1177/0963662510376707.

Banks, James A. 'The Lives and Values of Researchers: Implications for Educating Citizens in a Multicultural Society.' *Educational Researcher* 27, no. 7 (1998) 4–17.

Barbour, Ian G. *Religion and Science: Historical and Contemporary Issues*. San Francisco: HarperSanFrancisco, 1997.

———. *Religion in an Age of Science*. London: SCM, 1990.

———. 'Ways of Relating Science and Theology.' In *Physics, Philosophy, and Theology: A Common Quest for Understanding*, edited by Robert J. Russell, William R. Stoeger, and George V. Coyne, 21–48. Vatican: Vatican Observatory, 1988.

Bargal, David. 'Lewin, Kurt.' In *The SAGE Encyclopedia of Action Research*, edited by David Coghlan and Mary Brydon-Miller, 500–503. Thousand Oaks, California: SAGE, Inc, 2014.

Barkman, Linda Lee Smith. 'Muted Group Theory: A Tool for Hearing Marginalized Voices.' *Priscilla Papers* 32, no. 4 (Autumn 2018) 3–7.

Barnes, M. Elizabeth, E. Margaret Evans, Ashley Hazel, Sara E. Brownell, and Randolph M. Nesse. 'Teleological Reasoning, Not Acceptance of Evolution, Impacts Students' Ability to Learn Natural Selection.' *Evolution: Education and Outreach* 10, no. 1 (December 2017) 7. https://doi.org/10.1186/s12052-017-0070-6.

Barreto, Eric D. *Thinking Theologically: Foundations for Learning*. Minneapolis: Fortress, 2015.

Barrett, Justin L., and Roger Trigg. 'Cognitive and Evolutionary Studies of Religion.' In *The Roots of Religion: Exploring the Cognitive Science of Religion*, edited by Roger Trigg and Justin L. Barrett, 1–16. Ashgate Science and Religion Series. Farnham: Ashgate, 2014.

Bebbington, D. W. *Evangelicalism in Modern Britain: A History From the 1730s to the 1980s*. London: Unwin Hyman, 1989.

Bebbington, David W. 'Response: The History of Ideas and the Study of Religion.' In *Seeing Things Their Way: Intellectual History and the Return of Religion*, edited by Alister Chapman, John Coffey, and Brad S. Gregory, 240–57. Notre Dame: University of Notre Dame Press, 2009.

Beckwith, Francis J. 'Public Education, Religious Establishment, and the Challenge of Intelligent Design.' *Notre Dame Journal of Law, Ethics & Public Policy* 17, no. 2 (2003) 461–519.

Behe, Michael J. *Darwin's Black Box: The Biochemical Challenge to Evolution*. New York: Free, 1996.

'Being Christian in Western Europe.' Washington: Pew Research Center, 29 May 2018.

Bell, Judith. *Doing Your Research Project: A Guide For First-Time Researchers*. 6th ed. Maidenhead: Open University Press, 2014.

Bennett, Zoë. *Using the Bible in Practical Theology: Historical and Contemporary Perspectives*. Farnham: Ashgate, 2013.

Bennett, Zoë, Elaine Graham, Stephen Pattison, and Heather Walton. *Invitation to Research in Practical Theology*. Abingdon; New York: Routledge, 2018.

Berg, Bruce L. *Qualitative Research Methods for the Social Sciences*. 5th ed. Boston: Pearson, 2004.

Berger, Peter L., and Thomas Luckmann. *The Social Construction of Reality: A Treatise in the Sociology of Knowledge*. London: Penguin, 1966.

Bering, Jesse. *The God Instinct: The Psychology of Souls, Destiny, and the Meaning of Life*. London: Nicholas Brealey, 2011.

Berlinski, David. *The Devil's Delusion: Atheism and Its Scientific Pretensions*. New York: Basic Books, 2009.

Billingsley, Berry. 'Teaching and Learning about Epistemic Insight.' *School Science Review* 98, no. 365 (2017) 59–64.

Billingsley, Berry, Richard Brock, Keith S. Taber, and Fran Riga. 'How Students View the Boundaries Between Their Science and Religious Education Concerning the Origins of Life and the Universe.' *Science Education* 100, no. 3 (May 2016) 459–82. https://doi.org/10.1002/sce.21213.

Billingsley, Berry, Keith Taber, and Mehdi Nassaji. 'Scientism, Creationism or Category Error? A Cross-age Survey of Secondary School Students' Perceptions of the Relationships between Science and Religion.' *The Curriculum Journal*, 13 October 2020, curj.83. https://doi.org/10.1002/curj.83.

Biologic Institute. 'Biologic Institute.' Accessed 15 May 2020. http://www. biologicinstitute.org.

Blomberg, Craig L. 'The Miracles as Parables.' In *The Miracles of Jesus*, edited by David Wenham and Craig L. Blomberg, 327–59. Eugene: Wipf and Stock, 2003.

Boa, Kenneth D., and Robert M. Bowman. *Faith Has Its Reasons: Integrative Approaches to Defending the Christian Faith*. 2nd ed. Downers Grove: InterVarsity, 2005.

Bourdieu, Pierre, and Loïc J. D. Wacquant. *An Invitation to Reflexive Sociology*. Chicago: University of Chicago Press, 1992.

Bradley, Walter L. 'Phillip Johnson and the Intelligent Design Movement: Looking Back and Looking Forward.' In *Darwin's Nemesis: Phillip Johnson and the Intelligent Design Movement*, edited by William A. Dembski, 305–14. Downers Grove: InterVarsity, 2007.

Braun, Virginia, and Victoria Clarke. *Successful Qualitative Research: A Practical Guide for Beginners*. London: SAGE, 2013.

Religion & Society Research. 'British Evangelicals Are Not Fundamentalists', 19 July 2012. http://www.religionandsociety.org.uk/research_findings/featured_findings/ british_evangelicals_are_not_fundamentalists.

Brueggemann, Walter. *Theology of the Old Testament: Testimony, Dispute, Advocacy*. Minneapolis: Fortress, 1997.

Bryman, Alan. *Social Research Methods*. 4th ed. Oxford: Oxford University Press, 2012.

Building Deeper Relationship: Using Faith-Based Facilitation. London: Salvation Army International, 2010.

Bullock, C. Hassell. 'Wisdom, the "Amen" of Torah.' *Journal of the Evangelical Theological Society* 52, no. 1 (2009) 5–18.

Cameron, Helen, Deborah Bhatti, Catherine Duce, James Sweeney, and Clare Watkins. *Talking about God in Practice: Theological Action Research and Practical Theology.* London: SCM, 2010.

Cameron, Helen, and Catherine Duce. *Researching Practice in Ministry and Mission: A Companion.* London: SCM, 2013.

Cartledge, Mark J. 'The Use of Scripture in Practical Theology: A Study of Academic Practice.' *Practical Theology* 6, no. 3 (January 2013) 271–83. https://doi.org/10.11 79/1756073X13Z.00000000017.

Casanova, José. 'Rethinking Secularization: A Global Comparative Perspective.' *The Hedgehog Review* 8, no. 1–2 (Spring & Summer 2006) 7–22.

Champagne, Audrey B. 'Facts, Concepts, Principles, and Theories in Science, Assessment of: An Overview.' In *Encyclopedia of Science Education*, edited by Richard Gunstone, 427–28. Dordrecht: Springer, 2015.

Chandler, Dawn, and Bill Torbert. 'Transforming Inquiry and Action: Interweaving 27 Flavors of Action Research.' *Action Research* 1, no. 2 (October 2003) 133–52. https://doi.org/10.1177/14767503030012002.

Chapman, Alister, John Coffey, and Brad S. Gregory, eds. *Seeing Things Their Way: Intellectual History and the Return of Religion.* Notre Dame: University of Notre Dame Press, 2009.

Chapp, Larry. 'Is Nature Enough? Meaning and Truth in the Age of Science - By John F. Haught.' *Modern Theology* 23, no. 4 (October 2007) 642–45. https://doi. org/10.1111/j.1468–0025.2007.00420.x.

Chenoweth, Ben. 'The Vulnerability of the Literalist: A Critique of William R. Herzog II's Interpretation of the Parable of the Talents.' *Pacifica* 21 (2008) 175–91.

Churchland, Paul M. *Matter and Consciousness: A Contemporary Introduction to the Philosophy of Mind.* Rev. ed. Cambridge: MIT Press, 1988.

Clague, Alan. 'Militant Atheism and Biblical Literalism: Comrades-in-Arms for Promotion of Disharmony between the Science and Theology of Creation.' *Pacifica* 23, no. 1 (1 February 2010) 84–96. https://doi.org/10.1177/1030570X1002300105.

Clandinin, D. Jean, and F. Michael Connelly. *Narrative Inquiry: Experience and Story in Qualitative Research.* San Francisco: Jossey-Bass, 2000.

Clarke, Victoria, and Virginia Braun. 'Thematic Analysis.' In *Encyclopedia of Quality of Life and Well-Being Research*, edited by Alex C. Michalos, 6626–28. New York: Springer, 2014.

Clendenen, E. Ray. 'Textlinguistics and Prophecy in the Book of the Twelve.' *Journal of the Evangelical Theological Society* 46, no. 3 (2003) 385–99.

Coghlan, David, and Teresa Brannick. *Doing Action Research in Your Own Organization.* 2nd ed. London: SAGE, 2005.

Coleman, Gill. 'Action Research.' In *Methodologies for Practice Research: Approaches for Professional Doctorates*, edited by Carol Costley and John Fulton, 151–72. London: SAGE, 2019.

Collins, C. John. 'How to Think about God's Action in the World.' In *Theistic Evolution: A Scientific, Philosophical, and Theological Critique*, edited by J.P. Moreland,

Stephen C. Meyer, Christopher Shaw, Ann K. Gauger, and Wayne Grudem, 659–81. Wheaton: Crossway, 2017.

Collins, Francis S. *The Language of God: A Scientist Presents Evidence for Belief.* London: Pocket Books, 2007.

Commission on Religious Education. 'Commission on Religious Education | A New Vision for Religious Education in Schools.' Accessed 2 December 2020. https://www.commissiononre.org.uk/.

Conde-Frazier, Elizabeth. 'Participatory Action Research.' In *The Wiley-Blackwell Companion to Practical Theology*, edited by Bonnie J. Miller-McLemore, 234–43. Chichester: Wiley-Blackwell, 2012. https://doi.org/10.1002/9781444345742.ch22.

Conway, Lucian Gideon, Laura Janelle Gornick, Shannon C. Houck, Christopher Anderson, Jennifer Stockert, Diana Sessoms, and Kevin McCue. 'Are Conservatives Really More Simple-Minded than Liberals? The Domain Specificity of Complex Thinking: Ideology and Complexity.' *Political Psychology* 37, no. 6 (December 2016) 777–98. https://doi.org/10.1111/pops.12304.

Cook, Donald E. 'A Gospel Portrait of the Pharisees.' *Review & Expositor* 84, no. 2 (1987) 221–33.

Cooling, Trevor. *Worldviews in Religious Education.* London: Theos, 2020.

Costley, Carol. 'Research Approaches in Professional Doctorates: Notes on an Epistemology of Practice.' In *Methodologies for Practice Research: Approaches for Professional Doctorates*, edited by Carol Costley and John Fulton, 17–32. London: SAGE, 2019.

Costley, Carol, and John Fulton, eds. *Methodologies for Practice Research: Approaches for Professional Doctorates.* London: SAGE, 2019.

Coyne, Jerry A. *Faith versus Fact: Why Science and Religion Are Incompatible.* New York: Penguin, 2015.

———. *Why Evolution Is True.* Oxford: Oxford University Press, 2009.

'Creating A Multimedia Experience | Discovering Intelligent Design.' Accessed 6 May 2019. https://discovering.design/multimedia/.

Creswell, John W., and J. David Creswell. *Research Design: Qualitative, Quantitative, and Mixed Methods Approaches.* Fifth edition. London: SAGE, 2018.

Crick, Francis. *What Mad Pursuit: A Personal View of Scientific Discovery.* New York: Basic Books, 1988. http://public.eblib.com/choice/publicfullrecord.aspx?p=903645.

Cunningham, Joseph. 'Academic Discourse.' In *The SAGE Encyclopedia of Action Research*, edited by David Coghlan and Mary Brydon-Miller, 1–3. London: SAGE, 2014.

Curtis, Finbarr. 'The Secularity of Intelligent Design.' *The Hedgehog Review* 13, no. 2 (2011) 68–78.

Dawkins, Richard. 'Is it a Theory? Is it a Law? No, it's a Fact.' *Richard Dawkins Foundation*, 30 November 2015. https://www.richarddawkins.net/2015/11/is-it-a-theory-is-it-a-law-no-its-a-fact/.

———. *The Blind Watchmaker.* London: Longman, 1986.

———. *The God Delusion.* London: Bantam, 2006.

———. *The Greatest Show on Earth: The Evidence for Evolution.* London: Black Swan, 2010.

———. *The Selfish Gene.* New York: Oxford University Press, 1976.

De Gruchy, John. 'Kairos Moments and Prophetic Witness: Towards a Prophetic Ecclesiology.' *HTS Teologiese Studies / Theological Studies* 72, no. 4 (31 May 2016) 1–7. https://doi.org/10.4102/hts.v72i4.3414.

Deane-Drummond, Celia, ed. *The Evolution of Human Wisdom*. Lanham: Lexington, 2017.

Dembski, William A. *Intelligent Design: The Bridge between Science & Theology*. Downers Grove: InterVarsity, 1999.

———, ed. *Mere Creation: Science, Faith & Intelligent Design*. Downers Grove: InterVarsity, 1998.

———. *The Design Inference: Eliminating Chance through Small Probabilities*. Cambridge Studies in Probability, Induction and Decision Theory. Cambridge: Cambridge University Press, 2005.

———. *The Design Revolution: Answering the Toughest Questions about Intelligent Design*. Downers Grove: InterVarsity, 2004.

Dembski, William A., and James M. Kushiner, eds. *Signs of Intelligence: Understanding Intelligent Design*. Grand Rapids: Brazos, 2001.

Dembski, William A, and Michael Ruse, eds. *Debating Design: From Darwin to DNA*. Cambridge: Cambridge University Press, 2011.

Denscombe, Martyn. *The Good Research Guide: For Small-Scale Social Research Projects*. 4th ed. Open UP Study Skills. Maidenhead: Open University Press, 2010.

Denton, Michael. *Evolution: A Theory in Crisis*. Bethesda: Adler & Adler Publishers, 1986.

Dick, Bob. 'Action Research: Action and Research.' In *Doing Good Action Research*, 1–8. Southern Cross University, 2002.

———. 'Robust Processes: Action and Research (2)', Vol. 41, 2002. http://www.aral.com.au/DLitt/index.html.

———. 'What Can Grounded Theorists and Action Researchers Learn from Each Other?' In *The SAGE Handbook of Grounded Theory*, edited by Antony Bryant and Kathy Charmaz, 398–416. London: SAGE, 2007.

'Digital Millennials and the Bible: Produced in Partnership with Barna Group.' Swindon: Bible Society, 2018.

Dimock, Michael. 'Defining Generations: Where Millennials End and Generation Z Begins.' *Pew Research Center*, 17 January 2019. https://www.pewresearch.org/fact-tank/2019/01/17/where-millennials-end-and-generation-z-begins/.

———. 'Where Millennials End and Generation Z Begins | Pew Research Center.' Accessed 4 May 2019. https://www.pewresearch.org/fact-tank/2019/01/17/where-millennials-end-and-generation-z-begins/.

DiscoveryU. 'Discovering Intelligent Design.' Accessed 6 May 2019. http://discoveryu.thinkific.com/courses/discovering-intelligent-design.

'Doctor of Ministry Student Handbook (Part 5) Version 2.' Spurgeon's College; University of Chester, 2016.

Dodd, C. H. *The Parables of the Kingdom*. New York: Scribner, 1961.

Dreher, Jochen. 'The Social Construction of Power: Reflections Beyond Berger/Luckmann and Bourdieu.' *Cultural Sociology* 10, no. 1 (March 2016) 53–68. https://doi.org/10.1177/1749975515615623.

Dunn, James D. G. *Jesus Remembered*. Vol. 1. *Christianity in the Making*. Grand Rapids: Eerdmans, 2003.

Ecklund, Elaine Howard, David R. Johnson, Christopher P. Scheitle, Kirstin R. W. Matthews, and Steven W. Lewis. 'Religion among Scientists in International Context: A New Study of Scientists in Eight Regions.' *Socius: Sociological Research for a Dynamic World* 2 (31 August 2016) 237802311666435. https://doi.org/10.1177/2378023116664353.

Ecklund, Elaine Howard, Jerry Z. Park, and Katherine L. Sorrell. 'Scientists Negotiate Boundaries Between Religion and Science.' *Journal for the Scientific Study of Religion* 50, no. 3 (2011) 552–69.

Engel, James F., and Wilbert Norton. *What's Gone Wrong with the Harvest? A Communication Strategy for the Church and World Evangelism*. Grand Rapids: Zondervan, 1975.

Erduran, Sibel, Liam Guilfoyle, and Wonyong Park. 'Science and Religious Education Teachers' Views of Argumentation and Its Teaching.' *Research in Science Education*, 7 November 2020. https://doi.org/10.1007/s11165-020-09966-2.

Evans, Craig A. 'Jesus and the Spirits: What Can We Learn from the New Testament World?' *Transformation* 27, no. 3 (2010) 146–61.

'Evolution Resources from the National Academies.' Accessed 10 June 2019. http://www.nas.edu/evolution/TheoryOrFact.html.

'Explore Evolution | Who is This For?' Accessed 6 May 2019. http://www.exploreevolution.com/who_is_this_for.php.

Fanghanel, Joëlle. 'Investigating University Lecturers' Pedagogical Constructs in the Working Context.' York: Higher Education Academy, 2007.

Flew, Antony. *There is a God: How the World's Most Notorious Atheist Changed His Mind*. New York: HarperOne, 2007.

Florence, Anna Carter. 'A Parable Universe.' *Journal for Preachers* 38, no. 2 (2015) 3–8.

Fook, Jan. 'Reflective Models and Frameworks in Practice.' In *Methodologies for Practice Research: Approaches for Professional Doctorates*, edited by Carol Costley and John Fulton, 57–76. London: SAGE, 2019.

Forrest, Barbara, and Paul R. Gross. *Creationism's Trojan Horse: The Wedge of Intelligent Design*. New York: Oxford University Press, 2004.

Foster, John Bellamy, Brett Clark, and Richard York. *Critique of Intelligent Design: Materialism versus Creationism from Antiquity to the Present*. New York: Monthly Review, 2008.

Fraenkel, Jack R., Norman E. Wallen, and Helen H. Hyun. *How to Design and Evaluate Research in Education*. 8th ed. New York: McGraw-Hill, 2012.

Freire, Paulo. 'Conscientisation.' *CrossCurrents* 24, no. 1 (1974) 23–31.

———. *Pedagogy of the Oppressed*. Translated by Myra Bergman Ramos. London: Penguin, 1970.

Fuller, Steve. *Post-Truth: Knowledge as a Power Game. Anthem's Key Issues in Modern Sociology*. New York: Anthem, 2018.

Fulton, John, and Carol Costley. 'Ethics.' In *Methodologies for Practice Research: Approaches for Professional Doctorates*, edited by Carol Costley and John Fulton, 77–91. London: SAGE, 2019.

Garton, Sue, and Fiona Copland. '"I Like This Interview; I Get Cakes and Cats!": The Effect of Prior Relationships on Interview Talk.' *Qualitative Research* 10, no. 5 (October 2010) 533–51. https://doi.org/10.1177/1468794110375231.

Gauger, Ann, Douglas Axe, and Casey Luskin. *Science and Human Origins*. Seattle: Discovery Institute Press, 2012.

Gaventa, John, and Andrea Cornwall. 'Power and Knowledge.' In *The SAGE Handbook of Action Research: Participative Inquiry and Practice*, edited by Peter Reason and Hilary Bradbury, 2nd ed., 172–89. London: SAGE, 2008.

Gelernter, David. 'Giving up Darwin.' *Claremont Review of Books* XIX, no. 2 (Spring 2019) 104–9.

Gerth, H. H., and C. Wright Mills. *From Max Weber: Essays in Sociology*. The International Library of Sociology. Abingdon: Routledge, 1948.

Gibbs, Paul. 'Is Higher Education Inherently Good, Educative Practices Intrinsically Good and Universities Instrumentally Good? What Should We Hope For?' In *Higher Education and Hope*, edited by Paul Gibbs and Andrew Peterson, 223–39. London: Palgrave Macmillan, 2019.

Goldman, Alvin I. 'Truth and Realism.' In *The Nature of Nature: Examining the Role of Naturalism in Science*, edited by Bruce Gordon and William A. Dembski, 228–46. Wilmington: ISI, 2011.

Gonzalez, Guillermo, and Jay W. Richards. *The Privileged Planet: How Our Place in the Cosmos is Designed for Discovery*. Washington: Regnery, 2004.

Gordon, Bruce. 'The Rise of Naturalism.' In *The Nature of Nature: Examining the Role of Naturalism in Science*, edited by Bruce Gordon and William A. Dembski, 3–61. Wilmington: ISI, 2011.

Gordon, Bruce, and William A. Dembski, eds. *The Nature of Nature: Examining the Role of Naturalism in Science*. Wilmington: ISI, 2011.

Gould, Stephen Jay. 'Nonoverlapping Magisteria.' *Natural History* 106 (March 1997) 16–22.

———. *Rocks of Ages: Science and Religion in the Fullness of Life*. New York: Random House, 1999.

Graham, Elaine L., Heather Walton, and Frances Ward. *Theological Reflection: Methods*. London: SCM, 2005.

Grayling, A.C. 'The God Argument.' Text. *Radio National*, 26 March 2013. https://www.abc.net.au/radionational/programs/latenightlive/the-god-argument-ac-grayling/4594806.

Greenwood, Davydd J. 'An Analysis of the Theory/Concept Entries in the SAGE Encyclopedia of Action Research: What We Can Learn about Action Research in General from the Encyclopedia.' *Action Research* 13, no. 2 (June 2015) 198–213. https://doi.org/10.1177/1476750315573592.

'Guide to the General Data Protection Regulation (GDPR).' London: Information Commissioner's Office, 2018. https://www.gov.uk/government/publications/guide-to-the-general-data-protection-regulation.

Guillemin, Marilys, and Lynn Gillam. 'Ethics, Reflexivity, and "Ethically Important Moments" in Research.' *Qualitative Inquiry* 10, no. 2 (April 2004) 261–80. https://doi.org/10.1177/1077800403262360.

Hafer, Abby. *The Not-so-Intelligent Designer: Why Evolution Explains the Human Body and Intelligent Design Does Not*. Eugene, Oregon: Cascade, 2015.

Hamilton, James M. *God's Glory in Salvation through Judgment: A Biblical Theology*. Wheaton: Crossway, 2010.

Hammond, Michael. 'The Contribution of Pragmatism to Understanding Educational Action Research: Value and Consequences.' *Educational Action Research* 21, no. 4 (December 2013) 603–18. https://doi.org/10.1080/09650792.2013.832632.

Harris, Brian. 'Beyond Bebbington: The Quest for Evangelical Identity in a Postmodern Era.' *Churchman* 122, no. 3 (2008) 201–19.

Harris, Sam. 'Science Must Destroy Religion.' In *What Is Your Dangerous Idea?*, edited by John Brockman, 148–51. New York: Harper Perennial, 2007.

Hart, David Bentley. *Atheist Delusions: The Christian Revolution and its Fashionable Enemies*. New Haven: Yale University Press, 2009.

Hathcoat, John D., and Mark C. Nicholas. 'Epistemology.' In *The SAGE Encyclopedia of Action Research*, edited by David Coghlan and Mary Brydon-Miller, 302–6. London: SAGE, 2014.

Haught, John F. 'Darwin and Divine Providence.' *Sewanee Theological Review* 56, no. 4 (2013) 353–63.

Hays, Richard B. 'The Canonical Matrix of the Gospels.' In *The Cambridge Companion to the Gospels*, edited by Stephen C. Barton, 53–75. Cambridge Companions to Religion. Cambridge: Cambridge University Press, 2006.

Helskog, Guro Hansen. 'Justifying Action Research.' *Educational Action Research* 22, no. 1 (2 January 2014) 4–20. https://doi.org/10.1080/09650792.2013.856769.

Henning, John E., Jody M. Stone, and James L. Kelly. *Using Action Research to Improve Instruction: An Interactive Guide for Teachers*. Abingdon: Routledge, 2009.

Herzog, William R. *Parables as Subversive Speech: Jesus as Pedagogue of the Oppressed*. Louisville: Westminster; John Knox, 1994.

Hiebert, Paul G. *Transforming Worldviews: An Anthropological Understanding of How People Change*. Grand Rapids: Baker Academic, 2008.

Hillebert, Jordan. 'The Faith of a Physicist: Reflections of a Bottom-Up Thinker, John Polkinghorne.' *The Gifford Lectures*, 1 December 2014. https://www.giffordlectures.org/books/faith-physicist-reflections-bottom-thinker.

Holloway, Immy, and Lorraine Brown. *Essentials of a Qualitative Doctorate*. Qualitative Essentials. Walnut Creek: Left Coast, 2012.

Horn, Heather. 'Where Does Religion Come From?: A Conversation with Robert Bellah, Author of a New Book about Faith's Place in Evolution.' *The Atlantic*, 17 August 2011. https://www.theatlantic.com/entertainment/archive/2011/08/where-does-religion-come-from/243723/.

House, H. Wayne, ed. *Intelligent Design 101: Leading Experts Explain the Key Issues*. Grand Rapids: Kregel, 2008.

House, Paul R. 'Creation in Old Testament Theology.' *The Southern Baptist Journal of Theology* 5, no. 3 (2001) 4–17.

Howson, Chris. 'Liberation Theology.' In *The SAGE Encyclopedia of Action Research*, edited by David Coghlan and Mary Brydon-Miller, 507–10. London: SAGE, 2014.

Humanists UK. 'Humanists UK Welcomes Recommended New Subject "Religion and Worldviews".' Accessed 2 December 2020. https://humanism.org.uk/2018/09/09/humanists-uk-welcomes-landmark-commission-on-re-recommending-new-subject-religion-and-worldviews/.

Huxtable, Marie, and Jack Whitehead. 'Enhancing Educational Influences in Learning with a Living Educational Theory Approach to Pedagogical Action Research in Higher Education.' *Educational Action Research*, 15 June 2020, 1–18. https://doi.org/10.1080/09650792.2020.1779771.

Jean, Jason, and Yixi Lu. 'Evolution as a Fact? A Discourse Analysis.' *Social Studies of Science* 48, no. 4 (August 2018) 615–32. https://doi.org/10.1177/0306312718785773.

Johnson, Phillip E. 'Bringing Balance to a Fiery Debate.' In *Intelligent Design 101: Leading Experts Explain the Key Issues*, edited by H. Wayne House, 21–40. Grand Rapids: Kregel, 2008.

———. *The Wedge of Truth: Splitting the Foundations of Naturalism.* Downers Grove: InterVarsity, 2000.

Jones III, John E. 'Kitzmiller v. Dover Area Sch. Dist. Opinion, 400 F. Supp. 2d 707, 719 (M.D. Pa. 2005).' *American Civil Liberties Union.* Accessed 17 June 2019. https://www.aclu.org/legal-document/kitzmiller-v-dover-memorandum-opinion.

Kelemen, Deborah. 'Are Children "Intuitive Theists"?: Reasoning About Purpose and Design in Nature.' *Psychological Science* 15, no. 5 (1 May 2004) 295–301. https://doi.org/10.1111/j.0956-7976.2004.00672.x.

Kelemen, Deborah, and Cara DiYanni. 'Intuitions About Origins: Purpose and Intelligent Design in Children's Reasoning About Nature.' *Journal of Cognition and Development* 6, no. 1 (1 February 2005) 3–31. https://doi.org/10.1207/s15327647jcd0601_2.

Kelemen, Deborah, Natalie A. Emmons, Rebecca Seston Schillaci, and Patricia A. Ganea. 'Young Children Can Be Taught Basic Natural Selection Using a Picture-Storybook Intervention.' *Psychological Science* 25, no. 4 (April 2014) 893–902. https://doi.org/10.1177/0956797613516009.

Kember, David. *Action Learning and Action Research: Improving the Quality of Teaching and Learning.* London: Routledge, 2000.

Kemmis, Stephen, and Robin McTaggart. 'Participatory Action Research: Communicative Action and the Public Sphere.' In *Strategies of Qualitative Inquiry*, edited by N. K. Denzin and Yvonna S. Lincoln, 271–330. Thousand Oaks: SAGE, 2007.

Kemper, Gary, Hallie Kemper, and Casey Luskin. *Discovering Intelligent Design: A Journey into the Scientific Evidence.* Seattle: Discovery Institute Press, 2013.

Kinnaman, David. *You Lost Me: Why Young Christians Are Leaving Church, and Rethinking Faith.* Grand Rapids: Baker, 2011.

Kinnaman, David, and Mark Matlock. *Faith for Exiles: 5 Ways for a New Generation to Follow Jesus in Digital Babylon.* Grand Rapids: Baker, 2019.

Kistemaker, Simon J. 'Jesus as Story Teller: Literary Perspectives on the Parables.' *The Master's Seminary Journal* 16, no. 1 (2005) 49–55.

Klinghoffer, David. 'NASA Versus David Coppedge: Most Reprehensible Case of Anti-Intelligent Design Persecution Yet?' *Evolution News*, 20 December 2016. https://evolutionnews.org/2016/12/david_coppedge/.

Knowles, Michael P. 'Abram and the Birds in Jubilees 11: A Subtext for the Parable of the Sower?' *New Testament Studies* 41, no. 1 (January 1995) 145–51. https://doi.org/10.1017/S0028688500022992.

Kojonen, Erkki Vesa Rope. 'Intelligent Design: A Theological and Philosophical Analysis.' University of Helsinki, 2014.

Krauss, Lawrence M. *A Universe from Nothing: Why There Is Something Rather than Nothing.* New York: Free Press, 2012.

———. 'All Scientists Should Be Militant Atheists.' *The New Yorker*, 8 September 2015. https://www.newyorker.com/news/news-desk/all-scientists-should-be-militant-atheists.

Lawes, Caroline. *Faith and Darwin: Harmony, Conflict, or Confusion?* London: Theos, 2009.

Leach, Jane. 'Pastoral Theology as Attention.' *Contact* 153 (2007) 19–32.

Leidenhag, Mikael. 'The Blurred Line between Theistic Evolution and Intelligent Design.' *Zygon* 54, no. 4 (December 2019) 909–31. https://doi.org/10.1111/zygo.12556.

Lewis, C.S. *Miracles: A Preliminary Study.* London: Geoffrey Bles, 1947.

Lincoln, Yvonna S., and Egon G. Guba. 'Paradigmatic Controversies, Contradictions, and Emerging Confluences.' In *The SAGE Handbook of Qualitative Research*, edited by N. K. Denzin and Yvonna S. Lincoln, 3rd ed., 163–88. Thousand Oaks: SAGE, 2005.

Lipton, Peter. 'Inference to the Best Explanation.' In *A Companion to the Philosophy of Science*, edited by William H. Newton-Smith, 184–93. Blackwell Companions to Philosophy 18. Malden: Blackwell, 2000.

———. *Inference to the Best Explanation.* 2nd ed. International Library of Philosophy. Abingdon: Routledge, 2004.

———. 'What Good is an Explanation?' In *Explanation*, edited by Giora Hon and Sam S. Rakover, 43–60. Synthese Library 302. Dordrecht: Springer, 2001. https://doi.org/10.1007/978-94-015-9731-9.

Lloyd, John B. 'Everyday Intervention.' *Theology* 121, no. 6 (November 2018) 413–21. https://doi.org/10.1177/0040571X18794140.

Long, Robert. 'Religious Education in Schools (England).' Briefing Paper. House of Commons Library. London: House of Commons Library, 7 July 2016. researchbriefings.files.parliament.uk/documents/CBP-7167/CBP-7167.pdf.

'Lords Hansard Text for 18 Dec 200618 Dec 2006 (Pt 0006).' Accessed 17 June 2019. https://publications.parliament.uk/pa/ld200607/ldhansrd/text/61218w0006.htm.

Losch, Andreas. 'Critical Realism—A Sustainable Bridge Between Science and Religion?' *Theology and Science* 8, no. 4 (November 2010) 393–416. https://doi.org/10.1080/14746700.2010.517638.

———. 'On the Origins of Critical Realism.' *Theology and Science* 7, no. 1 (February 2009) 85–106. https://doi.org/10.1080/14746700802617105.

'Losing My Religion: Millennials and Faith Loss.' Accessed 5 December 2020. https://discipleshipresearch.com/2018/02/losing-my-religion-millennials-and-faith-loss/.

Lucas, Gavin. *Understanding the Archaeological Record.* Cambridge: Cambridge University Press, 2012.

Lugo, Luis. '"Nones" on the Rise: One-in-Five Adults Have No Religious Affiliation.' Washington: Pew Research Center, 9 October 2012. http://www.pewforum.org/Unaffiliated/nones-on-the-rise.aspx.

Luskin, Casey. 'Darwin Believers Hide Fears of Intelligent Design Behind a Wall of Denial and Ridicule.' *US News & World Report.* Accessed 28 June 2019. https://www.usnews.com/opinion/blogs/room-for-debate/2009/02/12/darwin-believers-hide-fears-of-intelligent-design-behind-a-wall-of-denial-and-ridicule.

Lykes, M. Brinton, and Amelia Mallona. 'Towards Transformational Liberation: Participatory and Action Research and Praxis.' In *The SAGE Handbook of Action Research: Participative Inquiry and Practice*, edited by Peter Reason and Hilary Bradbury, 2nd ed., 106–20. London: SAGE, 2008.

Lynch, Michael. 'Against Reflexivity as an Academic Virtue and Source of Privileged Knowledge.' *Theory, Culture & Society* 17, no. 3 (1 June 2000) 26–54. https://doi.org/10.1177/02632760022051202.

Madge, Nicola, and Peter J. Hemming. 'Young British Religious "Nones": Findings from the Youth On Religion Study.' *Journal of Youth Studies* 20, no. 7 (9 August 2017) 872–88. https://doi.org/10.1080/13676261.2016.1273518.

Maguire, Kate. 'Methodology as Personal and Professional Integrity: Research Designing for Practitioner Doctorates.' In *Methodologies for Practice Research: Approaches for Professional Doctorates*, edited by Carol Costley and John Fulton, 95–115. London: SAGE, 2019.

'Making Space for Millennials: A Blueprint for Your Culture, Ministry, Leadership and Facilities.' Ventura: Barna Group, 2014.

Mason, Jennifer. *Qualitative Researching*. 2nd ed. London: SAGE, 2002.

Masters, Janet. 'The History of Action Research.' In *Action Research Electronic Reader*, edited by I. Hughes, 1–8. on-line: University of Sydney, 1995. http://www.behs.cchs.usyd.edu.au/arow/Reader/rmasters.htm.

Maxwell, Joseph A. *A Realist Approach for Qualitative Research*. Thousand Oaks: SAGE, 2012.

———. 'Using Numbers in Qualitative Research.' Qualitative Inquiry 16, no. 6 (July 2010) 475–82. https://doi.org/10.1177/1077800410364740.

Maxwell, T. A. 'Philosophy and Practice – Why Does This Matter?' In *Methodologies for Practice Research: Approaches for Professional Doctorates*, edited by Carol Costley and John Fulton, 3–16. London: SAGE, 2019.

McDermott, John M. 'Jesus: Parable or Sacrament of God? An Ecumenical Discussion on Analogy and Freedom with E. Schweizer, K. Barth, and R. Bultmann.' *Gregorianum* 78, no. 3 (1997) 477–99.

McGarvey, Craig. 'Participatory Action Research: Involving "All the Players" in Evaluation and Change.' GrantCraft. Foundation Center, 2007.

McGinnis, Claire Mathews. 'The Old Testament.' In *The Blackwell Companion to Catholicism*, edited by James J. Buckley, Frederick Christian Bauerschmidt, and Trent Pomplun, 5–21. Oxford: Blackwell, 2007. https://doi.org/10.1111/b.9781405112246.2007.00002.x.

McGrath, Alister E. 'A Blast from the Past?: The Boyle Lectures and Natural Theology.' *Science & Christian Belief* 17, no. 1 (2005) 25–33.

———. *Darwinism and the Divine: Evolutionary Thought and Natural Theology*. Chichester: Wiley-Blackwell, 2011.

———. *Enriching Our Vision of Reality: Theology and the Natural Sciences in Dialogue*. London: SPCK, 2016.

———. 'New Atheism—New Apologetics: The Use of Science in Recent Christian Apologetic Writings.' Boyle Lecture. St Mary-le-Bow, Cheapside, 2014.

———. 'New Atheism—New Apologetics: The Use of Science in Recent Christian Apologetic Writings.' *Science & Christian Belief* 26, no. 2 (October 2014) 99–113.

———. *The Dawkins Delusion?: Atheist Fundamentalism and the Denial of the Divine*. London: SPCK, 2007.

McKernan, James. *Curriculum and Imagination: Process Theory, Pedagogy and Action Research*. London: Routledge, 2008.

McKitterick, Alistair. 'The Role of Teleology in Practical Theology.' In *Evangelicals Engaging with Practical Theology: Theology That Impacts Church and World*, edited by Helen Morris and Helen Cameron. Explorations in Practical, Pastoral and Empirical Theology. Abingdon: Routledge, Forthcoming.

———. 'The Theological Imperative Model for Practical Theology.' *Journal of European Baptist Studies* 16, no. 4 (September 2016) 5–20.

McLeish, Tom. *Faith and Wisdom in Science*. Oxford: Oxford University Press, 2014.

McNiff, Jean. 'Action Research for Professional Development', 2002. http://www.jeanmcniff.com/ar-booklet.asp.

———. 'My Story Is My Living Educational Theory.' In *Handbook of Narrative Inquiry: Mapping a Methodology*, edited by D. Jean Clandinin, 308–29. Thousand Oaks: SAGE, 2007.

———. *Writing up Your Action Research Project*. Abingdon: Routledge, 2016.

McNiff, Jean, and Jack Whitehead. *Action Research: Principles and Practice*. 2nd ed. London; New York: RoutledgeFalmer, 2002.

———. *All You Need to Know about Action Research*. London: SAGE, 2006.

Medawar, Peter. *The Limits of Science*. Oxford: Oxford University Press, 1984.

Mercer, Joyce Ann. 'Review of Practical Theology: An Introduction by Richard R. Osmer: Grand Rapids: Eerdmans, 2008.' *Theology Today* 67, no. 2 (July 2010) 234–39. https://doi.org/10.1177/004057361006700212.

Mertler, Craig A. *Action Research: Improving Schools and Empowering Educators*. 3rd ed. Thousand Oaks: SAGE, 2012.

Meyer, Stephen C. *Darwin's Doubt: The Explosive Origin of Animal Life and the Case for Intelligent Design*. New York, NY: HarperOne, 2013.

———. *Signature in the Cell: DNA and the Evidence for Intelligent Design*. New York: HarperOne, 2009.

Meyer, Stephen C., Scott Minnich, Jonathan Moneymaker, Paul A. Nelson, and Ralph Seelke. *Explore Evolution: The Arguments for and against Neo-Darwinism*. Melbourne; London: Hill House, 2009.

Miller-McLemore, Bonnie J. 'Introduction: The Contributions of Practical Theology.' In *The Wiley-Blackwell Companion to Practical Theology*, edited by Bonnie J. Miller-McLemore, 1–20. Wiley-Blackwell Companions to Religion. Chichester: Wiley-Blackwell, 2012.

Monton, Bradley John. *Seeking God in Science: An Atheist Defends Intelligent Design*. Peterborough: Broadview, 2009.

Moreland, J. P., and John Mark Reynolds, eds. *Three Views on Creation and Evolution*. Counterpoints. Grand Rapids: Zondervan, 1999.

Moreland, J.P. *Kingdom Triangle: Recover the Christian Mind, Renovate the Soul, Restore the Spirit's Power*. Grand Rapids: Zondervan, 2007.

———. *Scientism and Secularism: Learning to Respond to a Dangerous Ideology*. Wheaton: Crossway, 2018.

———. 'Theistic Evolution, Christian Knowledge and Culture's Plausibility Structure.' *Journal of Biblical and Theological Studies* 2, no. 1 (2017) 1–18.

Morris, Wayne. *Salvation as Praxis: A Practical Theology of Salvation for a Multi-Faith World*. London: Bloomsbury T&T Clark, 2014.

Morse, Janice M. 'Sampling in Grounded Theory.' In *The SAGE Handbook of Grounded Theory*, edited by Antony Bryant and Kathy Charmaz, 229–44. London: SAGE, 2007.

Moye, Richard H. 'In the Beginning: Myth and History in Genesis and Exodus.' *Journal of Biblical Literature* 109, no. 4 (1990) 577–98. https://doi.org/10.2307/3267364.

Müller, Gerd B. 'Why an Extended Evolutionary Synthesis Is Necessary.' *Interface Focus* 7, no. 5 (6 October 2017) 1–11. https://doi.org/10.1098/rsfs.2017.0015.

Muñoz-Guzmán, Carolina. 'Liberation Theology in Social Work.' In *International Encyclopedia of the Social & Behavioral Sciences*, 32–38. Elsevier, 2015. https://doi.org/10.1016/B978-0-08-097086-8.28051-3.

Murphy, Nancey. 'A Niebuhrian Typology for the Relation of Theology to Science.' *Pacific Theological Review* XVIII, no. 3 (1985) 16–23.

Nagel, Thomas. *Mind and Cosmos: Why the Materialist Neo-Darwinian Conception of Nature Is Almost Certainly False*. New York: Oxford University Press, 2012.

Niebuhr, H. Richard. *Christ and Culture*. San Francisco: Harper, 1951.

Nixon, Jon. 'Resources of Hope: Truth and Reason.' In *Higher Education and Hope: Institutional, Pedagogical and Personal Possibilities*, edited by Paul Gibbs and Andrew Peterson, 3–19. London: Palgrave Macmillan, 2019.

Noble, Denis. 'Physiology Is Rocking the Foundations of Evolutionary Biology.' *Experimental Physiology* 98, no. 8 (August 2013) 1235–43. https://doi.org/10.1113/expphysiol.2012.071134.

Pew Research Center: Religion & Public Life. '"Nones" on the Rise | Pew Research Center', 9 October 2012. https://www.pewforum.org/2012/10/09/nones-on-the-rise/.

Norman, Ralph. 'Theological Foundations of Action Research for Learning and Teaching.' *Discourse: Learning and Teaching in Philosophical and Religious Studies* 8, no. 1 (2008) 113–40. https://doi.org/10.5840/discourse20088112.

Norton, Lin. *Action Research in Teaching and Learning: A Practical Guide to Conducting Pedagogical Research in Universities*. London: Routledge, 2009.

———. 'Personal Communication', 2020.

———. 'The Case for Pedagogical Action Research in Psychology Learning and Teaching.' *Psychology Teaching Review* 20, no. 2 (2014) 3–11.

Notley, R. Steven. 'Reading Gospel Parables as Jewish Literature.' *Journal for the Study of the New Testament* 41, no. 1 (28 August 2018) 29–43. https://doi.org/10.1177/0142064X18788960.

'OARS Education—OARS Education.' Accessed 4 December 2020. https://oarseducation.com/.

O'Brien, Michael J., and R. Lee Lyman. *Applying Evolutionary Archaeology: A Systematic Approach*. New York: Kluwer Academic/Plenum, 2000.

Oliver, Paul. *The Student's Guide to Research Ethics*. 2nd ed. Maidenhead: McGraw-Hill; Open University Press, 2010.

Olson, Roger E. *How to Be Evangelical without Being Conservative*. Grand Rapids: Zondervan, 2008.

Osborne, Grant R. *The Hermeneutical Spiral: A Comprehensive Introduction to Biblical Interpretation*. Downers Grove: InterVarsity, 1991.

Osmer, Richard R. *Practical Theology: An Introduction*. Grand Rapids: Eerdmans, 2008.

Ospina, Sonia, Jennifer Dodge, Erica Gabrielle Foldy, and Amparo Hofmann-Pinil. 'Taking the Action Turn: Lessons from Bringing Participation to Qualitative Research.' In *The SAGE Handbook of Action Research: Participative Inquiry and Practice*, edited by Peter Reason and Hilary Bradbury, 2nd ed., 420–34. SAGE, 2008.

'Our Values—Moorlands College.' Accessed 17 April 2019. https://www.moorlands.ac.uk/our-values/.

Patterson, Richard. 'A Literary Look at Nahum, Habakkuk, and Zephaniah.' *Grace Theological Journal* 11, no. 1 (1991) 17–27.

Pattison, Stephen. 'Some Straw for the Bricks: A Basic Introduction to Theological Reflection.' *Contact* 99, no. 1 (1 February 1989) 2–9. https://doi.org/10.1080/13 520806.1989.11759678.

Patton, Michael Quinn. *Qualitative Research & Evaluation Methods: Integrating Theory and Practice*. 4th ed. Thousand Oaks: SAGE, 2015.

———. 'Sampling, Qualitative (Purposive).' In *The Blackwell Encyclopedia of Sociology*, edited by George Ritzer, 4006–7. Oxford: Blackwell, 2007.

Peacocke, A. R. *Creation and the World of Science*. The Bampton Lectures. Oxford: Clarendon, 1979.

'Pedagogical Action Research (PedAR) | Lin Norton.' Accessed 22 October 2020. https://www.linnorton.co.uk/pedagogical-action-research.

Center for Science and Culture. 'Peer-Reviewed Articles Supporting Intelligent Design.' Accessed 27 July 2020. https://www.discovery.org/id/peer-review/.

Peters, Donald. 'Vulnerable Promise from the Land (Mark 4:3b–8).' In *Jesus and His Parables: Interpreting the Parables of Jesus Today*, edited by V. George Shillington, 69–84. Edinburgh: T&T Clark, 1997.

Pharoah, Robin, Tamara Hale, and Becky Rowe. *Doubting Darwin: Creationism and Evolution Scepticism in Britain Today*. London: Theos, 2009.

Phelps, Renata, and Stewart Hase. 'Complexity and Action Research: Exploring the Theoretical and Methodological Connections.' *Educational Action Research* 10, no. 3 (September 2002) 507–24. https://doi.org/10.1080/09650790200200198.

Pike, Richard. '"Teach Children Evolution as Fact Not Theory" Says UK Chemistry Chief.' *Royal Society of Chemistry*, 25 April 2006. https://www.rsc.org/AboutUs/News/PressReleases/2006/Evolution.asp.

Pinker, Steven. 'Science Is Not Your Enemy.' *The New Republic*, 7 August 2013. https://newrepublic.com/article/114127/science-not-enemy-humanities.

Plantinga, Alvin. 'Games Scientists Play.' In *The Believing Primate: Scientific, Philosophical, and Theological Reflections on the Origin of Religion*, edited by Michael J. Murray and Jeffrey Schloss, 139–67. New York: Oxford University Press, 2009.

———. 'What Is "Intervention"?' *Theology and Science* 6, no. 4 (November 2008) 369–401. https://doi.org/10.1080/14746700802396106.

———. *Where the Conflict Really Lies: Science, Religion, and Naturalism*. New York: Oxford University Press, 2011.

Polkinghorne, J. C. 'Divine Action: Some Comments.' *Science & Christian Belief* 24, no. 1 (April 2012) 31–32.

———. *Science and Creation: The Search for Understanding*. London: SPCK, 1988.

———. *Science and Religion in Quest of Truth*. New Haven; London: Yale University Press, 2011.

Poole, Jennifer M., and Oliver Mauthner. 'Interviews.' In *The SAGE Encyclopedia of Action Research*, edited by David Coghlan and Mary Brydon-Miller, 463–65. London: SAGE, 2014.

Poplin, Mary S. *Is Reality Secular? Testing the Assumptions of Four Global Worldviews*. Downers Grove: InterVarsity, 2014.

Postans, Adam. 'Not a Single Pupil Took a Religious Education GCSE at This School.' *Bristol Post*, 1 July 2019. https://www.bristolpost.co.uk/news/local-news/not-single-pupil-took-religious-3027640.

Ramlo, Hannah. 'Beyond Millennials...' *PeoriaMagazines.com*, August 2017. https://www.peoriamagazines.com/as/2017/jul-aug/beyond-millennials.

Ramsay, Nancy J. 'Emancipatory Theory and Method.' In *The Wiley-Blackwell Companion to Practical Theology*, edited by Bonnie J. Miller-McLemore, 183–92. Wiley-Blackwell Companions to Religion. Chichester: Wiley-Blackwell, 2012.

Ratzsch, Del. 'Science and Religion.' In *The Oxford Handbook of Philosophical Theology*, edited by Thomas P. Flint and Michael C. Rea, 54–77. Oxford Handbooks in Religion and Theology. Oxford: Oxford University Press, 2009.

———. 'Teleological Arguments for God's Existence.' Accessed 6 April 2020. https://plato.stanford.edu/archives/win2010/entries/teleological-arguments/#IntDesIDMov.

Reason, Peter, and Hilary Bradbury. 'Concluding Reflections: Whither Action Research?' In *The SAGE Handbook of Action Research: Participative Inquiry and Practice*, edited by Peter Reason and Hilary Bradbury, 2nd ed., 695–707. London: SAGE, 2008.

———. 'Introduction.' In *The SAGE Handbook of Action Research: Participative Inquiry and Practice*, edited by Peter Reason and Hilary Bradbury, 2nd ed., 1–10. London: SAGE, 2008.

Reeves, Colin R. 'Bringing Home the Bacon: The Interaction of Science and Scripture Today.' In *Theistic Evolution: A Scientific, Philosophical, and Theological Critique*, edited by J.P. Moreland, Stephen C. Meyer, Christopher Shaw, Ann K. Gauger, and Wayne Grudem, 705–30. Wheaton: Crossway, 2017.

'Religion and Worldviews: The Way Forward; A National Plan for RE.' London: Commission on Religious Education, September 2018. religiouseducationcouncil.org.uk.

Rindge, Matthew S. 'Luke's Artistic Parables: Narratives of Subversion, Imagination, and Transformation.' *Interpretation: A Journal of Bible and Theology* 68, no. 4 (October 2014) 403–15. https://doi.org/10.1177/0020964314540406.

Ritchie, Jane, and Jane Lewis. 'Generalising from Qualitative Research.' In *Qualitative Research Practice: A Guide for Social Science Students and Researchers*, edited by Jane Ritchie and Jane Lewis, 263–86. London: SAGE, 2003.

Root, Andrew. *Christopraxis: A Practical Theology of the Cross*. Minneapolis: Fortress, 2014.

———. *Exploding Stars, Dead Dinosaurs, and Zombies: Youth Ministry in the Age of Science*. Minneapolis: Fortress, 2018.

Rowley, Jennifer. 'Data Analysis.' In *The SAGE Encyclopedia of Action Research*, edited by David Coghlan and Mary Brydon-Miller, 239–42. London: SAGE, 2014.

Rue, Penny. 'Make Way, Millennials, Here Comes Gen Z.' *About Campus: Enriching the Student Learning Experience* 23, no. 3 (August 2018) 5–12. https://doi.org/10.1177/1086482218804251.

Sands, Justin. 'Introducing Cardinal Cardijn's See–Judge–Act as an Interdisciplinary Method to Move Theory into Practice.' *Religions* 9, no. 4 (14 April 2018) 129. https://doi.org/10.3390/rel9040129.

Saroyan, Alenoush, Cynthia Weston, Lynn McAlpine, and Susan Cowan. 'The Final Step: Evaluation of Teaching.' In *Rethinking Teaching in Higher Education: From a Course Design Workshop to a Faculty Development Framework*, edited by Alenoush Saroyan and Cheryl Amundsen, 115–30. Sterling: Stylus, 2004.

Saunders, Nicholas. *Divine Action and Modern Science*. Cambridge: Cambridge University Press, 2002.

Schimmel, Solomon. *The Tenacity of Unreasonable Beliefs: Fundamentalism and the Fear of Truth*. Oxford: Oxford University Press, 2008.

Schweizer, Eduard. *Jesus, the Parable of God: What Do We Really Know about Jesus?* Princeton Theological Monograph Series 37. Eugene: Pickwick, 1994.

'Science and Religion: What Teachers Believe.' Portsmouth Point: Belief, December 2013.

'Scientists – Dissent from Darwin.' Accessed 18 June 2019. https://dissentfromdarwin. org/scientists/.

Scott, Eugenie C. 'Creationism and Intelligent Design.' In *How Evolution Shapes Our Lives*, edited by Jonathan B. Losos and Richard E. Lenski, 284–99. Princeton: Princeton University Press, 2016.

Segal, Robert A. 'Myth.' In *The Blackwell Companion to the Study of Religion*, edited by Robert A. Segal, 337–55. Blackwell Companions to Religion. Oxford: Blackwell, 2006.

Seidman, Irving. *Interviewing as Qualitative Research: A Guide for Researchers in Education and the Social Sciences*. 3rd ed. New York: Teachers College Press, 2006.

Shapiro, Robert. *Origins: A Skeptic's Guide to the Creation of Life on Earth*. Toronto: Bantam, 1987.

Shermer, Michael. *Why Darwin Matters the Case against Intelligent Design*. New York: Holt, 2006.

Sire, James W. *Habits of the Mind: Intellectual Life as a Christian Calling*. Downers Grove: InterVarsity, 2000.

Barna Group. 'Six Reasons Young Christians Leave Church', 2011. https://www.barna. com/research/six-reasons-young-christians-leave-church/.

Somekh, Bridget. 'Action Research.' In *The SAGE Encyclopedia of Qualitative Research Methods*, edited by Lisa M. Given, 4–7. Thousand Oaks: SAGE, 2008.

Christians in Science. 'Southampton Previous Events.' Accessed 9 August 2020. http:// www.cis.org.uk/resources/articles-talks-and-links/general-science-and-faith/ central-south-previous-events/.

Staune, Jean. 'Introduction.' In *Science & the Search for Meaning: Perspectives from International Scientists*, edited by Jean Staune, 3–11. West Conshohocken: Templeton Foundation, 2006.

Sternberg, Richard. 'How My Views on Evolution Evolved', 2008. http://www. richardsternberg.com/pdf/sternintellbio08.pdf.

Stolberg, Tonie, and Geoff Teece. *Teaching Religion and Science: Effective Pedagogy and Practical Approaches for RE Teachers*. Abingdon: Routledge, 2011.

Susskind, Leonard. *The Cosmic Landscape: String Theory and the Illusion of Intelligent Design*. London: Little Brown, 2005.

Sweeney, James, and Clare Watkins. 'Theological Action Research.' In *The SAGE Encyclopedia of Action Research*, edited by David Coghlan and Mary Brydon-Miller, 776–77. London: SAGE, 2014.

Swinton, John, and Harriet Mowat. *Practical Theology and Qualitative Research*. 2nd ed. London: SCM, 2016.

Taylor, Charles. 'The Polysemy of the Secular.' *Social Research* 76, no. 4 (2009) 1143–66.

Teece, Geoff. 'The Aims and Purpose of Religious Education.' In *Learning to Teach Religious Education in the Secondary School: A Companion to School Experience*, edited by L. Philip Barnes, 3rd ed., 1–14. Learning to Teach Subjects in the Secondary School Series. Abingdon: Routledge, 2018.

Tenneson, Michael, David R. Bundrick, and Matthew S. Stanford. 'A New Survey Instrument and Its Findings for Relating Science and Theology.' *Perspectives on Science and Christian Faith* 67, no. 3 (September 2015) 200–222.

————. 'Faith and Science Integration: Surveys and Findings.' In *Faith & Science Conference: Genesis & Genetics: Proceedings of the 2014 Faith & Science Conference*, edited by David R. Bundrick and Steve Badger, 319–52. Springfield, MO: Logion, 2014.

Thaxton, Charles B., Walter L. Bradley, and Roger L. Olsen. *The Mystery of Life's Origin: Reassessing Current Theories*. New York: Philosophical Library, 1984.

Evolutionary Informatics. 'The Evolutionary Informatics Lab.' Accessed 15 May 2020. https://www.evoinfo.org/.

Oxford University Museum of Natural History. 'The Great Debate.' Accessed 20 July 2020. https://oumnh.ox.ac.uk/great-debate.

Thorvaldsen, Steinar, and Ola Hössjer. 'Using Statistical Methods to Model the Fine-Tuning of Molecular Machines and Systems.' *Journal of Theoretical Biology* 501 (September 2020) 110352. https://doi.org/10.1016/j.jtbi.2020.110352.

Barna Group. 'Three Spiritual Journeys of Millennials.' Accessed 3 May 2019. https://www.barna.com/research/three-spiritual-journeys-of-millennials/.

Tomlin, Graham. 'The Telos of Theological Education.' *Theological Education* 51, no. 2 (2018) 113–25.

Torrance, Andrew B. 'Should a Christian Adopt Methodological Naturalism?' *Zygon, How to Do Religion and Science?*, 52, no. 3 (September 2017) 691–725. https://doi.org/10.1111/zygo.12363.

Toulmin, Stephen. 'Is Action Research Really "Research"?' *Concepts and Transformation* 1, no. 1 (January 1996) 51–61. https://doi.org/10.1075/cat.1.1.05tou.

Treier, Daniel J. 'Theology as the Acquisition of Wisdom: Reorienting Theological Education.' *Christian Education Journal* 3NS, no. 1 (1999) 127–39.

Trigg, Roger. *Rationality and Religion: Does Faith Need Reason?* Oxford: Blackwell, 1998.

Turner, Bryan S. 'Introduction: A New Agenda for Social Theory?' In *The New Blackwell Companion to Social Theory*, edited by Bryan S. Turner, 1–16. Blackwell Companions to Sociology. Chichester: Wiley-Blackwell, 2009.

Van Leeuwen, Raymond C. 'Liminality and Worldview in Proverbs 1–9.' *Semeia* 50 (1990) 111–44.

Vasileiou, Konstantina, Julie Barnett, Susan Thorpe, and Terry Young. 'Characterising and Justifying Sample Size Sufficiency in Interview-Based Studies: Systematic Analysis of Qualitative Health Research Over a 15-Year Period.' *BMC Medical Research Methodology* 18, no. 1 (December 2018) 148. https://doi.org/10.1186/s12874-018-0594-7.

Volf, Miroslav. *Exclusion and Embrace: A Theological Exploration of Identity, Otherness, and Reconciliation*. Nashville: Abingdon, 1996.

Ward, Pete. *Liquid Ecclesiology: The Gospel and The Church*. Leiden: Brill, 2017. https://doi.org/10.1163/9789004347359.

Warnick, Bryan R., and C. David Fooce. 'Does Teaching Creationism Facilitate Student Autonomy?' *Theory and Research in Education* 5, no. 3 (2007) 357–78. https://doi.org/10.1177/1477878507081761.

Watkins, Clare. *Disclosing Church: An Ecclesiology Learned from Conversations in Practice*. Abingdon: Routledge, 2020.

Wells, Samuel. *Improvisation: The Drama of Christian Ethics.* London: SPCK, 2004.

West, John G. *Darwin Day in America: How Our Politics and Culture Have Been Dehumanized in the Name of Science.* Wilmington: ISI, 2015.

West, Richard L., and Lynn H. Turner. *Introducing Communication Theory: Analysis and Application.* 6th ed. New York: McGraw-Hill Education, 2018.

Evangelical Alliance. 'What Is the Engel Scale?' Accessed 18 September 2020. https://www.eauk.org/what-is-the-engel-scale.

Whitehead, Jack. 'Creating a Living Educational Theory from Questions of the Kind, "How Do I Improve My Practice?"' *Cambridge Journal of Education* 19, no. 1 (1 January 1989) 41–52. https://doi.org/10.1080/0305764890190106.

———. 'Living Theories.' In *The SAGE Encyclopedia of Action Research*, edited by David Coghlan and Mary Brydon-Miller, 514–17. London: SAGE, 2014.

Wier, Andy. 'From the Descriptive to the Normative: Towards a Practical Theology of the Charismatic-Evangelical Urban Church.' *Ecclesial Practices* 4, no. 1 (17 May 2017) 112–32. https://doi.org/10.1163/22144471-00401002.

Wilkinson, David. *Science and Apologetics: How Can We Defend Our Faith in the Light of Modern Science?* Thinking About . . . Christians in Science, n.d.

Willard, Dallas. *Personal Religion, Public Reality?: Towards a Knowledge of Faith.* London: Hodder & Stoughton, 2009.

———. 'The Bible, the University, and the God Who Hides.' In *The Bible and the University*, edited by David Lyle Jeffrey and C. Stephen Evans, 8:17–39. Milton Keynes: Paternoster, 2007.

Wolf, Richard, Greg Langley, Kirti Pandey, Michelle Willys, and Petra Brandes. 'Millennials: Work, Life and Satisfaction.' Munich: Allianz, 16 November 2017.

Woodhead, Linda. 'The Rise of "No Religion" in Britain: The Emergence of a New Cultural Majority.' *Journal of the British Academy* 4 (2016) 245–61.

Wright, Andrew. *Christianity and Critical Realism: Ambiguity, Truth, and Theological Literacy.* New Studies in Critical Realism and Spirituality. London: Routledge, 2013.

Wright, N. T. 'Jerusalem in the New Testament.' In *Jerusalem Past and Present in the Purposes of God*, edited by P. W. L Walker, 2nd ed., 53–77. Carlisle: Paternoster, 1994.

———. *The New Testament and the People of God.* Christian Origins and the Question of God 1. London: SPCK, 1992.

Yerxa, Donald A. 'Phillip Johnson and the Origins of the Intelligent Design Movement, 1977–1991.' *Perspectives on Science and Christian Faith* 54, no. 1 (2002) 47–52.

Zimmerman, Paul A. 'Discovering Intelligent Design: A Journey into the Scientific Evidence by Gary Kemper, Hallie Kemper, and Casey Luskin.' *Concordia Theological Quarterly* 77, no. 3–4 (2013) 363–65.